APPLYING CROSS-CUR
APPROACHES CREATIV___.

The Connecting Curriculum

Applying Cross-Curricular Approaches Creatively explores how we can make connections in the classroom through our own and our children's lives, supporting teachers in becoming more personally involved in decisions about the style of teaching and learning and the substance of curriculum in schools. With a focus on personal reflection and discussion, examining and sharing our life's narrative, it offers educators inspiration, guidance and resources to deliver a truly integrated curriculum creatively. It examines key topics such as:

- Educationalists with an interest in cross-curricular and creative approaches
- Planning for and creating creativity
- Choosing cross-curricular themes
- Mind-full approaches to teaching and learning
- Assessing creative and integrated learning
- Your role as a researcher in the classroom

Applying Cross-Curricular Approaches Creatively is an essential text for those wishing to plan a coherent curriculum with cross-curricular elements and one that is able to sustain their enthusiasm for a lifetime in education. It places the 'basics' of genuine motivation, engagement and participation at the core of its arguments for meaningful learning for all children. Filled with autobiographical accounts and case studies, and with ready-to-use ideas for creative lessons, this uplifting book challenges us to return to curriculum breadth and balance and away from a 'one size fits all' approach.

Jonathan Barnes is Visiting Senior Research Fellow in Education at Canterbury Christ Church University, UK.

THE LEARNING TO TEACH IN THE PRIMARY SCHOOL SERIES

Series Editor: Teresa Cremin, The Open University, UK

Teaching is an art form. It demands not only knowledge and understanding of the core areas of learning, but also the ability to teach these creatively and foster learner creativity in the process. *The Learning to Teach in the Primary School Series* draws upon recent research which indicates the rich potential of creative teaching and learning, and explores what it means to teach creatively in the primary phase. It also responds to the evolving nature of subject teaching in a wider, more imaginatively framed 21st century primary curriculum.

Designed to complement the textbook *Learning to Teach in the Primary School*, the well informed, lively texts in this series offer support for student and practising teachers who want to develop more creative approaches to teaching and learning. Uniquely, the books highlight the importance of the teachers' own creative engagement and share a wealth of research-informed ideas to enrich pedagogy and practice.

Titles in the series:

For a full list of titles in this series, please visit www.routledge.com

APPLYING CROSS-CURRICULAR APPROACHES CREATIVELY

Jonathan Barnes

LONDON AND NEW YORK

First published 2018
by Routledge
2 Park Square, Milton Park, Abingdon, Oxon OX14 4RN

and by Routledge
711 Third Avenue, New York, NY 10017

Routledge is an imprint of the Taylor & Francis Group, an informa business

British Library Cataloguing-in-Publication Data
A catalogue record for this book is available from the British Library

Library of Congress Cataloging-in-Publication Data
A catalog record for this book has been requested

ISBN: 978-1-138-20092-0 (hbk)
ISBN: 978-1-138-20095-1 (pbk)
ISBN: 978-1-315-51361-4 (ebk)

Typeset in Times New Roman and Helvetica Neue
by Apex CoVantage, LLC

CONTENTS

SERIES EDITOR'S FOREWORD

Teresa Cremin

Over recent decades, teachers working in accountability cultures across the globe have been required to focus on raising standards, setting targets and 'delivering' prescribed curricula and pedagogy. In this period, the language of schooling, as Mottram and Hall (2009: 109) assert, has predominantly focused upon 'oversimplified, easily measurable notions of attainment'. They argue that this has had a standardising effect, prompting children and their development to be discussed 'according to levels and descriptors' rather than as children – as unique individuals and unique learners.

Practitioners, positioned as passive recipients of the prescribed agenda, appear to have had their hands tied, their voices quietened and their professional autonomy both threatened and constrained. At times, the relentless quest for higher standards has obscured the personal and affective dimensions of teaching and learning, fostering a mindset characterised more by compliance and conformity than curiosity and creativity.

However, creativity too has been in the ascendant in recent decades; in many countries efforts have been made to re-ignite creativity in education, since it is seen to be essential to economic and cultural development. In England, this impetus for creativity can be traced back to the National Advisory Committee on Creative and Cultural Education (NACCCE, 1999), which recommended a core role for creativity in teaching and learning. Primary schools in England were encouraged to explore ways to offer more innovative and creative curricula (DfES, 2003) and new national curricula in Scotland and Wales also foregrounded children's critical and creative thinking. Additionally, initiatives such as Creative Partnerships, an English government-funded initiative to nurture children's creativity, inspired some teachers to reconstruct their pedagogy (Galton, 2010, 2015). Many other schools and teachers, encouraged by these initiatives, and determined to offer creative and engaging school experiences, have exercised the 'power to innovate' (Lance, 2006). Many have proactively sought ways to shape the curriculum responsively, appropriating national policies in their own contexts and showing professional commitment and imagination, despite, or perhaps because of, the persistent performative agenda (e.g. Craft et al., 2014; Cremin et al., 2015; Neelands, 2009, Jeffrey and Woods, 2009).

Schools continue to be exhorted to be more innovative in curriculum construction and national curricula afford opportunities for all teachers to seize the space, exert their professionalism and shape their own curricula in collaboration with the young people with whom they are working. Yet for primary educators, tensions persist, not only because the dual policies of performativity and creativity appear contradictory, but also perhaps because teachers' own confidence as creative educators, indeed as creative individuals, has been radically reduced by the constant barrage of change and challenge. As Csikszentmihalyi (2011) notes, teachers lack a theoretically underpinned framework for creativity that can be developed in practice; they need support to develop as artistically engaged, research-informed curriculum co-developers. Eisner (2003) asserts that teaching is an art form, an act of improvisation (Sawyer, 2011), and that teachers benefit from viewing themselves as versatile artists in the classroom, drawing on their personal passions and creativity as they teach creatively.

As Joubert also observes:

Creative teaching is an art. One cannot teach teachers didactically how to be creative; there is no fail-safe recipe or routine. Some strategies may help to promote creative thinking, but teachers need to develop a full repertoire of skills which they can adapt to different situations.

(Joubert, 2001: 21)

However, creative teaching is only part of the picture, since teaching for creativity also needs to be acknowledged and their mutual dependency recognised. The former focuses more on teachers using imaginative approaches in the classroom (and beyond) in order to make learning more interesting and effective, the latter, more on the development of children's creativity (NACCCE, 1999). Both rely upon an understanding of the notion of creativity and demand that professionals confront the myths and mantras which surround the word. These include the commonly held misconceptions that creativity is the preserve of the arts or arts education, and that it is confined to particularly gifted individuals.

Creativity, an elusive concept, has been multiply defined by educationalists, psychologists and neurologists, as well as by policy makers in different countries and reserachers in different cultural contexts (Glăveanu et al., 2015). Debates resound about its individual and/or collaborative nature, the degree to which it is generic and/or domain specific, and the differences between the 'Big C' creativity of genius and the 'little c' creativity of the everyday. Notwithstanding these issues, most scholars in the field believe it involves the capacity to generate, reason and critically evaluate novel ideas and/or imaginary scenarios. As such, it encompasses thinking through and solving problems, making connections, inventing and reinventing, and flexing one's imaginative muscles in all aspects of learning and life.

In the primary classroom, creative teaching and learning have been associated with innovation, originality, ownership and control (Woods and Jeffrey, 1996; Jeffrey, 2006), and creative teachers have been seen in their planning and teaching, and in the ethos which they create, to afford high value to curiosity and risk taking, to ownership, autonomy and making connections (Craft et al., 2014; Cremin et al., 2009;

Cremin, 2015). Such teachers often work in partnership with others: with children, other teachers and experts from beyond the school gates (Cochrane and Cockett, 2007; Davies et al., 2012; Thomson et al., 2012). These partnerships offer new possibilities, with teachers acquiring some of the repertoire of pedagogic practices – the 'signature pedagogies' that artists use (Thomson and Hall, 2015).

Additionally, in research exploring possibility thinking, which Craft (2000) argues drives creativity in education, an intriguing interplay between teachers and children has been observed. In this body of work, children and teachers have been involved in immersing themselves in playful contexts, posing questions, being imaginative, showing self-determination, taking risks and innovating – together (Burnard et al., 2006; Cremin et al., 2006;Chappell et al., 2008; Craft et al., 2012; Cremin et al., 2013). As McWilliam (2008) argues, teachers can choose not to position themselves as the all-knowing 'sage on the stage', or the facilitator- like 'guide on the side'. They can choose, as creative practitioners do, to take up a role of the 'meddler in the middle', co-creating curricula in innovative and responsive ways that harness their own creativity and foster that of the children. A new pedagogy of possibility beckons.

This series *Learning to Teach in the Primary School*, which accompanies and complements the edited textbook *Learning to Teach in the Primary School* (Cremin and Burnett, 2018, fourth edition), seeks to support teachers in developing as creative practitioners, assisting them in exploring the synergies between and potential for teaching creatively and teaching for creativity. The series does not merely offer practical strategies for use in the classroom, though these abound, but more importantly seeks to widen teachers' and student teachers' knowledge and understanding of the principles underpinning creative approaches, principles based on research. It seeks to mediate the wealth of research evidence and make accessible and engaging the diverse theoretical perspectives and scholarly arguments available, demonstrating their practical relevance and value to the profession. Those who aspire to develop further as creative and curious educators will find much of value to support their own professional learning journeys and markedly enrich their pedagogy and practice right across the curriculum.

ABOUT THE SERIES EDITOR

Teresa Cremin is a Professor of Education (Literacy) at the Open University and a Fellow of the Royal Society of the Arts, the Academy of Social Sciences, and the English Association. She is also a Trustee of the UK Literacy Association, co-editor of the journal *Thinking Skills and Creativity*, and co-convenor of the British Educational Research Association's Special Interest Group on Creativity. Teresa has been a Board member of BookTrust and the Poetry Archive, a Director of the Cambridge Primary Review Trust, and President of UKLA and UKRA.

Her work involves research, publication and consultancy in literacy and creativity. Many of Teresa's current projects seek to explore the nature and characteristics of creative pedagogies, including for example those fostering reading for pleasure, creative writing, immersive theatre, children's storytelling and story acting. Teresa is also passionate about (and still researching) teachers' own creative development and their identity positioning in the classroom as readers, writers, and artistically engaged educators and humans.

Teresa has written and edited nearly 30 books. Forthcoming and current volumes include: *Experiencing Reading for Pleasure in the Digital Age* (Sage, 2018); *Writer Identity and the Teaching and Learning of Writing; Storytelling in Early Childhood: Enriching Language, Literacy and Culture*, (Routledge, 2017, edited collections); *Teaching English Creatively* (Routledge, 2015); *Researching Literacy Lives*: *Building home school communities* (Routledge, 2015); *Building Communities of Engaged Readers: Reading for Pleasure* (Routledge, 2014), and *Writing Voices: Creating Communities of Writers* (Routledge, 2012).

REFERENCES

Burnard, P., Craft, A. and Cremin, T. (2006) Possibility thinking. *International Journal of Early Years Education*, Vol. 14, No. 3, pp. 243–262.

Chappell, K., Craft, A., Burnard, P. and Cremin, T. (2008) Question-posing and question-responding: The heart of possibility thinking in the early years. *Early Years*, Vol. 283, pp. 267–286.

Cochrane, P. and Cockett, M. (2007) *Building a Creative School: A Dynamic Approach to School Improvement*. Stoke on Trent: Trentham Books.

Craft, A. (2000) *Creativity Across the Primary Curriculum*. London: Routledge.

Craft, A., Cremin, T., Burnard, P., Dragovic, T. and Chappell, K. (2012) Possibility thinking: Culminative studies of an evidence-based concept driving creativity? *Education 3–13: International Journal of Primary, Elementary and Early*, Vol. 41, No. 5, pp. 538–556.

Craft, A., Cremin, T., Hay, P. and Clack, J. (2014) Creative primary schools: Developing and maintaining pedagogy for creativity. *Ethnography and Education*, Vol. 9, No. 1, pp. 16–34.

Cremin, T. (2015) Creative teachers and creative teaching and, in A. Wilson (ed.) *Creativity in Primary Education*. London: SAGE Publications, pp. 33–44.

Cremin, T., Barnes, J. and Scoffham, S. (2009) *Creative Teaching for Tomorrow: Fostering a Creative State of Mind*. Deal: Future Creative.

Cremin, T., Burnard, P. and Craft, A. (2006) Pedagogy and possibility thinking in the early years. *International Journal of Thinking Skills and Creativity*, Vol. 1, No. 2, pp. 108–119.

Cremin, T. and Burnett, C. (eds.) (2018) *Learning to Teach in the Primary School* (4th ed.). London: Routledge.

Cremin, T., Chappell, K. and Craft, A. (2013) Reciprocity between narrative, questioning and imagination in the early and primary years: Examining the role of narrative in possibility thinking. *Thinking Skills and Creativity*, Vol. 9, pp. 136–151.

Cremin, T., Glauert, E., Craft, A., Compton, A. and Stylianidou, F. (2015) Creative little scientists: Exploring pedagogical synergies between inquiry-based and creative approaches in early years science. *Education 3–13, International Journal of Primary, Elementary and Early Years Education*, Special issue on creative pedagogies, Vol. 43, No. 4, pp. 404–419.

Csikszentmihalyi, M. (2011) A systems perspective on creativity and its implications for measurement, in R. Schenkel and O. Quintin (eds.) *Measuring Creativity*. Brussels: The European Commission, pp. 407–414.

Davies, D., Jindal-Snape, D., Collier, C., Digby, R., Hay, P. and Howe, A. (2012) Creative environments for learning in schools. *Thinking Skills and Creativity*. http://dx.doi.org/10.1016/j.tsc.2012.07.004.

Department for Education and Skills (DfES) (2003) *Excellence and Enjoyment: A Strategy for Primary Schools*. Nottingham: DfES.

Eisner, E. (2003) Artistry in education. *Scandinavian Journal of Educational Research*, Vol. 47, No. 3, pp. 373–384.

Galton, M. (2010) Going with the flow or back to normal? The impact of creative practitioners in schools and classrooms. *Research Papers in Education*, Vol. 25, No. 4, pp. 355–375.

Galton, M. (2015) 'It's a real journey – a life changing experience': A comparison case study of creative partnership and other primary schools. *Education 3–13:International Journal of Primary, Elementary and Early Years Education*, Vol. 43, No. 4, pp. 433–444.

Glăveanu, V., Sierra, Z. and Tanggaard, L. (2015) Widening our understanding of creative pedagogy: A North – South dialogue. *Education 3–13. International Journal of Primary, Elementary and Early Years Education*, Special issue on creative pedagogies, Vol. 43, No. 4, pp. 360–370.

Jeffrey, B. (ed.) (2006) *Creative Learning Practices: European Experiences*. London: Tufnell Press.

Jeffrey, B. and Woods, P. (2009) *Creative Learning in the Primary School*. London: Routledge.

Joubert, M. M. (2001) The art of creative teaching: NACCCE and beyond, in A. Craft, B. Jeffrey and M. Liebling (eds.) *Creativity in Education*. London: Continuum.

Lance, A. (2006) Power to innovate? A study of how primary practitioners are negotiating the modernisation agenda. *Ethnography and Education*, Vol. 1, No. 3, pp. 333–344.

McWilliam, E. (2008) Unlearning how to teach *Innovations in Education and Teaching International* Vol 45, No.3, pp. 263-269.

Mottram, M. and Hall, C. (2009) Diversions and diversity: Does the personalisation agenda offer real opportunities for taking children's home literacies seriously? *English in Education*, Vol. 43, No. 2, pp. 98–112.

National Advisory Committee on Creative and Cultural Education (NACCCE) (1999) *All Our Futures: Creativity, Culture and Education*. London: Department for Education and Employment.

Neelands, J. (2009) Acting together: Ensemble as a democratic process in art and life. *Research in Drama Education*, Vol. 14, No. 2, pp. 173–189.

Sawyer, K. (ed.) (2011) *Structure and Improvisation in Creative Teaching*. New York: Cambridge University Press.

Thomson, P. and Hall, C. (2015) 'Everyone can imagine their own Gellert': The democratic artist and 'inclusion' in primary and nursery classrooms. *Education 3–13. International Journal of Primary, Elementary and Early Years Education*, Special issue on creative pedagogies, Vol. 43, No. 4, pp. 420–432.

Thomson, P., Hall, C., Jones, K. and Sefton-Green, J. (2012) *The Signature Pedagogies Project: Final Report*. London: Creativity, Culture and Education, available at: www.creativetallis.com/uploads/2/2/8/7/2287089/signature_pedagogies_report_final_version_11.3.12.pdf (accessed 1.6.12).

Woods, P. and Jeffrey, B. (1996) *Teachable Moments: The Art of Creative Teaching in Primary Schools*. Buckingham: Open University Press.

ACKNOWLEDGEMENTS

In the spirit of this book, I must first thank my probably long-dead primary school teachers: Mrs Bettice, Mr Rochelle, Mr Darnell, Mr Clements and Mr Maynard. Two secondary school educators, Edmund Semmonds in music and Charles Dixon in art, worked to maintain the environment of confident enthusiasm and curiosity my parents and primary teachers had established. All these teachers in some way introduced me to the values of beauty, joy, participation and meaningful communication and helped me find my passions.

Those introductions prepared me to meet the love of my life Cherry, whose beauty, joyful engagement with life and ease with creativity and communication allowed me to flourish. She has tolerated – even encouraged – months of me being glued to a computer as I have constructed this product of a fulfilled life in education. She also led, and leads, me towards a global perspective on a values-creating and truly connected curriculum. With Cherry I have lived and worked in Kenya, Malaysia, Rwanda and India and for shorter periods Tanzania, Japan, Indonesia, France and Germany. The joy of sharing life in those places and confirming common humanity and shared values has sustained both of us through the most difficult times. She is my constant and ever-refreshing example of how to be.

I must also thank the co-pedagogs who have inspired me in my last 15 years as a teacher and educator. Specifically I thank: Adam Annand, Alex Ntung, Andrea Ramos, Angeline Conaghan, Beatrice Bamurange, Catherine Carden, Dan File, Danella Essart, Danny Rikh, David Wheway, Glen Sharp, Graham Birrell, Grenville and Anne Hancox, Hope Azeda, Ian Shirley, Ibrahim Ssemambo, Ken and Matt Miles, Krishna Moorthy, Linden West, Mike Fairclough, Robert McCrea, Rosemary Walters, Sam Bailey, Stephen Clift, Stephen Scoffham, Teresa Cremin, Tony Booth, Trish Vella-Burrows, Vanessa Young and Viv Wilson – all of them and many more have encouraged me in different ways, but chiefly they have shown me what compassion and kindness is.

Our children – Jacob with his passion for music, words, languages, friendship and awesome spaces; Esther's strength in artistic invention, poetry, song, colour and creativity itself; Naomi's love and dedication to family, friends, food and emotional intelligence; and Ben's great ability to share the joys of sport and cooking with those that need them most – have constantly affirmed the emotionally sustaining importance of connecting and creative experience. Their lives, and example, their patience with me and their un-conditional love has sustained both Cherry and me through the painful years that coincided with the writing of this book. Last, I thank our grandchildren – Isaac, Theo, Tess, Charlie, Bella and Daisy – who have shown again and again how discovering their own ways of being creative unlocks positivity in them, too: some of their pictures decorate the front cover.

INTRODUCTION

Teaching and learning are highly personal activities. No two teachers or learners are alike. This ultra-diversity within and between us is a prime source of human creativity and the basis of our hope for the future. The curricula and pedagogies adopted by individual teachers and schools can either encourage or impede that hope and creativity. A central argument of this book is that teachers should be much more personally involved in decisions about the style of teaching and substance of curriculum in schools.

I argue that autobiographical reflection and discussion can and should be part of the daily practice and continuing development of teachers. Reflecting on, examining, refining and sharing our life's narrative can help us make wiser choices and sustain us through the inevitable challenges of life in and out of education.

This book is written for all kinds of teachers. It is meant to support and challenge parents, students of childhood studies, education or teaching, established teachers, head teachers, managers, governors and all those interested in the experience and learning of 4–11-year-olds. Its case for emotionally relevant, extended cross-curricular approaches and frequent opportunities for creative practice is formulated to enhance the experience of children *and their teachers* in primary academies and schools across the UK.

CROSS-CURRICULAR APPROACHES

An obvious starting point in considering cross-curricular approaches in schools is to ask, "*What is the problem with subject-based learning?*" For some children there *is* no problem; pure and separated subject teaching is the right way forward for them. For many more, it is clear that traditional methods are not working and the frequently observed 'long tail of under-achievement' remains. Despite nearly 30 years' attention to standards and targets, the percentages of those not achieving expected results in the 'core subjects' (English, maths) remains similar. High level thinking and learning in what were called the 'foundation' subjects (academic subjects that are not mathematics, English and sometimes science), becomes less common, less valued (Scoffham and Barnes, 2017). Until 2012, the Office for Standards in Education, Children's

Services and Skills (Ofsted) made detailed reports on the foundation subjects. These reports often catalogued low or falling standards but since 2012 there have been no primary separate subject reports on the foundation subjects. The apparent decline in deep exposure to the foundation subjects is made worse by the significant reduction of Initial Teacher Education (ITE) and local authority in-service training time devoted to history, geography, religious education (RE), art and design, design/technology, music and physical education (PE). So in many schools, rigorous separate subject teaching outside the core subjects appears in a state of decline.

Underachievement in the foundation subjects may arise from a combination of the heavy demands of the core subjects and poor motivation, weakened confidence, undemanding targets and poorly developed teacher knowledge in the foundation subjects. When the core subjects dominate curriculum time, children with the potential to shine in 'lower status' subjects may quickly become disaffected and de-motivated. Curriculum breadth and balance was promised in the various iterations of the English National Curriculum and equal time allocations for all subjects were recommended by the Cambridge Primary Review (Alexander, 2010), but would a fairer and deeper exposure to *all* subjects transform school experience for many children? Philosophy of education arguments like this can and should help school communities consider the right course of action to raise achievement and motivation.

Every school will come to different conclusions on its aims and general direction. I hope that this book will engender meaningful debates about the curriculum, ethical, moral, social, spiritual and physical environments and methods of teaching in many schools and seminar groups. I also know that there can and should be no 'one-size-fits-all' curriculum answer for the diverse communities served by schools. This book therefore offers a wide range of solutions to the overarching question of how we can enrich the education experience of *all* children. It will ask the reader to consider the role of creativity and a connecting curriculum in answering that question.

Defining cross-curricular teaching and learning

Cross-curricular links occur all the time in life outside school. Virtually every problem we face requires the perspectives of a number of subject-disciplines to solve it. Most objects that surround us are the product of multi-disciplinary teams. Questions, themes, experiences and the environments around us can be understood, interpreted, examined or shared using the language, skills and knowledge of any of the established curriculum subjects. *Cross-curricular teaching and learning relies on making links between two or more traditional curriculum subjects in response to an authentic experience, problem, theme or question so that new learning occurs in each subject.*

I have identified eight different kinds of cross-curricular learning each with a different purpose and character (Barnes, 2015):

- Tokenistic
- Hierarchical
- Single transferrable subject-discipline
- Thematic
- Inter-disciplinary

- ■ Multi-disciplinary
- ■ Opportunistic
- ■ Double focus

Cross-curricular learning is often used as a motivator, or to offer more depth to a theme than a single subject could do. Although primary teachers are trained across the curriculum, primary school curricula are rarely truly integrated – most make links between separate subjects for specific purposes and short time periods. This book will deepen understanding about different types of cross-curricular learning. It will recommend extended use and more experimentation with curriculum integration as a means of making school education meaningful to and successful for more children.

At no point will this book suggest that the curriculum should be exclusively cross-curricular. Cross-curricular learning and separate subject learning are not opposites. Pure subject teaching is necessary to provide the vocabulary, knowledge and skills that can be put to work in solving problems. Good cross-curricular learning often requires that the child (*and their teacher*) possesses specific knowledge and skills in the subject-disciplines that will be linked. Cross-curricular contexts can also be where those separate subject skills and knowledge are learned. Good subject knowledge and skills are often best tested and expressed when they are applied to real-world problems. Secure separate subject learning provides the raw materials with which learning is put to use in the real world.

CREATIVE APPROACHES

Creativity implies originality, imagination, some kind of outcome and a judgement of relative value or usefulness. It involves often unexpected connection making. Creativity can be taught. It can be measured. It is the birthright of every child and teacher. In a school setting generating creative responses usually requires a positive atmosphere of security, confidence and an openness to what Anna Craft (2005) called 'possibility thinking'. Providing the optimum conditions for creativity in teaching, the curriculum and in the daily experience of children needs careful consideration, and will be a theme that runs throughout the chapters. The quality of the learning environment is the responsibility of the teacher; therefore, great attention will be given to thinking about your own personal experience and understanding of creativity and how cross-curricular approaches can help develop it.

In introducing the concept of a 'connecting curriculum', this book offers original, imaginative and hopefully valuable approaches to the work of teaching that will help you build meaningful links between subjects, individuals, experiences and the objects that surround us. A connecting curriculum ultimately aims to make life for teachers and children richer, fuller and happier by establishing affirmative and sustaining connections between what happens in school and what is happening in the rest of life.

THE STRUCTURE OF EACH CHAPTER

One of the original features of this book is that it uses autobiography – the reader's and the author's – as the starting point for thinking about curriculum and creativity.

A repeated pattern of autobiography, biographical fragments, research, theory, case studies and practical advice will connect the chapters and illustrate the importance of connectivity itself.

a) Autobiography

Each chapter will begin with a few autobiographical paragraphs. A range of snapshots from my 45 years in education will illustrate large and small points in the subsequent text. Experience in teaching all age ranges on four continents has led me to believe there may be some universals about effective education. I have loved every one of my years in education, and in the light of negative reports on the recruitment and retention of teachers, I became interested in researching how teachers might sustain a similarly positive life in education.

The autobiographical paragraphs lead to questions about your biography. Such reflections are intended to prompt you to call up significant stories from your own life. Asking yourself for the sources of the fundamental values that drive you, lead your decisions and provide your aims in life may be an unfamiliar question. I have found, however, that when teachers are asked to consider significant and formative memories and relate autobiographical stories, this can unlock motivation, energy, focus and commitment in ways that generalised exhortation cannot.

b) Readers' biographical fragments

Space in the text has been provided throughout to contain your written and reflective key personal stories. Questions and provocations will, I hope, lead to the rediscovery of important (often early) life events that have helped shape character and values. Time to reflect on questions of meaning are, I suggest, central to effective and creative teaching and deep learning. Many teachers are denied the opportunity to find meaning in their work-life because of outside pressures, but through this book I want to encourage teachers to discover resilience and fulfilment in their profession. I believe cross-curricular pedagogies can do this, but not alone. First a teacher should strive to discover the unique contributions they bring to education. They should also be given multiple opportunities to develop more knowledge and experience in the things they love. This book will therefore provide guided opportunities to think or wonder and perhaps revisit the values, skills and passions that led you towards teaching in the first place. The teacher who is supported to sustain, even build their idealism will, I believe, more easily discover the energy and capacity to be a knowledgeable, dynamic, fulfilled practitioner.

c) Research and theory

Teachers are called to be habitual researchers. In each chapter, the themed theoretical and research positions of others will be outlined so that you can consider pertinent research questions. Cross-curricular and creative approaches are increasingly the subject of practitioner research. Teachers and other education decision-makers should be aware of the research that informs choices on subjects, themes, methods, groupings, contexts, environments, interactions and evaluations. They should also have seriously considered the educational theory behind pedagogical and curricular decisions thrust on them and the stated aims of their school. The first three chapters mainly concern theory and aspects of education history, and the remaining chapters offer themed and practical suggestions for applying cross-curricular and creative approaches in the school.

d) Philosophical considerations

The Philosophy of Education has been eradicated from most ITE courses in the UK. Yet questions on the nature and purpose of education remain. What schooling should be like, what should be taught, who should be taught and why we should value education are time-honoured, deeply philosophical questions. This book is not the place for a general introduction to educational philosophy but in exposing and examining the sources of my own beliefs about cross-curricular and creative approaches I hope to stimulate the reader to think about their responses. Many chapters will contain a section where the (sometimes opposing) views of past and present thinkers and practitioners are summarised and examined.

e) Case studies

Multiple case studies will illustrate the chapter themes. Successful and powerful cross-curricular activity occurs across the country and at all ages. The case studies show a way forward, suggesting ways in which the novice teacher can develop a personal style and response. Case studies are essential because they offer real illustrations translatable by you to a wide range of the real-world, real-classroom contexts. They are taken from a range of different types of school: nurseries, children's centres, academies and independent schools, as well as local authority primary schools.

f) Practical exercises

Chapters 4–10 contain many practical suggestions. Using the summaries of guidance, thought-provoking questions and exercises for seminars, staff development or ITE modules, teachers can consider how ideas from this book can be put in practice in *their* setting. Professional development, parent discussion and seminar groups can be enlivened through structured analysis after trying out some of the cross-curricular and creative ideas and approaches highlighted in this book. The emotionally relevant, sensory, practical, motivating outcomes of effective cross-curricular and creative teaching and learning will be evidenced when you look at the engaged faces, relaxed postures and good relationships that occur when children are truly involved. My life in education has convinced me that such effective and engrossing teaching starts with sharing and building upon the narratives and lives of every participant.

This book arises from a deep belief that school is where we learn to live peacefully and productively with our neighbours. Schools should positively reflect the diversity within ourselves and in our societies, our complex inter-relationships, technologies and the multiple connections we depend on. Schools are the only places in a position to model for all young people the human values of respect, justice, tenacity, humility, caring, generosity, sharing trust and the welcome of strangers. The curriculum can be the vehicle through which we show what generosity looks like in historical, sporting or geographical contexts. It can give children experience of demonstrating care through RE, drama and song and can inspire genuinely felt humility, respect or awe in the way it teaches science, art or technology. Mathematics, English and languages can introduce children to beauty and diversity as well as logic and rubrics.

Children and teachers spend many of their waking hours living and perhaps learning and applying such values in school. Creative and cross-curricular attention to these values will help those in education make personal and positive sense of their world and hopefully start changing it for the better.

If you want to contribute to positive change in the intellectual, social, psychological, material, moral and spiritual lives of children in school, I suggest you start by getting to know yourself better.

REFERENCES

Alexander, R. (2010) (Ed.) *Children, their world, their education: Final report of the Cambridge Primary Review*. Abingdon: Routledge.

Barnes, J. (2015) *Cross-curricular learning 3–14,* London: Sage.

Craft, A. (2005) *Creativity in schools: Tensions and dilemmas*. Abingdon: Routledge.

Scoffham, S. and Barnes, J. (2017) The humanities in English primary schools: struggling to survive. *Education 3-13,* Vol.35, pp. 298–308.

CONNECTING AUTOBIOGRAPHY AND CREATIVITY

SUMMARY

This chapter expands on the claim that autobiography offers a valuable tool for teachers. A summary of memories of my own primary schooling is followed by an invitation for you to think about your own as the starting point of creatively connecting personal and professional life. I will introduce the idea of using brief autobiographical vignettes called 'Key Stories' to help identify the driving forces that can sustain a fulfilling life in education. Case studies from the lives of other teachers will introduce the idea that a teacher's own story can positively influence the emerging biographies of children.

MY STORY

Introducing you to six years in my own primary education might help illustrate the links between autobiography and the pedagogical and curricular decisions we make as teachers.

Between 7 and 11 years I was taught by five exceptional teachers. Four were men, witty, gentle, urbane and rapidly retrained after service in World War II. Each teacher transported me via their enthusiasms to worlds undreamed of within my London working class family. My first teacher, Mrs Bettice, was warm and caring and shared slides of her travels throughout Europe, opening for me a lifetime's fascination with maps, iconic buildings and landscapes. At 7, I learned about the Auvergne, the ruins and fountains of Rome, palaces and canals in Venice, Renaissance arts in Florence. She sent me around all the junior classes to show my freehand map of the world. At 8 and 9, Mr Darnell retold Greek myths that inspired clay models of the characters and a papier maché Greek boat. The following year, Mr Rochelle dramatically told modern stories and taught us poems in his warm Welsh accent. He helped us construct a working model of a Welsh coal mine, with tunnels, shafts, lifts, winding gear and train tracks. He linked us via class loads of letters to the captain of the 'Sugar Transporter' – a merchant ship sailing between the West Indies and London. The captain responded to each child on airmail paper. One day a parcel of coconuts, conch shells, Jamaican coins, stamps, a jam jar of

Sargasso seaweed and black and white postcards of his ship arrived at our school after we visited the Royal Docks to meet him.

Mr Maynard taught us art and music – only those two subjects. In his spare time, he wrote operettas – a mix of Gilbert and Sullivan and Leonard Bernstein. He enthusiastically persuaded us to take part in ambitiously staged versions of them. Mr Maynard introduced us to Benjamin Britten's music through singing his song arrangements – I still remember them word for word. As a class we sang Bernstein's songs and choruses from 'West Side Story' well before it was a film. My last class teacher, Mr Clements, showed me how to see and paint all the different greens in a tree. He pinned my painting of a waterfall at the front of the school hall near the portrait of a dead but very popular teacher, Mr Vivien. Mr Clements (we never knew Christian names) also led the 'school journey' to an ex-army camp deep in the Sussex landscape where in my red and navy school cap and tie, I encountered Downland, escarpments, forests, rivers, water voles, pygmy shrews, a swimming grass snake and how to identify a dozen birds from their calls. Fifty-five years later I recall the faces, hairstyles, stance, clothes and attitudes of each of these teachers with gratitude.

I was the first in my family to get a place in grammar school. The affirmation I felt was immense. Mr Maynard knew I sang in a church choir and encouraged me to audition for the school choir. I 'got in' and felt proud of myself. At 11, under the direction of Mr Semmonds (who chain-smoked through every music lesson even as he played intense Chopin piano sonatas), I sang my heart out in choral evensongs each week in the local teacher training college chapel. The next summer we sang for two weeks in place of the regular choristers of St Paul's Cathedral – the building itself affirmed me.

St Paul's also provided an experience that concretised my love of history, music, art and religion. One summer afternoon at 3:10, waiting for the daily procession into the choir stalls, I found myself transported, transformed by a kind of sensory overload. For a few moments the combination of loud organ music, baroque paintings, cavernous, echoing architecture, golden mosaics, bright stained glass windows and meaningful ceremony overwhelmed me. The effect on me was so powerful that I can readily conjure up the warmth of the bright sun on my shoulder through the yellow stained glass window to my right; still sense the cold shiny marble feet of the sculpture of John Donne standing on his funeral urn above me; still see/feel/hear the ringing dome and black and white flagstones vibrating to the thunderous 32-foot reeds of the organ as it played Olivier Messiaen's Dieu parmi nous – 'God amongst us'. I understood what, dieu parmi nous meant – I felt it for just a few seconds.

Such moments are unpredictable. In the cathedral at the same time were 25 other 12-year-olds – as far as I know, none shared my transformational experience. The primary teachers that prepared me for this experience were just doing their daily job. My age-mates remember different things from the same setting. None have spent the rest of their lives championing cross-curricular approaches to learning as I have. But I know my lifetime's absorption in the multiple connections between art, music, history, place, spirituality, poetry, story and drama stems from the chance collision of people, places, things, perceptions and emotions on that day in St Paul's.

The story sounds too rosy, and of course is. The narrative I honed for 55 years censors my fear of the head teacher, glosses over a harsh caning he gave for play-fighting in the corridor and my thrashing with a slipper for some other forgotten misdemeanour. Strangely, I have forgotten what his face was like. It ignores the threatening and dull teachers of my grammar school and the crises of the teenage years. The affirmative narrative established in my primary years massively outweighs those negative experiences; it sustained and continues to sustain me. The events, places, objects and people I describe might seem pre-ordained to supply the prerequisites of resilience to any child. I am acutely aware, however, that the smallest change in the story would have sent my life in a different direction. The discoveries, achievements, unexpected affirmations, chance encounters, unpredicted joys and positive accidents of my early life helped me flourish. Others sharing the same place, people and time – I think almost daily of my friend John who killed himself – found no such fulfilment.

Writing down parts of a very ordinary life like that above, helped me identify the themes and approaches examined throughout this book. I found common threads in my narrative that have coloured my beliefs across curriculum and life. These recurring themes included:

- The unplanned and multiple sources of learning
- An expectation and exploitation of the unexpected
- The strong influence of social, spiritual, physical, emotional and intellectual environments
- The value of bringing together different subjects, minds and methodologies
- The importance of breadth and balance in the school experience
- An interest in connections across the curriculum and into everyday life
- A love of creativity
- An awareness of the role of the existential or spiritual in learning

My interest in establishing positive social, spiritual, physical, emotional and intellectual environments in schools arose directly from the unique environment I occupied between 1958 and 1963. The same years generated my enduring passion for creativity and connectivity.

Your experience is important and equally deserving of analysis.

YOUR STORY

You have another story. You probably remember teachers who powerfully influenced you. Some 'teachers' will have been relatives, carers, teaching assistants, mentors or never-met heroes or heroines in stories. Some may have been qualified. School influences can also be wholly negative, (about 25% of the prospective teachers I interview were led towards teaching because they wanted to repair the damage inflicted by teachers). Most, however, choose teaching because of the positive influence of a teacher. Use Table 1.1 to relate a fragment of your education story. Write a little about those who inspired or encouraged you, or who awoke interests you retain today. If you were not inspired or were even harmed by a teacher, your narrative will be different but no less valuable. Ask yourself what was missing in your school that would have generated motivation, inspiration, affirmation and security. Why did you still choose teaching?

If appropriate, share your thoughts and memories and discuss commonalities and differences with colleagues. You may not want to share details in a public context and might need to talk with someone, professional or otherwise, privately – no personal experience is unimportant. Think about the often unintentional impact you have or will have on your own students. As honestly as you can, try to answer some of the questions.

Table 1.1 Questions to frame your educational story

What were the names of teachers who were special to you?
What interests did this teacher/these teachers spark, encourage, develop, affirm in you?
About what age were you?
What specific school experiences do you remember with pleasure?
Were you taken to any memorable places? Where? What did you do there?
What positive learning experiences happened outside the classroom?
What curriculum subjects were special to you?
Were there teachers who discouraged or impaired your learning?
What approaches did they take that disheartened you?
What aspects of your schooling do you want to avoid as a teacher yourself?
What are the most successful teaching approaches for you?
Were you inspired by someone who was not a teacher? Who? What inspired you?
What lessons generated the most engagement for you?
Why do you think this was?
On reflection, do you find you were not inspired in any particular direction?
Can you say why this might be?

After answering some of these questions, consider and perhaps talk about the passions and interests that would be right to share with children.

Table 1.2 A personal summary of the sources of your interests in education

My interests and passions	The possible source(s) of my interests and passions

---

USING AUTOBIOGRAPHY TO MAKE
US BETTER TEACHERS

The time-honoured advice 'Know thyself' is appropriate in many contexts. For teachers, this maxim can help identify a unique profile of strengths, weaknesses, passions, aversions, metaphors, illustrations, knowledge about and experience of. Autobiography – the written stories from your life – is one way towards knowing yourself. Your story is a resource to which you have deep and privileged access.

Auto-ethnography uses the systematic study of aspects of your life story as the basis of research. Auto-ethnographic approaches are commonly used in arts research, but increasingly address questions relating to careers in public serving professions. Critics of auto-ethnography, like Delamont, characterise it as the "essentially lazy – literally lazy and intellectually lazy, ... selfish and ultimately fatuous study [of] ... uninteresting and inconsequential lives" (2007: 2). I argue, however, that all lives are consequential and interesting, and that systematic and self-critical, self-study can achieve great depth, relevance and special usefulness in professions aimed at supporting others. Auto-ethnography aims to generate personal change and promote positive action by helping us identify potential sources of resilience and fulfilment.

Auto-ethnography uncovered the sources of hope and other inclusive values for me. It helped me recognise the importance of these values in maintaining optimism in the face of situations that may have led towards despair. Autobiographical approaches can help you reaffirm and sustain your fundamental values against the pressures to compromise, dilute or dismiss them.

Autobiography has important social functions too. Sharing autobiographical fragments holds communities together. A mature understanding of self is key to what Goleman (1996) called the 'emotionally intelligent' individual essential to healthy communities. Yet in a society which prizes individuality, little time in education or education research is given to understanding how identity is constructed and sustained, or how it contributes to the common good (Hicks, 2006; Layard and Dunn, 2009). If self-understanding helps us develop a fuller understanding of others, then for teachers it should heighten sensitivity to the emerging selves of children and the value of a supportive social and cultural environment (Bruner, 1990).

Autobiography attempts to validate and *justify* the way that life has gone for us (Bruner, 2004). This observation reminds us of one of the dangers of auto-ethnography, however: the tendency to weave events into a glossy, romanticised story. We must strive for honesty, and perhaps sharing parts of our autobiography can help us do this. Bruner also asserts that, "we become the autobiographical narratives by which we 'tell about' our lives" (Bruner, 2004: 694). If a teacher's dominant narrative is one of care for children and their learning, then it is incumbent on schools to help them build their capacity to enrich that narrative.

Culture impacts strongly on autobiography. Culture is the shared language, behaviour and beliefs of the groups to which we 'belong'; it influences who we are. Cultures continually limit and steer our choices, and the narratives we create inevitably draw on those of others. Therefore, in telling our personal story we should always be aware of the intersecting stories of others. In examining my own life, I soon recognised how tiny interventions from others sent it in unpredictable directions. By examining the complex and delicate fusion of physical, social, emotional and psychological influences of life, I discovered that values easily traceable to my childhood formed one of life's few constants.

IDENTIFYING THE VALUES THAT SUSTAIN YOU

Values can sustain us. They may be defined as "deeply held beliefs that act as guides to action at all levels of life" (Booth, 2005: 151), and provide meaning and purpose. Values offer the map and compass with which to negotiate our way. Ideally our jobs allow and encourage us to make full use of those aids, but when they are taken away, interfered with or disabled, we become lost and dispirited. Consider your own guiding values. Some will be selfish and exclusive – beliefs in the importance of your own health, wealth, family and happiness understandably lie behind many day-to-day choices. Other values may be more idealistic and outward-looking – I call these 'virtuous values'. Virtuous values are those that guide us towards becoming what we might call our 'best selves'. The Classical virtues were: faith, love, hope, justice, courage, temperance and prudence. Virtuous behaviour involves many other aspects of moral goodness as judged by our culture. Virtue is often compromised by external pressures, and increasingly teachers report diminishing opportunities to live and cultivate the virtuous values they expressed in their job or university interviews.

We cannot avoid having values. We are, however not always conscious of them, nor do they always align with one another. We rarely talk about them, but because they define and drive our large and small choices, it is important that we think about them. Our values, inclusive or exclusive, influence the kind of teacher and person we are, the resources we use and the environments we create.

Values link fundamental beliefs and action. If someone believes in 'fairness' or 'equality', for example, it should affect their choice of food, holiday destination, job, friends, transport, entertainment, partner and clothing. If 'prestige' or 'success' is a dominant value, then your choices are likely to be different. You may have been asked about your guiding values when you applied for a place on an Initial Teacher Education (ITE) course or attended a job interview. Coherent expressions of relevant values are considered important indicators of suitability for a post, but often in real-life job settings, they are not referred to again.

I have suggested values often stem from childhood experience. That is why in Chapters 3 and 4 you will read of educationalists' early lives. Children gain values through observation and events that resonate with them, as well as through direct teaching. Teachers, schools, curricula and friends may introduce values contrary to those of home, and these conflicting messages may result in discomfort or feelings of guilt. Both adults and children feel uneasy when forced into values compromise, values denial or values contradiction, so open 'values discussion' should form a frequent part of classroom and staffroom interaction.

Try to identify the key beliefs that drive and direct your actions. Values are often condensed into single words like *love, kindness, equality, justice, community* or short phrases like *environmental sustainability* or *communication across cultures*. You may find it helpful to isolate four or five key values that guide your personal and public life. A simple method of doing this is to draw around your hand and write one of your guiding values in each digit of the outline (Figure 1.1).

Discuss them with a colleague and try to agree on the wording of two values you share. In larger group settings, you may wish to widen the discussion and see if the whole group can agree on two or three values.

Your values will define what you take from this book. The developing values and life experience of the children in your class will similarly affect what they gain from your

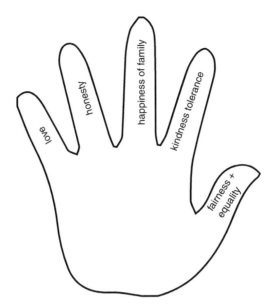

■ **Figure 1.1** The values hand

teaching. Learning involves constant negotiation between teacher values and learner values. To succeed in 'school' learning, the child may have to accept some of the values their teacher represents, but equally the teacher should be familiar with and accommodate the values of the child, (Freire, 1992). For both teachers and children, living and working within 'meaningful goals' is, according to Ryff (1989), a prime component of happiness. When we live life 'in the direction of our values' (McNiff and Whitehead, 2005: 29), we tend to feel more satisfied, more fulfilled. When our jobs allow us to express and share our values, particularly our virtuous values, we may feel high degrees of job satisfaction (Barnes, 2013). Personal happiness among teachers is a vital resource for education but can often seem in short supply.

Threats to teachers' values

Excessive workloads, problems with pupil behaviour, high accountability regimes and school inspections have led many teachers to report exhaustion, lack of fulfilment, demoralisation (YouGov/NUT, 2015, for example). Google 'Trends' searches indicate high interest in articles and news items on 'teacher stress' or 'leaving teaching', while interest in 'Teacher job satisfaction' is low. Between 25% (NFER, 2016) and 53% of teachers in the UK (YouGov/NUT, 2015) say they are considering leaving the profession because of the pressures. Currently, 11% actually do leave before their retirement date and a high percentage of postgraduate teachers leave teaching within their first five years in the classroom. Studies reveal significant numbers of teachers with 'low' or 'very low' morale (YouGov/NUT, 2015) and though some (for example, NFER, 2016) offer more encouraging interpretations, pessimism and lack of motivation among teachers is a common theme in education research and discourse. The need to address both pupil *and* teacher happiness is therefore great because each affects the output of the other.

GOOD TEACHING AND TEACHER AUTOBIOGRAPHY

Ideally life beyond the classroom contributes to your personal well-being and capacity to operate as an effective manager of learning. Interests outside school make us more knowledgeable and since we probably think more deeply in these areas, it is likely that we can use them to help children's thinking and learning. Recently I asked a sample of teachers to share their personal interests and explain how they incorporated them into their curriculum (Table 1.3).

When teaching personally significant themes, teachers claimed that enthusiasm came more easily and classes responded more positively.

Case Study 1 shows how one person's interest influenced a whole curriculum.

Case Study 1.1 West Rise, Eastbourne – a Bronze Age environment

A school head teacher fascinated in archaeology took over a junior school at the edge of marshland just 10 minutes' walk from its playground. The marsh, a site of Special Scientific Interest (SSI), was of great archaeological interest having beneath its surface evidence of a large Bronze Age settlement. It has become the focus of the whole junior curriculum in the school. In an email, Mike Fairclough, the head, describes a few ways the marsh is used in the curriculum in his school:

> The Marsh is an area of 120 acres of wetland and two lakes and forms part of the school grounds. 3000 years ago the area was the site of the second largest Bronze Age settlement in Europe. We are building a Bronze Age village on-site with the children and use the environment as a place in which children learn about this exciting period in their history.
>
> The Marsh is also home to a million honey bees in the school's "Bee Sanctuary". The children are taught about the magical world of bees and help to look after them.
>
> We hold a Countryside Management day every year on The Marsh. The day allows children to experience clay pigeon shooting, target practice, fly fishing and working with gun dogs. The emphasis is on environmental sustainability and conservation, whilst giving the children the opportunity to shoots clays, for which Britain holds the Olympic Gold Medal.
>
> Archery, bird watching, foraging, farming and paddle boarding are included in the wide variety of rich experiences which the children at West Rise enjoy on The Marsh.

In addition to these activities, children write and perform songs about the marsh, construct professional-looking information panels about its flora and fauna, learn to row coracles across one of the lakes, feed and tend the resident herd of water buffalo, make bronze and have constructed round houses and a log causeway. It will come as no surprise that such powerful experiences motivate deep thinking and lasting learning across the whole curriculum. These extraordinary experiences also provide the children with a huge range of stories that will last a lifetime.

(West Rise website: www.westrisejunior.co.uk/)

■ Table 1.3 Teachers' enthusiasms across the curriculum (with thanks to Dan File and Elham Church of England Primary School)

Teachers' personal interests	Theme explored in school this year	Values developed	Subjects most obviously involved (English is involved in each)
Gardening	Nature	Conservation/love of nature/variety/diligence	Geography/history, mathematics
Singing	'Added to many themes through the year'	Empathy, beauty, collaboration	Choir ('I've got a song for everything')
Being a Parent	'Alters the style of all my teaching'	Community, care, family, empathy	Personal Social and Health Education (PSHE)/citizenship (but 'It affects the way I teach everything according to my daughter')
Art	Ice and snow	Beauty, freedom, self-expression	art
Creativity	Toys (watch/design and make bird feeders)	Individuality, originality	All subjects
My spiritual self	'Applies across all themes . . .'	Spirituality Care, compassion	PSHE, SMSC, RE, citizenship
My Locality	Emergency services Transport	Conservation, learning, sustainability	Geography/history
My Family	'Referred to throughout the curriculum'.	Community, care, family	PSHE, SMSC, RE, citizenship
Conversation	'An essential skill in most themes'	Empathy, respect, communication,	English (and all subjects, really)
History	Space	Tradition	Art, science, mathematics
Shakespeare	School musical	Justice, fairness, respect	PE, SMSC, citizenship
Nature	Rivers	Kindness, sustainability generosity, sensitivity, communication,	RE, SMSC
Dance	School musical/PE	Teamwork, equality,	PE
Music	Choir	Beauty, joy	Music, drama
People	Everything	Communication, community	PSHE, citizenship
Theatre	School musical/role play	Communication, beauty, equality, perseverance,	English (especially drama)
Science	Weather theme/what's it made of?	Truth	Science/geography
Languages	MFL	Communication	English MFL

KEY STORIES

Key Stories are short, self-contained, frequently told, first-person vignettes that capture an important turning point in life. Key Stories are often related to our lifelong values. They may illustrate the early days of certain beliefs or abilities; perhaps the first recognition of a personal interest, passion or approach. We tend to share Key Stories in relaxed social occasions or when we want to communicate what is *really* important to us. Our close friends may have heard them several times. Sometimes we privately reiterate such stories to ourselves to reaffirm what we stand for; they redirect us towards the person we would like to be. The autobiographical vignettes at the beginning of each chapter are Key Stories that help me understand where my values come from – you probably have some too.

Key Stories from teachers

Humans are storytelling creatures, universally able to invent metaphors, parables, fantasies and riveting tales (Brown, 1992). Some are simply entertaining, but Key Stories are more fundamental and carry fundamental values. Thinking about your Key Stories can help you identify specific contributions you can make to your school.

My research using autobiographical and biographical conversations with teachers over a 10-year period, collected scores of Key Stories – important fragments of autobiography significant and particular to their tellers. They shared a number of interesting commonalities. Each story:

▨ Recorded an experience that led to significant *and lasting* thought or action
▨ Concerned an event in early life – typically between 5 and 14 years
▨ Occurred away from home and often independent of a primary carer
▨ Involved strong emotions and is retold in a compelling, enthusiastic way
▨ Had been frequently retold
▨ Was regarded by the teller as an early sign of a continuing value or passion
▨ Was promoted to the status of *Key Story* years after it occurred

Consider the following short Key Story told by a non-teacher.

Text Box 1.1 *A sample Key Story: Leo's Key Story*

I must have been three or four, and you know I was fixated on the Peter Pan story and specially on Captain Hook. Well this playschool teacher knew of my fascination and liked my drawings of Hook. She helped me to make a moving screen using a cereal box, the cardboard tubes from paper towels and a stuck together loop of my Peter Pan drawings. The tubes poked through each side of the cereal box so they could tightly hold the loop of three or four different drawings. The playgroup teacher cut a screen out of one side of the box so that when I turned the tube at the top, my drawings moved from right to left like the pictures on a TV screen. Also I recall that she and the other teachers were helping all the kids equally to make different things so there was a real sense that they were encouraging us based on our own individual needs and desires . . . I remember thinking that so clearly.

(Personal communication, May 2017)

Leo is now 29, a self-employed film maker, assisting in making TV films, adverts and videos for online music magazines, websites and institutions. He records his travels, relationships and incidents in intricate drawings, detailed notes and musical compositions. When asked to list his core values, he replied:

> I think I would say my deepest values would involve a sense of humanity, not quite sure how to sum that up and not sure if it's a value really but I mean a sense of altruism and benevolence towards others. Honesty would be another one. Creativity. Fairness or justice would be another. I think humour would be a value too. Thanks for asking me this question. It made me think.

What does Leo's Key Story tell you about him? Do his values feed back to his story? How do Leo's values relate to yours? Does the story have a message for teachers?

Beatrice, a Rwandan veterinarian and manager, shared this story:

> When I was 8 or 9 I lived in Burundi and my home was near the Sisters of Mercy, I watched them working and I got to hear about Mother Teresa. . . . I used to envy them so much and said to my mother, "do you know what? I am going to work with mother Teresa when I grow up." She was happy about it but said no more. At that time I had a brother and he was in hospital, but when I went to visit him I saw that many children around him had no visitors and no food was brought to them, so I went straight home and made food and brought it to the other kids who were sick. I did this many times.

in 2010 with no teaching experience or money, Beatrice, a member of the community that suffered most gravely in the genocide of the 1990s, founded a happy, successful and popular primary school for 200 poor rural children just outside Kigali. Using the expressed values of love, accountability, diligence and integrity, Beatrice uses the school to heal the community by bringing the formerly warring communities together. Through their children she spends her life building trust so that communities with a bitter and tragic past can forge a hopeful future.

Bringing a cherished past event into the present, and discussing the values it exemplifies can help teachers breathe life into their sessions and discover new ways of improving the experience of children (West and Reid, 2016; Bainbridge, 2016).

Storytelling is risky. Personal stories may be misunderstood, inappropriate, embarrassing, even dangerous in certain circumstances. The stories teachers share with each other and especially with children must therefore be examined carefully and in the light of the highest moral values of society and the school. Revealing a personal story to anyone outside the safety of family or friendship can make us feel exposed and vulnerable, so great care and sensitivity should be exercised when we are trusted with those of others. Ridicule, unkind laughter, incomprehension, disbelief, disinterest or disagreement can threaten, damage, even destroy these precious creations.

Chow, a Malaysian, newly qualified teacher, shared the following story with his class to demonstrate that "every word and every action they take influences others whether they realise it or not":

> ## Text Box 1.2 *Chow's Key Story*
>
> *When I was 9 years old I had an opportunity to sit with a 12-year-old girl on the school bus. I felt really nervous as she was pretty good looking. She was eating a packaged snack and was seated by the open window. When she finished, guess what she did?* [at this point in the story Chow gives students the chance to guess what she did and they usually guess the girl threw the empty packet out of the window] . . . *She folded the wrapper nicely and placed it carefully in her pocket. That single incident is the only reason that I have never littered to this day. She said nothing, wasn't showing me deliberately, she was just doing her own thing.*

Your Key Stories

By now, stories of your own may have come to mind. It might help discussion or reflection to write one of these stories in the following text box. Your story may be about how you came to have a particular interest, approach or value. Say where you were, who was involved, your age, how you felt and why is this story important to you.

Write your chosen Key Story here.

> ## Text Box 1.3 *Your Key Story 1*

Key Stories can be negative, too. In interviews I have heard of destructive, demoralising, denigrating, dismissive teachers who made harmful and lasting impressions on individuals. Most common are the stories of teachers telling young people they were *unable* to sing or draw, catch, run, spell, count, think or speak 'properly'. Some readers will instantly remember that teacher. A past teacher's discouragement may continue to replay in the mind well into adulthood, making it difficult to overcome lack of confidence. It is for today's teachers to ensure that the Key Stories formed in their classes are affirmative and empowering.

Negative stories often have more impact than positive ones, (Fredrickson and Tugade, 2004; Fredrickson and Branigan, 2005). We all live with disappointments, difficulties and depressing situations but there are clearly differences in how individuals deal with them. Damaging events can provoke optimistic, stoic, fatalistic or pessimistic, sad and angry responses, and we may experiment with several coping strategies in such situations. Studies have found, however, that those who habitually take more negative views display less resilience. Unfortunately, consistent negativity appears to put us at significantly more risk of health-damaging, life-shortening stress (e.g., Fredrickson, 2005; Montgomery and Rupp, 2005; Fredrickson, 2009). This research should, I believe, encourage teachers to minimise negative responses and build on the positive with children.

Teachers are not therapists. Too much emphasis on personal, psychological 'problems' can, as Ecclestone and Hayes (2009) have suggested, slow progress, confine children's natural resilience and hamper their ability to recover from setbacks. In what Furedi (2009) has called our 'uncertain age', TV and other aspects of popular culture may well have 'invited' young people towards 'ill-health' through frequent exposure to the difficulties in relationships and poor mental health suffered by celebrities or reality show contestants. Nonetheless, it is clear from neuroscientific studies that stress, fear, prolonged unhappiness and anxiety result in changes to body and brain that impact negatively upon learning. Difficulties with memory and information processing can result from trauma or abuse in a child's life, but recent studies reveal that much lower levels of *prolonged* anxiety can also have detrimental effects on learning too (Metz et al., 2016). Periods of challenge and stress are of course an integral part of deeper, transferrable and lasting learning, but prolonged and unmitigated pressure is likely to be damaging. Though teachers should avoid medical diagnoses, they *can* work to ensure that positive stories predominate in their classrooms.

Teachers have a responsibility to be optimistic. If they want pupils to be engaged, motivated, achieving and happy, it is reasonable to expect teachers to be working towards becoming happy, motivated, achieving people themselves (Freire, 1992).

Teachers are themselves under significant stress much of the time. Teacher mental illness is a major cause of absenteeism and the number of days (and jobs) lost through mental illness is rising (Gov. UK, 2017). If we want teachers to stay in the profession, then more attention should be paid to their own well-being. We know that those with a tendency towards negative responses are more likely to suffer 'burnout' or other mental, physical and economic consequences of stress. Teacher well-being may well depend on first discovering what makes them unhappy, sad or fearful, Montgomery and Rupp suggest that:

> [U]nderstanding and uncovering negative emotions related to external stressors is the first step towards a better performance, a higher degree of professional satisfaction, and, consequently, a higher level of teacher retention.
>
> (Montgomery and Rupp, 2005: 483)

The autobiographical approach throughout this book maps out an accessible and practical route towards the aim to be a better teacher. As Bainbridge argues:

> The process of becoming an educational professional is essentially one of identity and role formation that requires the expectations and fantasies of the past to negotiated in the present.
>
> (Bainbridge, 2016: 2)

CONCLUSION

Thinking about your autobiography can make you a better teacher. The events you identify as important in your life's journey often reveal the things you value most. In teaching, what you most value influences the curriculum and pedagogy choices you make. A high degree of self-knowledge is necessary if you are to sustain a fulfilling life in education. Knowing yourself can build your capacity to learn and grow, give and accept, empathise and lead – qualities essential to effective teaching. Sharing the Key Stories that have signposted the direction of your journey and suggested its destination will help you to change relationships into friendships and become part of a team that caringly serves and supports children. You need supporting, too. Staff development programmes that allow space to promote staff friendships, staff discussions (and action) on fundamental values, and multiple opportunities to find and build your creative strengths are vital features of a successful school.

REFERENCES

Bainbridge, A. (2016) *On Becoming an Education Professional: A Psychosocial Exploration of Developing an Educational Professional Practice*. Baisingstoke: Palgrave.

Barnes, J. (2013) *What sustains a life in education?* Unpublished PhD thesis, Canterbury Christ Church University.

Booth, T. (2005) Keeping the future alive: Putting inclusive values into action. *FORUM*, Vol. 47, Nos. 2 & 3, pp. 151–157.

Brown, D. (1992) Human universals, in S. Pinker (ed.) *The Blank Slate*. London: Penguin.

Bruner, J. (1990) *Acts of Meaning*. London: Harvard University Press.

Bruner, J. (2004) Life as narrative. *Social Research*, Vol. 71, pp. 691–710.

Delamont, S. (2007) Arguments against auto-ethnography. *Qualitative Researcher*, Issue 4, presented at *British Educational Research Association Conference*, Cardiff, available at: www.cardiff.ac.uk/socsi/qualiti/QualitativeResearcher/QR_Issue4_Feb07.pdf (accessed 24.10.17).

Ecclestone, K. and Hayes, D. (2009) *The Dangerous Rise of Therapeutic Education*. London: SAGE Publications.

Fredrickson, B. (2009) *Positivity*. New York: Crown.

Fredrickson, B. and Branigan, C. (2005) Positive emotions broaden the scope of attention & thought – action repertoires. *Cognition & Emotion*, Vol. 19, No. 3, pp. 313–332.

Fredrickson, B. and Tugade, M. (2004) Resilient individuals use positive emotions to bounce back from negative experiences. *Journal of Personality & Social Psychology*, Vol. 80, No. 2, pp. 326–333.

Freire, P (1992) *Pedagogy of the oppressed*. New York: Continuum.

Furedi, F. (2009) *Wasted: Why Education Isn't Educating*. London: Continuum.

Goleman, D. (1996) *Social Intelligence: The New Science of Human Relationships*. New York: Arrow.

Gov. UK (2017) *Thriving at work*, available at: www.gov.uk/government/publications/thriving-at-work-a-review-of-mental-health-and-employers (accessed 25.10.17).

Hicks, D. (2006) *Lessons for the Future: The Missing Dimension in Education*. London: Routledge.

Layard, R. and Dunn, C. (2009) *A Good Childhood*. London: Penguin.

McNiff, J. and Whitehead, J. (2005) *Action Research for Teachers*. Abingdon: Fulton.

Metz, C., Elzinger, B. and Schwabe, L. (2016) Stress, fear and memory in healthy individuals, in D. Bremner (ed.) *Posttraumatic Stress Disorder: From Neurobiology to Treatment*. Atlanta, GA: Wiley Blackwell.

Montgomery, C. and Rupp, A. (2005) *A meta analysis for exploring the diverse causes and effects of stress in teachers*, available at: http://files.eric.ed.gov/fulltext/EJ728362.pdf (accessed 24.10.17).

National Federation for Education Research NFER (2016) *Should I stay or should go?*, available at: www.nfer.ac.uk/publications/LFSA01/LFSA01.pdf (accessed 24.10.17).

Ryff, C. (1989) Happiness is everything or is it? Explorations on the meaning of psychological well-being. *Journal of Personality Social Psychology*, Vol. 57, No. 6, pp. 1089–1081, available at: http://aging.wisc.edu/pdfs/379.pdf (accessed 25.10.17)

West, L. and Reid, H. (2016) *Constructing Narratives of Continuity and Change: A Transdisciplinary Approach to Researching Lives*. Abingdon: Routledge.

YouGov/NUT (2015) *Teacher survey on government education policy*, available at: www.teachers.org.uk/news-events/press-releases-england/nutyougov-teacher-survey-government-education-policy

A POSITIVE PEDAGOGY AND A CONNECTING CURRICULUM

SUMMARY

This chapter will introduce two linked concepts: 'positive pedagogy' and the 'connecting curriculum'. Both terms will be used throughout this book and involve an approach to education that places personal relevance plus intellectual, physical, psychological and social well-being at the centre of decisions. I will argue that creative and cross-curricular learning must relate closely and thoughtfully to the real everyday lives of the children and community you serve. Such an approach generates and sustains positive attitudes toward the self and learning. Evidence on the relationships between connection making, creativity and well-being will be briefly reviewed together with the suggestion that positive pedagogy can significantly increase the chances of constructive events and deep engagement in daily school life.

INTRODUCTION

Here is a Key Story of mine.

I was 30 years old, teaching and living with my family in Bali, Indonesia. One morning I was walking on a dirt road between delicately terraced padi fields which followed the contours of a hillside. My 4-year-old son was holding hands with me. Suddenly he jumped with both feet into a muddy puddle and splashed greenish fetid water all over my white shirt, legs and shorts. I was really cross with him and started telling him off. Unseen by me a young Balinese young man of about 20 was walking towards us as this incident happened. The man was on his way to a Hindu temple, bare-chested, wearing a sarong and with a white frangipani behind his ear. He was carrying some fruit and rice offerings in a decorated silver bowl. As he got closer he smiled and greeted us (I was still cross and brushing off the mud) and gently said, 'You should never be angry with a child in Bali – they are the nearest thing we have to God.' Shaken and moved by this gentle and unexpected upbraiding, I went on my way with my son. I never met the stranger again, never knew his name but have never forgotten his impact on me.

My friends and family would not be surprised that I retell this story here. They are familiar with its message and I hope recognise some of the ways that I have responded to it. It contains several features important to me: it occurred in a foreign land, involves beauty, kindness, spirituality and wisdom, communication across a cultural divide, a distinctive landscape and family. Communication, the spiritual, beauty, wisdom, family, and kindness are values I prize highly. Such incidents have led me increasingly toward a belief that teaching and curriculum should aim at positive experience. Academic and scientific research has helped me justify and explain these beliefs.

POSITIVE AND CREATIVE LEARNING ENVIRONMENTS FOR ALL

The environments we occupy influence our story. The difficulty is that each of us perceive the same physical and emotional environment differently. In his ground-breaking book on thinking, learning and the emotions, Antonio Damasio makes a passing comment on the environments we share. From a neuroscientific perspective, he observes: "few if any perceptions of any object or event, actually present or recalled from memory, are ever neutral in emotional terms" (Damasio, 2003: 93). This suggests, for example, that the chair you are sitting on and the very floor on which you rest your feet will provoke slightly different emotional responses/memories or associations for each person sitting on the same chair, resting on the same floor.

Feel the chair beneath you. Look at its colour, patterns, joins or worn parts. Does it have a smell? Is there anything about chair or fabric that reminds you of a feeling, another thing, past event, place, person, object or happening? Any, even very minor, connections between this minor aspect of your environment and present feelings or memory of a past experience or person will confirm that these connections are exclusive to you, part of what Pinker (2002) calls your 'unique environment'.

The idea of a unique environment affects our understanding of diversity. The specific physical, emotional and relational setting in which *only you* exist, the things that *only you* saw, heard, touched, smelt, tasted, thought, felt, connected or remembered, make your mind different than anyone else's. Pinker makes the point that we do not even share that environment with our identical twin who shared the same womb, house, family and the same street and school.

If even objects hold different associations for each person, then a classroom – a collection of objects – becomes an environment full of potential connections for every child and adult using it. The view, the seats, desks, posters, pens, pencils, books, tablets and curtains all mean something very slightly different to each person. Add the different cultural environments represented in each class and the uniquely perceived *emotional* surroundings created by teacher, assistants and other pupils, and the range of personal responses becomes enormous. The idea that the settings we construct as teachers can be received in 30 different ways is a powerful, starting point for thinking about a creative and connecting curriculum.

Beginning with creativity

Creativity is a defining human capability. Whatever age or ability we are, when we discover where and how we are most able to exercise our creative abilities, we tend to feel good. When we share thinking and creating with diverse others we often experience great satisfaction (Clift and Camic, 2016). Psychologists and neuroscientists have provided ample evidence of strong connections between feelings of happiness and the processes of seeking, discovering and inventing (e.g., Csikszentmihalyi, 1997; Pangsepp, 1998; Damasio, 2003; McGilchrist, 2010). The champions of research into creativity in schools have similarly connected personal and educational well-being to shared and personal involvement in creative activity (Craft, 2000, 2005; Abbs, 2003; Thomson et al., 2012). The question for teachers is how they can generate and promote creativity within the curriculum – this is discussed in detail in Chapter 6.

I have proposed that well-planned and well-delivered cross-curricular approaches are an effective way towards creativity in schools (Barnes, 2015c). If we define creativity as "imaginative activity fashioned so as to produce outcomes that are both original and of value" (National Advisory Committee on Creative and Cultural Education (NACCCE), 1999: 30), any original, valued, imaginative and productive connections between everyday life and the curriculum subjects can be called creative. Making links *between* curriculum subjects is particularly productive in generating such creativity.

Positive pedagogy

Most teachers want their classrooms to be positive places. Stephen Scoffham and I (Scoffham and Barnes, 2009) coined the term 'positive pedagogy' to describe what an affirmative approach to building an environment for learning might be like. Through adopting a positive pedagogy teachers seek to avoid the 'social engineering' that Ecclestone and Hayes (2009: 145) warn against but simply be human and humane in the multifarious contacts of the day. A positive pedagogue encourages children themselves to draw positive messages from their interactions with ideas, others, subjects and experiences. The use of the word 'pedagogy' signifies an interest beyond just teaching, to include all aspects of learning influenced by teachers. Pedagogy involves the room, furniture, equipment, relationships, curriculum choices, attitudes to what and who is taught, styles of teaching, planning, feedback and the aspects of ourselves we share with the children.

The idea of a unique environment could make the coherent and positive education of 30-plus children seem an impossibility. This is why values, aims and research are so important in teaching. I suggested in Chapter 1 that teachers should be clear about the values they hold and work towards, living them in their lives and work in school. Positive pedagogy depends on well-articulated aims and fulfilled teachers in settings where emotional, physical, sensory and intellectual connections are constructive (Ofsted, 2013; Barnes and Scoffham, 2017). Three issues feed into a positive pedagogy:

▨   Knowing ourselves: the role of autobiography in helping us become better people
▨   Building a positive social, emotional and physical environment in class
▨   Linking positivity, creativity and cross-curricularity in the 'connecting curriculum'

Knowing ourselves: the role of autobiography

The ancient aphorism, 'Know thyself' penned by Plato, suggests an important starting point for change. Knowing yourself in the context of education can begin with completing some of the autobiographical exercises already recommended. Sharing aspects of ourselves with others helps us refine our thoughts and understand our motivations in order to provoke positive change in our thoughts and actions. Sharing such personal stuff is not easy. We generally only share our personal stories in very secure contexts. School management will need to work hard to help staff as well as children to become confident sharers of selfhood. Humour, spontaneity, risk taking, invention, willing participation and ease with vulnerability within a workplace require a degree of trust whether we are old or young (Barnes and Shirley, 2007). The autobiographical stories you select as sharable parts of your identity may explain the seeds of the activities, attitudes and accomplishments that contribute to feelings of fulfilment – your passions. The joyful, flourishing and rewarding parts of life I experienced as a primary school child have motivated my best contributions to children's lives (Robinson and Aronica, 2012). Your passion may involve a particular skill set, like football, arithmetic, classification, running, drawing, mapping, pottery or choral singing; it might equally involve less subject-oriented talents – like being good at forming, mending or understanding relationships. You could be excellent at self-understanding or memory, or have a particular ability to show empathy, kindness, compassion or hope. You may have a passion for justice or fairness, take pride in your reliability or show a strong ability to be generous or forgiving. Your passions, generously shared, can energise your pedagogy, whatever your story. A Rwandan teacher and theatre director, brought up in a refugee camp in Uganda, put it like this:

> I came from a family of scientists, but I attribute what I am as an artist to a priest/ teacher Father Grimes who encouraged us to grace our living with arts and skills. The artist in me came out first I suppose in school through contemporary African dance introduced by that teacher, I must have been about 14. He took art so seriously and was so disciplined about it. . . . He really recognised my passion for art. We performed Shakespeare plays in full costume and the plays of modern African writers and did school productions in the National Theatre of Uganda. I loved it, you had to leave school and got cake! . . . After school my teacher suggested I applied to do a degree in music, dance and drama and specialised in community-based theatre. I wrote a play about social justice and took it to the villages around and Rwanda radio took it seriously. I started a festival at the genocide memorial, tapping on friends for finance. From that time art became a spiritual thing for me, the need to laugh and to share with each other, to have a break from everyday life and just be human beings playing together – you don't perform the story, you feel the story, when you get to that place creativity flows.
>
> (Hope Azeda, personal communicaation, 19.09.2016)

Like Father Grimes, teachers who identify and celebrate their own creative strengths are likely to notice similar abilities in children. Teachers often praise children who show strengths that they have themselves (Sternberg, 1997). Attributes very different from our own, however, may seem less important, even unnoticeable, and we run the risk of denying some children the opportunity to feel success. Self-reflection can help us identify our more rigid or dismissive mindsets. Working closely with others means that they can cover our 'blind spots' – those things that others can see when we do not.

Reflect on skills and abilities you once had but have now been neglected or abandoned. Think also about the things you are *not* good at, or do not like. Honesty about each other's areas of weakness may help us appreciate and affirm those that excel in areas that are often not recognised, like social, intellectual, imaginative, intrapersonal, spiritual, practical or creative abilities. Share your list of abilities and difficulties with a trusted colleague. Positive pedagogy implies an intention to give equal attention and affirmation to those whose talents you do not share and those whose skills are not 'academic'.

I think I'm quite good at . . .	*I think I'm not very good at . . .*

Building a positive social, emotional and physical environment in class

Positive classroom environments begin with the first interaction of the day at the gates of the school or classroom door. Greetings that notice the new shoes, lost teeth or changed hairstyle, that are interested in the health of a hamster or an aunt's weekend visit – these small interactions have always helped teachers construct an atmosphere of security and belonging. Equally, the way you respond to questions, comments, challenges, mistakes and successes throughout the day establishes the underlying emotional tone of a class. A caring, attentive ethos may not, however, be enough to promote desirable traits like progress, creativity, self-motivation, diligence and engagement. Positivity alone is insufficient.

Both children and adults need to flourish and *feel* that they are flourishing. The evidence is that many children in primary schools in the UK and USA do not experience healthy intellectual, psychological, social and physical growth (Marmot, 2010). Many have a negative mindset (Dweck, 2012) and lack the combination of economic and social advantage, enjoyment and challenge, that result in good development. These things are particularly evident in the lives of children with 'Special Educational Needs and Disabilities' (SEND) who in my experience respond quickly and usually highly positively to having their own creativities recognised and affirmed. Often the discovery of a creative strength results in positive changes elsewhere in their lives.

The four yearly *Health Behaviour in School Aged Children* (HBSC) reports of the World Health Organisation (WHO) suggests some worrying comparisons between British school children and those in many other European countries. The most recent HBSC report records, for example, that only 37% of Scottish 11-year-olds (compared to 78% of

Albanians of the same age) say they 'like school a lot'. At 11 years, 30% of English children report feeling 'pressured' by school work (compared to 9% in Sweden), 80% of them find their peers 'kind and helpful' (compared to 90% in Macedonia) (WHO, 2016). There are many interpretations of such differences, but HBSC comparisons across the developed world indicate some particularly unhealthy trends among British and American children. Not liking school, feeling pressured and not trusting one's peers are indicators of lack of flourishing and associated with poor performance in school and reduced life satisfaction (WHO, 2016). Hugely increased general wealth and security over the last 70 years has made very little difference to comparative measures of well-being in the UK or USA.

Feelings of well-being are essential to good learning. A Public Health England survey stated:

> It is widely recognised that a child's emotional health and wellbeing influences their cognitive development and learning, as well as their physical and social health and their mental wellbeing in adulthood.
>
> (Lavis and Robson, 2015)

Fixed and narrow interpretations of intelligence and knowledge, as well as stress, have consistently been shown to result in under performance in school and life (e.g., Gardner, 1993; Sternberg, 1997; Perkins, 2002; Dweck, 2015, 2012). A combination of high percentages of poorly motivated children, stressed teachers and limiting definitions of achievement results in lost potential and unhappy school lives for many. In the HBSC report, children's feelings of personal growth and fulfilment correlate closely with good family and friends relationships and perceived success in school. 'Academic' children (i.e. those confident and quick in language, logic and memory) are likely to feel good about school since it prizes and celebrates the things they are good at. For a school or classroom to positively affect *every* child and especially those with SEND or other barriers to learning, we must look wider than subjects and reductive definitions of intelligence and diversity. Over the last 15 years, a range of psychologists (for example Csikszentmihalyi, 2002; Diener, 2009; Gilman et al., 2009; Seligman, 2011), have used their research to suggest (like their 18th century forbears and non-western educationalists such as Makiguchi) establishing happiness or well-being as a major aim of schooling. Some UK and US schools have taken up the challenge (e.g., Wellington College and Ashley Primary School websites).

Definitions of happiness or well-being vary. In 1989, Carol Ryff's research linked well-being with feelings of self-acceptance, environmental mastery, positive relations with others, autonomy, purpose in life and personal growth (Ryff, 1989). Csikszentmihalyi (1997) links feelings of happiness with deep engagement or 'flow'. Seligman (2011) sees well-being as involving: 'feeling good', a sense of accomplishment, authentic (and positive) connections and a purposeful existence. Some argue that aiming at happiness is illusionary and easily exclusive – that simple 'contentment' is a more realistic aim (Bloch, 2015).

A positive pedagogy embraces definitions of well-being ranging between mild interest and contentment to moments of elation. It is founded on ideas that a school should place its highest value on the flourishing of every child and adult within a supportive, inclusive community. If you were defining what a school founded on well-being would look like, what would you say?

Discuss the following statement with a group of four or five others:

Table 2.1 Caring for well-being: what are the implications?

Caring for well-being:

What would a **curriculum**
for well-being look like?

What would a **teaching style** aimed
at well-being be like?

What **teacher attitudes** would
generate well-being ?

How could we **plan**
for well-being?

How can we use **assessment** to
add to well-being?

How can our **classroom arrangement**
add to well-being ?

How can **resources**
enhance well-being?

The school that cares for the well-being of every child (Table 2.1) should be one that offers a positive emotional, physical, social and intellectual environment, and a wide range of equally-valued subjects and activities in which all children can find success.

In your discussions, itemise the implications of a positive pedagogy across the life and work of the school.

A connecting curriculum

The *connecting curriculum* depends upon recognising and celebrating the diversity within and between us. It purposely seeks the links upon which creativity depends. It is a curriculum that helps children and teachers collaborate to connect their lives with curriculum subjects and to each other. It also aims to link the personal history and present of each of us with positive experiences, discoveries and outcomes. Thus, a connecting curriculum ties together not just the curriculum subjects to the lives of all those in school, but attempts positively to link the different layers of experience within our own lives. This broad connection making provides the underpinning of cross-curricular learning.

Cross-curricular learning occurs when the thought processes, skills, language and dominant values of two or more curriculum subjects are used to throw light upon and understand a single experience, theme, problem or question. As in all school learning, the progressive acquisition of new skills and knowledge is expected when cross-curricular approaches are used. Although throughout this book the social, personal, motivational and joyful aspects of cross-curricular learning will be stressed, it is important to recognise that school learning should also enhance subject standards and progression in all children. For this reason, the subjects should be named as their perspectives are used to throw light on an issue, question or theme.

Connections between cross-curricularity, creativity and well-being are observable across time and culture (Barnes, 2015a, b). My interest in these connections started with a small scale research collaboration (Grainger et al., 2004). Observing the practice of ITE colleagues representing subjects across the curriculum, we noted that student teachers found the most effective, memorable and engaging sessions were those that employed personal stories, humour, risk taking, cognitive challenge or conflict, metaphors, extemporary asides and illustrations – each factors that made some kind of connection. Our research uncovered aspects of creativity in the most memorable parts of the ITE sessions observed (geography, English and music sessions). We observed both tutors and students making connections through:

■ Confident improvisation
■ Humour
■ Friendly responses
■ Original and practical illustrations
■ Anecdotes
■ Multiple opportunities for reflection
■ New thinking
■ A preference for collaborative contributions

In the minds of students, personal anecdotes played a particularly important role in connecting them with the subject matter on offer. So the successful connecting curriculum not only makes effective connections and measurable progress in and between subjects, but connects learners and teachers on many levels. Similar responses arose from related staff development programmes I have led in Malaysia, India, Rwanda and Tanzania.

There are dangers in a connecting curriculum, however. Poorly planned and controlled cross-curricular work can result in what Roth (2001) calls a 'bland broth' of weak, unspecific, vague and untransferrable learning. The 'Three Wise Men' report of 1992 (Alexander et al., 1992) warned against the 'highly questionable dogmas' that then existed in primary education which included widely used but poorly understood cross-curricular or 'topic based' methods weakened by poor subject knowledge, unclear objectives and little sense of progression. Primary teachers today must continue to address fears of 'dismantling the subject-disciplines' (Ecclestone and Hayes, 2009: 145), and hold fast to what is valuable about subject teaching. As Gardner (2004) argued, the individual subject-disciplines may prove to be among the greatest inventions of the last two millennia. Insights regarding the concept of 'place' contributed by the subject of geography, for example, are different from but not superior to those offered by history, science, modern languages, English, art, music, RE, PE, mathematics, design/technology or citizenship. Each discipline has its heroes, history, language, skills and attitudes; each has shaped our present world. Rather than abandoning or diminishing the subject-disciplines they should be strengthened and given parity of prestige (NACCCE, 1999; Alexander, 2010). Enhanced, more equal subject teaching in the primary years should not come at the expense of cross-curricular approaches – it should stimulate and feed them. My first cross-curricular approach addresses this issue.

There are also false ways of connecting the subjects of a curriculum. These are methods that might look like cross-curricular learning but actually only add to learning in one subject. This I call 'token connectivity' (Figure 2.1). One subject (usually a foundation subject), is used to enhance learning in another (usually 'core') subject. Genuine connections are not made between them and no growth is expected in the subsidiary subject.

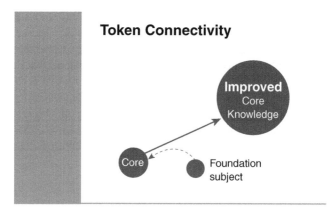

Token Connectivity

▨ **Figure 2.1** Token connectivity – when the connection between subjects is not genuine; one subject simply adds colour to what is considered a 'more important' subject – no progress is made in this subject

HIERARCHICAL CROSS-CURRICULAR LEARNING

Hierarchical relationships in the curriculum habitually place some subjects above others in importance. Using two subjects hierarchically to help understand an issue, answer a question or study a theme means that the intended progress in *one* subject is significantly greater or considered more important than progress in the second (Figure 2.2). For example, a teacher may want her reception class to understand the definition of a square. A collection of square and rectangular shapes and objects may have been collected, children may be involved in classifying, drawing, signing, identifying squares in the environment and may have traced around shapes in a workbook. They will have been tested on their concept of a square. Several sessions may have been devoted to this work. On the last 'squares' session the teacher may introduce the song *Frere Jacques* with the words:

> *Find four corners,*
> *Find four corners,*
> *Sides the same,*
> *Sides the same,*
> *Put them all together*
> *Put them all together*
> *Square's my name*
> *Square's my name* (MacGregor, 2005)

The connection between song and the mathematics learning is clear. Musically, children will have learned to put new words to a tune they already know and perhaps improved their ability to sing in tune, some, but not a great deal of musical progress will have been made. The main focus of the music will have been to enhance children's mathematical understanding.

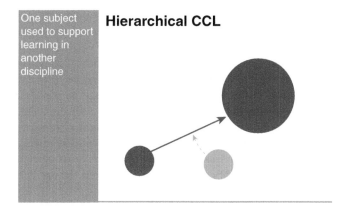

■ **Figure 2.2** Hierarchical cross-curricular learning: some progress is made in two or more subjects, but the learning focus is really on the 'superior' subject

MULTI-DISCIPLINARY CROSS-CURRICULAR LEARNING

Many ways of making effective connections between curriculum subjects will be introduced in this book. The most straightforward kind of cross-curricular learning uses context *only* to motivate thinking in two or more subjects. This method I call multi-disciplinary cross-curricular learning (Figure 2.3). It involves planning and using a powerful learning experience to be interpreted independently through the mindsets and skills of two different subjects. A visit to the school pond can, for example, be illuminated through introducing skills and knowledge of science and *quite separately* (and possibly on another occasion) be the subject of a descriptive writing or poetry session. Subject learning is progressed separately – but both are linked to the same physical context. Progression in two subjects can often be measured more easily using a multi-disciplinary approach.

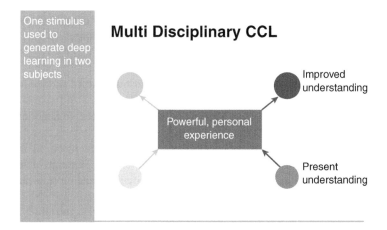

■ **Figure 2.3** Multi-disciplinary cross-curricular learning: learning targets in two or more subjects are achieved by using a single experience to generate motivation for learning in each of the two subjects separately

Multi-disciplinary approaches can be used for almost any response to an experience. Both the natural world and the made environment can be interpreted through the eyes of every curriculum subject. Think again of the chair you are sitting on. It is the product of design and technology, of course, but also of science, history, mathematics and art. The tree outside your window may be interpreted through another language or the languages of art and poetry, music, dance, movement, science or mathematics. It may become a symbol in RE, a stimulus for PE or an issue for citizenship. The satisfaction felt by the designer of maker of your chair was at least partly drawn from knowing they had successfully applied the knowledge and skills of many subject-disciplines. Indeed, everything that surrounds us and most day-to-day challenges require cross-curricular inputs or interpretations. The multi-disciplinary approach gives children the joy of engaging starting points for learning and the teacher the satisfaction of being able to double-use a visit, visitor or special event in school.

SUSTAINING A CREATIVE, CONNECTING AND POSITIVE CURRICULUM

Connective activity in schools can also *result* in positive environments. Roberts (2006) and more recently Thomson et al. (2012) and Robinson (2016) suggest that positive outcomes like improved relationships, self-image, confidence, commitment, concentration – even school attendance – frequently result from extended contact with creative practitioners and focused periods of creative connections across the disciplines.

Values can be seen as the 'prime mover' and sustainer of creative and positive action. If the values you identified earlier truly guide your decisions about teaching and learning, then ideas like beauty, love, fairness, empathy, knowledge, tenacity, peace, justice, friendship, honesty, hope or joy (and many more) should lead your decisions on resources, relationships, curriculum and pedagogy. In my doctoral research, participants found that identifying and expressing the personal stories connected with their most valued values was crucial in influencing conditions toward well-being and creativity in their work places (Barnes, 2013).

Values, cross-curricular experience and positivity combine to engender, sustain and grow creativity. Thus, we may imagine a virtuous spiral (Figure 2.4) developing as follows:

1   The teacher identifies and reflects on their own values and the influences that generated them.
2   The teacher shares Key Stories and values with peers to negotiate guiding values for a positive pedagogy.
3   An ethos of challenge, friendliness, humour, invention, affirmation and values-consciousness begins to develop among staff (e.g., Cremin et al., 2009).
4   Relationships between teachers and children become more meaningful, active, creative and engaged (Csikszentmihalyi, 1997).
5   Children are more likely to experience what Csikszentmihalyi calls 'flow' resulting from increased capacity for commitment, attention, resilience and original thinking.

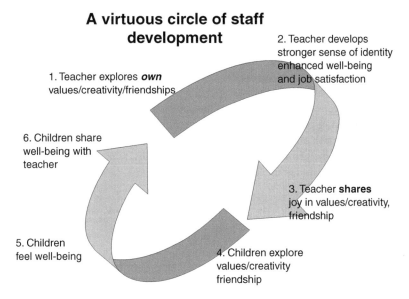

A virtuous circle of staff development

1. Teacher explores *own* values/creativity/friendships

2. Teacher develops stronger sense of identity enhanced well-being and job satisfaction

3. Teacher **shares** joy in values/creativity, friendship

4. Children explore values/creativity friendship

5. Children feel well-being

6. Children share well-being with teacher

■ **Figure 2.4** A virtuous spiral of creativity in schools

6   Relationships, self-image, ability to build (and build on) connections are enhanced (Fredrickson, 2009).
7   The classroom becomes one where both pupils and teachers share an increased sense of well-being. These feelings of well-being provide the impetus for increased creative action and the cycle repeats at a higher level.

Schools are right to promote academic, sporting and artistic excellence, but encouragement alone is inadequate. A sense of healthy *growth* is a vital component of flourishing in all people. Dweck (2016: 8–12) has collected strong evidence that the development of a 'growth mind-set' is needed to promote healthy and sustained educational progress. Encouraging intellectual, social or psychological growth goes well beyond simple 'reward and punishment' strategies, and Dweck highlights the need for teachers to help young people to:

■   Show *resilience*
■   *Respond* confidently
■   Value *diversity* and diverse responses
■   Understand *process*
■   Maintain *diligence*
■   Seek and find *alternative strategies*
■   Know how the *brain* works
■   Recognise the ways we *learn best*

She suggests that teaching these skills should become part of every pedagogy and we discuss the implications of these thoughts throughout the rest of this book.

CONCLUSION

The two new concepts introduced in this chapter – the connecting curriculum and a positive pedagogy – are introduced because both can effectively promote creativity. Whether you are a child or an adult, the discovery of where you can be most creative, most inventive, original and imaginative is an important event. Your creative strengths provide you with a sense of meaning and joy which, if nurtured and developed, can last a lifetime. The chances of discovering personal strengths are greatly heightened if primary schools provide children with a rich and varied palette of subject and activity options. Finding and developing a passion in the primary years can, and often does, make a huge and positive difference to choices and attitudes for the rest of life.

REFERENCES

Abbs, P. (2003) *Against the Flow*. Abingdon: Routledge.

Alexander, R., Rose, J. and Woodhead, C. (1992) *Three wise men report*, available at: www. educationengland.org.uk/documents/threewisemen/ (accessed 24.10.17).

Alexander, R. (2010) (Ed.) *Children, their world, their education: Final report of the Cambridge Primary Review*. Abingdon: Routledge.

Ashley C of E Primary School website, available at: www.ashleyschool.org.uk/home/harmony/ the-principle-of-health-wellbeing (accessed 27.10.17).

Barnes, J. (2013) *What sustains a life in education?* Unpublished PhD thesis, Canterbury Christ Church University.

Barnes, J. (2015a) 'Creativity and promoting well-being in children and young people through education' in Clift, S. and Camic, P. (eds.) (2015) *Oxford Textbook of Creative Arts, Health and Wellbeing,* Oxford: Oxford University Press.

Barnes, J. (2015b) 'An Introduction to Cross-Curricular Learning' in Driscoll, P., Lambirth, A. and Roden, J. (eds.) *The Primary Curriculum: A Creative Approach*, London: Sage.

Barnes, J. (2015c) *Cross-Curricular Learning 3–14,* London: Sage.

Barnes, J. and Scoffham, S. (2017) The humanities in English primary schools: Struggling to survive. *Education 3–13*, Vol. 43, No. 3, pp. 298–308, doi:10.1080/03004279.2017.129 6918

Barnes, J. and Shirley, I. (2007) Strangely familiar: Cross-curricular & creative thinking in teacher education. *Improving Schools*, Vol. 10, No. 2, pp. 289–306.

Bloch, S. (2015) *Happiness is an illusion, here's why you should seek contentment instead*, University of Melbourne, discussion statement, available at: http://theconversation.com/ happiness-is-an-illusion-heres-why-you-should-seek-contentment-instead-43709

Clift, S. and Camic, P. (eds.) (2015) *Oxford Textbook of Creative Arts, Health and Wellbeing,* Oxford: Oxford University Press.

Craft, A. (2000) *Creativity Across the Primary Curriculum: Framing and Developing Principles and Practice*. Abingdon: Routledge.

Cremin,T., Barnes,J. and Scoffham, S (2009) *Creative Teaching for Tomorrow: Fostering a Creative State of Mind*. Deal: Future Creative.

Csikszentmihalyi, M. (1997) *Creativity: Flow and the Psychology of Discovery and Invention*. New York: Harper Collins.

Csikszentmihalyi, M. (2002) *Flow: The Classic Work on How to Achieve Happiness*. New York: Ebury Press.

Damasio, A. (2003) *Looking for Spinoza: Joy, Sorrow & the Feeling Brain*. Orlando, FL: Harcourt.

Diener, E. (2009) *Culture and Well-Being, the Collected Works of Ed Diener*. London: Springer.

Dweck, C. (2012) *Mindset: How You Can Fulfill Your Potential.* New York: Constable & Robinson Limited.

Dweck, C. (2016) *Mindset: The New Psychology of Success.* New York: Random House.

Ecclestone, K. and Hayes, D. (2009) *The Dangerous Rise of Therapeutic Education.* London: SAGE Publication.

Frederickson, B. (2009) *Positivity: Groundbreaking Research Reveals How to Embrace the Hidden Strength of Positive Emotions, Overcome Negativity and Thrive.* New York: Crown.

Gardner, H. (1993) *Frames of Mind: The Theory of Multiple Intelligences* (2nd ed.). London: Fontana.

Gardner, H. (2004) *Changing Minds: The Art & Science of Changing Our Own & Other People's Minds.* Boston, MA: Harvard Business School.

Gilman, R., Scott-Huebner, E. and Furlong, M (eds.) (2009) *Handbook of Positive Psychology in Schools.* New York: Routledge.

Grainger, T., Barnes, J. and Scoffham, S. (2004) A creative cocktail: Creative teaching in ITE. *Journal of Education in Teaching (JET)*, Vol. 30, No. 3, pp. 243–253.

Lavis, P. and Robson, C. (2015) *Promoting children and young people's emotional health and wellbeing: A whole school and college approach*, available at: http://cypmhc.org.uk/sites/cypmhc.org.uk/files/Promoting%20CYP%20Emotional%20Health%20and%20Wellbeing%20Whole%20School%20Approach.pdf (accessed 24.10.17).

MacGregor, H. (2005) *Tom Thumb's Musical Maths: Developing Maths Skills with Simple Songs.* London: A and C Black.

Marmot, M. (2010) *Fair society healthy lives*, available at: www.parliament.uk/documents/fair-society-healthy-lives-full-report.pdf (accessed 24.10.17).

McGilchrist, I. (2010) *The Master and His Emissary: The Divided Brain and the Making of the Western World.* London: Yale.

NACCCE (National Advisory Council on Creative & Cultural Education) (1999) *All Our Futures: Creativity, Culture & Education.* London: DfEE.

Ofsted (2013) *Not yet good enough: Personal, social, health and economic education in schools*, available at: file:///Users/jb1142/Downloads/Not%20yet%20good%20enough.pdf (accessed 24.10.17).

Pangsepp, J. (1998) *Affective Neuroscience: The Origins of Animal & Human Emotions.* New York: Oxford University Press.

Perkins, D. (2002) *The Eureka Effect: The Art & Logic of Breakthrough Thinking.* New York: Norton.

Pinker, S. (2002) *The Blank Slate.* London: Penguin.

Roberts, P. (2006) *Nurturing Creativity in Young People: A report to Government to inform future policy,* London: DCMS/DES.

Robinson, K. (2016) *Creative Schools: Revolutionizing Education From the Ground Up.* London: Penguin.

Robinson, K. and Aronica, L. (2012) *The Element: How Finding Your Passion Changes Everything.* London: Penguin.

Roth, M. (2001) The metamorphosis of Columbus, in S. Wineburg and P. Grossman (eds.) *Interdisciplinary Curriculum: Challenges to Implementation.* New York: Teachers' College Press.

Ryff, C. (1989) Happiness is everything or is it? Explorations on the meaning of psychological well-being. *Journal of Personality Social Psychology*, Vol. 57, No. 6, pp. 1089–1081.

Scoffham, S. and Barnes, J. (2009, August) Transformational experiences & deep learning: The impact of an intercultural study visit to India on UK initial teacher education students. *Journal of Education for Teaching*, Vol. 3, pp. 257–270, available at: www.informaworld.com/smpp/title~db=all~content=t713430265~tab=issueslist~branches=35 – v3535 (accessed 24.6.11).

Seligman, M. E. P. (2011) *Flourish: A Visionary New Understanding of Happiness and Well-Being.* London: Nicholas Brealey.

Sternberg, R. (1997) *Successful Intelligence.* New York: Plume.

Thomson, P., Hall, C., Jones, K. and Sefton-Green, J. (2012) *The Signature Pedagogies Project: Final Report.* Newcastle: CCE.

Wellington College website, available at: www.wellingtoncollege.org.uk/pastoral-care/well-being/ (accessed 25.10.17).

World Health Organisation (2016) *Growing Up Unequal: The Health Behaviour of School Aged Children Report.* Geneva: World Health Organisation.

A HISTORY OF CROSS-CURRICULARITY

SUMMARY

This chapter introduces some key ideas, movements and characters in the history and philosophy of education. It will concentrate on traditions and approaches where diverse modes of learning are integrated. Starting with reflections on my own primary education, I will suggest relationships between educationalists' beliefs and their biographical and educational experiences. The historical overview serves as a reminder that what we now call 'cross-curricular' approaches have characterised education thinking across time and cultures.

INTRODUCTION: AUTOBIOGRAPHY APPLIED TO THE HISTORY OF EDUCATION

We are all subject to history. My own primary schooling briefly described in Chapter 1 happened in a specific historical period – shortly after World War II, in a period when British colonialism was being challenged and in the early years of the Welfare State. It took place and during a brief period of national optimism and idealism captured by events like the Festival of Britain, the coronation of Elizabeth II and the rebuilding of the bombed Coventry Cathedral. That buoyant period ended with the Cold War and the Cuban Missile Crisis in 1962, but the hopefulness of the preceding 10 years coloured the curriculum, pedagogy and environments I encountered as a child. The walls of my school were decorated with high quality reproductions of the work of 20th century artists, we learned the music of living composers, pottery and craft exhibitions toured our classrooms. We played in genuine 'bombsites' but also Battersea Park with its Festival Garden, tree walks and public sculptures by Henry Moore and Barbara Hepworth. We felt part of new and confident architecture of the South Bank, Centre Point and Millbank Tower.

Education in London in the late 1950s and early 1960s was characterised by free milk, vaccinations against polio, vitamins, cod liver oil capsules, the possibility of free tertiary education and egalitarian challenges to the grammar school system. The curriculum I encountered placed culture art, music, drama, poetry, dance, craft literature, games, geography and history at the same level of importance as grammar and arithmetic. This characterisation emerged from the practice of the teachers described in Chapter 1 and was probably driven by their experience of war and dreams for a better future. It may also have arisen from contemporary education theory and policy – at that time, Herbert Read and John Berger were influencing arts education while Piaget and Bruner were championing constructivism and 'discovery methods'. Primary education (at least in parts of London) was already familiar with the approaches recommended by the Plowden report. For me education was fun, liberating and engaging; relevant subjects bled into each other and none seemed superior to the rest. Themes like mining, poetry, legends, travel and love were explored from many angles – indeed, I have difficulty in identifying what subjects were applied to the themes; I just know that I was wholly engrossed.

As you read the following summaries of different educational trends, try to identify the sources of the curricular and pedagogical choices that characterised your primary education.

CROSS-CURRICULAR APPROACHES OF THE PAST

Through education, societies or cultures pass on (or draw out) the knowledge, attitudes and skills they most value. The curriculum is the vehicle for releasing, parcelling up and allocating the knowledge and skills considered important. Pedagogy concerns the ways knowledge and skills are communicated and/or delivered by individuals.

Traditional approaches

Responsibility for education in traditional societies is shared among elders, parents (usually fathers with boys, mothers with girls, or mothers with all children up to the age of 4 or 5), extended family members, slightly older age-mates, shamans, priests or pastors. Religion plays a major part in the education of many children around the world. Traditional education in rural communities often uses stories that capture the values, morality or history of the clan or tribe. Education may involve attendance at ceremonies, observing or working alongside older community members, play-hunting, play-planting, collecting, tending, herding, milking, putting out bush fires, house construction and other aspects of rural life. Practical and cultural education is essential to the social, economic, physical and psychological survival of the community.

Alex Ntung, son of a cattle herder from South Kivu in East Congo, describes his education before entering a westernised school in Uvira:

> The birth of every new child in our village was an important educational event for us. It involved many families who brought gifts in special baskets. It was more than just a celebration of a new born baby but a message to other children about how special they are as respected members of the community.
>
> A new born baby was never allowed out of the hut before the official name-giving ceremony, after the mother's customary seven-day confinement. A few weeks later there was a christening.
>
> Both ceremonies were of great importance with loud singing and dancing. As children, we regarded these traditional events in very special way. They were powerful messages about our expected roles as children, in family, clan and community. These cultural messages were reinforced by:

■   Overhearing adults talking about the great choice of the name the new baby had been given.

■   Knowing that we are greater than the cows because we were named on the seventh day whereas a female cow would have to wait for a name relating to its motherhood until after its first its first calf.

It was great for us to know that we were much more important than the animals our community love so much.

The choice of a child's name was also educational. Names are often based on the expected good character and the child's anticipated role in the society. My family-given name is Mvuka Ntungane which means 'born to be of fair justice' [and] my wife's name is Mukinanyana which means 'the one that dances joyfully like the calves'. Other popular names translate as: 'leader', 'one who hates doing wrong things', 'one who knows how to speak for others', 'one who is compassionate', 'one who is gracious', 'one who is a helper', 'one who makes us proud'.

All learning had to be relevant to life. Between the ages of 4 and 10, just after the evening meal, and independently, we would be excited and impatient about going outside to 'play with the moon and stars'. Every day, we looked forward to the night and every night we looked forward to the day because of the wide range of traditional activities that brought joy and learning. In the night time we role-played games involving community and family leadership. Most of the games were rooted in the strong moral and values-based tradition of our cattle herding life style.

In the night, after the outdoor activities, we would head to any grandmothers' hut (all older women, often widows, were our grandmothers). We would be told powerful stories. The stories would make us laugh so much and sometimes would make us cry, but the grandmothers were careful to ensure that such stories left ever-lasting and good moral messages and didn't negatively affect us psychologically. Every story would start with a declaration to ensure that it would not lead to negative learning or bad attitude. The declaration at the beginning of every story was "hara-baye ntihakabe hapha imbga nimbeba hakira inka ningoma." Which means, "Once upon time something happened that should never happen again, if such thing ever returns may it only affect a rat but save people, drums and cows." A story with a bad character would end with another declaration, 'sinje wohera wohera'. Which means that 'may none of us ever do or be such a thing'.

Between 4 and 10 years old, we were assigned roles rather than specific tasks. We were expected to fulfil social and cultural responsibilities appropriate to children. Such roles were performed informally alongside adults, for example milking, fetching water, building huts, making milk pots, growing crops and participation in traditional ceremonies and rite of passage rituals. The rituals were in form of dramas that acted out good and bad values and ended by praising good values.

Our rituals communicated strong messages that placed humans above materials and animals. They reinforced the idea that materials should be a resource for humanity and our livelihood. From about the age of 8 onwards at around midday, after the morning activities, we joined the adults in what was called the 'green field' – a special place. Here men would gather and discuss and re-tell stories of elders and remind us that, 'those who are not interested in talking to a father [all men of their biological father's age group] would never know what their grandfathers said'. The 'green field' also provided an opportunity to learn about a system of a community justice called, 'justice amongst the grass'. In these sessions, leaders known and respected for their integrity, wisdom and abilities had the role of communicating fairness, discussing and resolving conflicts between families, individuals and communities. It was through informal moments in the green field that we learned about ceremonial speeches, the dos and don'ts of community life, being morally right, fairness and equality, impartiality, being truthful and the idea of not taking sides.

Before Christianity, we had our own god. As part of this belief, we were fascinated by the nature's beauty and diversity. We attributed characters and qualities to particular parts of nature. We learned through informal activities for example, how nature responds and reacts through the weather. Through this knowledge we could read and predict events, tell times and meteorological signs accurately. The stories about nature were highly relevant to our geographical areas. We would know for example the character of a river; how far we could play or not play in the area near it. Without modern medical facilities, we would be told about bio-diversity and how it was a source of medicines and cures. We would be told about special trees, the forest itself and the trees that were king and queen of the forest in way that almost humanised the forest.

We loved working alongside the adults but loved being independent still more. We spent time in the forest searching for fruits, swimming in the rivers and preparing traps for quails and searching for honeybees. Such independence gave us a wider view of the world around us and our ability to live symbiotically with it.

Values and moral education was the highest priority. We learned this through stories, proverbs, expressions, legends, metaphors, analogies and herder's poetry. Each oral form applied to our life as cattle herders, and was relevant across all aspects of our lives. Most of the words used by elders were words that were more than simple communication, they carried moral and cultural significance.

As we grew, we learned. Through herding cattle for instance we learned about gender relations, courage, responsibility and accountability. We learned about our society, its kinship system and family genealogy. We were able to recite our ancestry lines as far as fifteen ancestors and their connections with the rest of the clans through their sisters who married into other clans. For me this was a perfect way to imbue a sense of community and interconnection. Every boy child was given the responsibility to carry his clan identity with the highest moral standards, and reflecting these in interactions with others. We learned that every action impacted on our family and community and therefore we should think carefully about our actions.

In our language a hero is someone who does the right thing. Heroism involved behaving in the right way and negative actions were understood to have implications well beyond the action itself. For example, the word 'stealing' in our language is understood as 'killing or destroying friendship'. As herders, we learned through stories that leadership does not only belong to a 'leader' but is a word that could be applied to other aspects of the moral life. We were taught songs that expressed moral and spiritual values and conduct, social norms, integrity, humanity, compassion, helping others in danger, welcoming visitors.

As boy younger than 9, I learned the concept of mathematics through herding. I was able every morning to register more than a hundred cows without having to count them. I would group them in age category, character, male and female. By this process I was also able to conduct a diagnosis of any illnesses or injuries by simple observation. My understanding of number or health was applied across my life, to personal health and that of my friends, to distances, areas, trade and money. Although life was in a kind of wilderness we learned about arts too, but creativity was often for necessity rather than pleasure, for example we made useful and decorated milk pots so we could tell whose was whose. Making music with with musical instruments was different, my dad used to play traditional songs on his flute every morning at 5 o'clock just for the pleasure of it.

Our oral tradition meant that we retained information by its emotional connection. We learned history from grandparents, religion through ceremonies and services. Geography was made personal through searching for good pasture.

This testimony represents an integrated and informal approach to education, familiar across many cultures and times. Modern approaches often separate education from the rest of life. Children in traditional societies still play and work alongside adults living their everyday lives (Rogoff, 2003). Alex describes 'junior' participation in important ceremonies, early responsibility for essential daily tasks, trust, risk, freedom, clear rules and sanctions, communal responsibility independence and lack of close supervision. Traditional education has little formality and no special building, writing or planning, but the curriculum is complete, complex and effective in preparing the young for life in a homogenous society.

Ancient education systems

City-based societies in the ancient world also sought to legitimise social and authority structures through instructing children on the fundamental beliefs of the culture. Like the pastoralists in today's Africa, ancient Greeks in Sparta and Athens and Confucian scholars in China emphasised morals, mainly through stories. Morals were enshrined in laws and conventions written and learned by pupils hoping for administrative or political positions in adulthood. Egyptian scribes and priests taught ethics, virtue and manners as well as hieroglyphics.

As far as we can tell, combinations of contrasting thought processes were encouraged in classical Greek, Egyptian and Chinese systems. 'Wisdom' in ancient Egypt fused ethics, morality, morals, manners and religion. Ancient Greeks combined natural and physical sciences, and rhetoric included religion, language, drama, debate, citizenship, creative writing, and politics. Dance and music were taught together (in Sparta, apparently to help soldiers become more agile).

Formal education in the ancient world was generally restricted to boys from affluent families, but democratisation in Greece meant that increasingly poorer males became eligible. Girls were usually educated at home by their mothers so they could fulfil what were regarded as 'womanly' roles, including running the family business.

In periods of peace and prosperity, combinations of the disciplines characterised the creative high points of civilisation (Csikszentmihalyi, 2002). The Greco/Roman/Egyptian cultural interactions of the 1st and 2nd centuries, the 9th century Tang Dynasty in China, Aztec Mexico in the 15th century and Moghul India in the 17th century each combined arts, technologies, religion and sciences to produce magnificent environments and beautiful objects. The period we call The Renaissance is perhaps the most well-known example of integrated approaches to learning.

Renaissance education

Individual contributions to ideas were more evident during the Renaissance. Great humanists like Dante, Petrarch, Erasmus and Vittoria de Feltre sought inspiration from each other, as well as the pre-Christian cultures of ancient Greece and Rome. Rather than focus exclusively on Christian liturgy and literature, humanist teachers examined classical concepts of virtue and truth. Petrarch discovered and used the ancient Roman Cicero's letters; others sought out philosophical, scientific, mathematical, astrological and geographical tomes from the long lost libraries of Alexandria, Constantinople and Rome. The emphasis of education changed from a God or Bible-centred one, to more liberal and earthly human foci. In the schools of the period, humanistic studies (*Studia humanitatis*) or liberal arts (*Artes Liberales*) involved grammar, rhetoric, history, poetry, mathematics, moral philosophy and music – a general and not a vocational education. Physical education included dance, movement and sport. Greek and Latin were taught as essential to accessing the learning of the ancients.

The aim of Renaissance education was *humanitas* – knowledge of how to live as a cultivated and educated member of society. Wisdom, eloquence, wide general knowledge and aesthetic sensibility were the markers of the educated man (pupils were almost all male), but the men – and a few aristocratic women – still represented a rich minority (Black, 2001). The invention of the printing press by Gutenburg in 1436 challenged the monopoly of the rich and powerful (Man, 2010).

By about 1500, over 20 million books had been printed and distributed throughout present day Germany, Netherlands, Italy, Spain and France. Erasmus alone sold 750,000 copies of his writings during his lifetime (Man, Ibid.*)*.

Desiderius Erasmus (1467–1536)

Erasmus was a celebrity, prolific writer and considered one of the most educated and wise men of his time (Jardine, 1993). Educated in Italy and France, he travelled throughout Europe and was a master of Greek, Latin and the *studia humanitatis*. Significantly, he used the printed word to spread his ideas on the secular good life and a Christianity lived rather than blindly believed. Through books, edifying prints and pamphlets, education could reach beyond the courts and palaces to the lives of small scale land owners, farmers, merchants, shopkeepers and business people, women as well as men. Erasmus's critical and scholarly approaches to Biblical translation and church law, his editions of ancient Greek masterpieces like Ptolomy's *Geografia* and his religious support of Luther illustrate his breadth of knowledge. Erasmus was a 'Renaissance Man' in the same mould as Petrarch, Leonardo da Vinci and Michelangelo: educated across the curriculum and able to see his world through many different lenses.

By the 17th century, humanistic and religiously focussed education developed in tandem throughout Europe and the Americas. Separated disciplines were united via the light they threw on the underlying beliefs of humanism or various interpretations of Christianity. In what became known as 'The Enlightenment', rational approaches began to challenge medieval religious ideas and feudal hierarchies.

Enlightenment and education

'The Enlightenment' describes a period of philosophical, economic, political scientific, intellectual change between the mid-17th century and the beginning of the 19th century. It was led by philosophers such as Descartes, Diderot and Voltaire in France, Spinoza in Holland, Kant in Germany, and Locke, Bacon and Adam Smith in Britain. Enlightenment was founded on ethics, questioning and rational argument rather than authoritarian decrees and compliance. Its ideas arose from and interlinked with the scientific and industrial revolutions. Changes from medieval to enlightenment thinking led to revolution in France, central Europe, and America, and provoked gradual moves toward universal education. Enlightenment ideas emphasised reason, preached religious tolerance, supported the separation of church and state, opposed absolute monarchy and espoused beliefs in freedom, dissent and scientific method. Such thoughts influenced pedagogy, curriculum and society which have lasted until today, but this revolution has its roots in individual biographies.

BIOGRAPHIES AND EDUCATIONAL CHANGE

Brief biographies of some significant figures of Enlightenment philosophy illustrate a close relationship between life stories and the values that led change in 'Western' education.

Jan Comenius (1592–1670)

Comenius, an orphaned and poor child brought up by his grandfather, was among the first educationalists to spread Enlightenment ideas. He was religious and eventually became a bishop in his non-conformist church. Though he was Czech, Comenius lived and worked in France, England, Poland, Hungary, Sweden and Holland. His educational and philosophical writings in German, Czech and Latin were translated into many European languages soon after completion. His seminal book *The Great Didactic* expanded his beliefs in 'natural education', the idea that teachers should follow the inborn progression of children's physically active interests in things around them rather than rely on adult and abstract conceptions of grammars, theorems and rules. His *Janua Linguarum Reserata* ('The Gate of Languages Unlocked') was a collection of useful facts about the world for use in schools, presented in parallel Greek, Latin and Czech texts so that pupils could compare the meanings of words as they learned Latin and/or Greek. Comenius aimed at universal and full-time education for all young people, and believed it should show the connections between all things. He published over 50 textbooks on various aspects of knowledge. His *Orbis Sensualium Pictus* ('The Visible World in Pictures') published in 1658 was enlivened with examples from both local and pan-European cultures and was the first school book where illustrations were used as part of pedagogy. It was used in schools throughout Europe for two centuries. Comenius believed there were basic principles through which knowledge in farming, philosophy, science, botany, zoology, language, logic and music were linked. His work included the ideas that:

- Learning foreign languages brings humans together
- Using objects to generate questions and ideas is more effective than simply using words
- The environment of the child should be used as an educational resource

> ■ Learning should be enjoyable
> ■ Education should be universal and lifelong (Murphy, 1995)
>
> Comenius' division of education into kindergarten, elementary, secondary, college and university still forms the basis of education systems throughout the West.

The invention of printing combined with new philosophies brought education to a new public. The first Encyclopaedias – truly cross-curricular publications – were compiled in England (Chambers *Cyclopaedia* in 1728) and France (Diderot's *Encyclopedie* 1758), and were quickly popular. Within a few years, they had begun to achieve their aim of changing the way people thought. The first edition of Diderot's work sold over 4,250 copies in France alone. It was published in 28 volumes and contained almost 72,000 articles and 3,100 illustrations by the leading thinkers, artists and scientists of the day (Blom, 2005). The encyclopaedia claimed to be a "systematic dictionary of the sciences, arts and crafts", and placed knowledge in the hands of secular writers like Voltaire and Rousseau, wresting control of education from the hands of the church. The goal of Diderot's encyclopaedia was to:

> assemble all the knowledge scattered on the surface of the earth, to demonstrate the general system to the people with whom we live, & to transmit it to the people who will come after us, so that the works of centuries past is not useless to the centuries which follow, that our descendants, by becoming more learned, may become more virtuous & happier.
>
> (Berger, 2016)

Reprints, new editions and translations of the encyclopaedias fed education well into the 19th century.

Jean-Jacques Rousseau (1712–1778)

Rousseau was born in Geneva. His mother died within days of his birth. He was brought up by his father, a well-read clockmaker who read French novels and Classical texts with him as he worked. At the age of 11 or 12, Rousseau was fostered by his uncle and, after a perfunctory education, apprenticed to an engraver whose harsh treatment caused him to run away and seek safety away from Geneva. By 15, he was informally adopted by a Catholic woman in northern Italy. His female guardian converted him to Catholicism, educated him in philosophy, musical composition and performance, and eventually took him as a lover. His autobiographical works suggest a somewhat confused, lonely, hypochondriac and isolated young man. He became perhaps the most influential educational thinker of The Enlightenment.

Rousseau lived most of his adult life in France becoming a leader of intellectuals, friend of Diderot and a respected musician and composer who had revolutionary ideas about religion and education. His educational ideas were expressed in the five volumes of *Emile* (Rousseau, 1776). Contrary to his Calvinistic upbringing with its beliefs in the fundamental sinfulness of all human beings, Rousseau believed that humans were naturally good and that society gradually corrupted childhood innocence. The education system outlined in *Emile* suggested that by controlling the environment within which the child was educated, society's negative influence could be minimised until the individual was more capable of rational and good moral choices. Rousseau's educational philosophy was founded upon a concern for the individual's right to freedom and happiness. He advocated individualised and 'child-centred' approaches to education, reflecting the diversity of each soul.

Rousseau's ideas were cross-curricular, too. In the idealised world of *Emile*, everything was linked to the child's sensory and emotional development. We read of Emile playing freely in the outdoors, within a wholly natural environment, developing his senses, discovering and making connections while his tutor supports and facilitates rather than instructs. As Emile approaches puberty the focus changes and he learns physical, dextrous skills like carpentry in order to develop manual and constructive abilities. Formalised education only begins in the teenage years when Emile's dedicated tutor supports and extends his curiosity and introduces history and religion in a sceptical, free thinking and questioning context. As a young adult, Emile learns about the corrupting influence of society.

Significantly Rousseau reminds us of the scant control parents and teachers had over the outcomes for their children:

> [O]ur power is largely illusory, for who can hope to direct every word and deed of all with whom the child has to do.
>
>   Viewed as an art, the success of education is almost impossible since the essential conditions of success are beyond our control. Our efforts may bring us within sight of the goal, but fortune must favour us if we are to reach it.
>
> Jean-Jacques Rousseau (1762)

In Book 5, Emile meets Sophie, whose education has been similar though angled towards the gendered roles typical of the period. They learn about love and friendship and their respective roles in adult life together.

Johann Pestalozzi (1746–1827)

Pestalozzi also experienced, loss, exile and poverty in his early life. He was brought up by an impoverished widowed mother and her housemaid, but also was highly influenced by his pastor grandfather who actively cared for the poor and sick of the locality. The values Pestalozzi developed in these years shaped his philosophy and contribution to education. He adopted a similar romantic approach to that of Rousseau, but rather than concentrating on polemic, Pestalozzi put forward detailed advice on regular teaching and a practical focus on the role of schools. In his own teaching, he observed that education was most successful when learning tasks were practical and broken down into small steps and basic elements. Life experience and the influence of his grandfather showed Pestalozzi the importance of sympathy and care for individuals and engendered his belief in social justice. Pestalozzi was passionate about the education of the poor and particularly orphans. Like Rousseau he expressed his philosophy in story or letter form. His book *How Gertrude Teaches Her Children* (Pestalozzi, 1801) was influential throughout his native Switzerland. Pestalozzi linked moral and intellectual education with personally selected goals, sensory engagement, individual differences, physical education and outdoor activity – cross-curricular learning with a single aim – *fitness for life*.

> Lead your child by the hand to the great scenes of nature; teach him on the mountain and in the valley. There he will listen better to your teaching; the liberty will give him greater force to surmount difficulties. But in these hours of liberty it should be nature that teaches rather than you. Do not allow yourself to prevail for the pleasure of success in your teaching; or to desire in the least to proceed when nature diverts him; do not take away in the least the pleasure which she offers him. Let him completely realize that it is nature that teaches, and that you, with your art, do nothing more than walk quietly at her side. When he hears a bird warble or an insect hum on a leaf, then cease your talk; the bird and the insect are teaching; your business is then to be silent.
>
> Pestalozzi diary entry (1774–02–15)

Friedrich Froebel (1782–1852)

Froebel lived and worked in Germany and Switzerland. Like Comenius, Rousseau and Pestalozzi, he lost a parent early and was brought up by others. In adolescence, Froebel showed a strong interest in plants, animals and construction. He took a range of practical jobs including forestry, but eventually in his early 20s, Froebel became a tutor. Whilst working in a school he met Pestalozzi, and this meeting consolidated Froebel's progressive ideas about pedagogy. Like Pestalozzi, he was religious with a strong social conscience. With friends, Froebel founded a school in Germany and later an education institute to carry forward his ideas. He wrote pamphlets, launched an education magazine and brought together experience and theory in *The Education of Man* in 1826. In the gendered language of the time Froebel stated that education's purpose was:

> to encourage and guide man as a conscious, thinking and perceiving being in such as way that he becomes a pure and perfect representation of that divine inner law through his own personal choice.
>
> Froebel (1826: 2)

Childhood experience of personal loss, Christianity and the natural world link Froebel's life with the biographies and philosophies of Comenius, Rousseau and Pestalozzi. These features are evident in the metaphors, examples and recommendations employed throughout his writings. For example:

> We grant space and time to young plants and animals because we know that, in accordance with; the laws that live in them, they will develop properly and grow well; young animals and plants are given rest, and arbitrary interference with their growth is avoided, because it is known that the opposite practice would disturb their pure unfolding and sound development; but the young human being is looked upon as a piece of wax, a lump of clay which man can mould into what he pleases.
>
> Froebel (1826: 8)

Froebel's contribution is strongly linked with Early Years education. He developed toys for young children, basic shapes and forms with which they could construct imaginary worlds and interact with each other. He founded a number of popular nursery schools whose success led the Swiss government to ask him to establish nurseries throughout the country. His term for nursery, 'kindergarten', links childhood both physically and metaphorically with the garden. Education outdoors, free, active, following nature and playful characterised Froebel's approach. Singing, playing games, constricting patterns from nature or pattern books, building with Froebel's 'gifts' (the geometric building blocks) and gardening formed the core of kindergarten activities. His ideas spread through writings, song books and pamphlets, but also depended on the patronage of aristocratic and progressive families in 19th century Germany, Switzerland, the Netherlands, Britain and the USA.

19th century influences on cross-curricular learning

In many ways, education became a tool of industrialisation. The rapid spread of factories, transport, trade and colonialisation required schools to produce a quickly and uniformly educated population. Instruction in the separated subjects – mathematics, language, geography, history, religion and increasingly science and technology – was the shortcut to a literate and numerate workforce. The personalised, cross-curricular, nature-based ideals of The Enlightenment were inefficient – unfit for the conformist, practical, industrial purposes of education.

Some 19th and early 20th century thinkers, however, held to the wisdom of the Enlightenment and continued to argue for broader, more connected approaches to education. A brief summary of their early years suggests why these 19th century philosophers and psychologists thought as they did.

John Dewey (1859–1952)

Dewey understood the disadvantaged. His father was a small scale grocer and his mother an evangelical Christian with a deep care for the poor. An elder brother died tragically shortly before John's birth – the calamity of his death perhaps contributing to Dewey's shy, self-consciousness nature. Dewey initially identified as an active Christian, though later declared himself an atheist and co-founded an influential humanist association. Friendships with prominent philosophers and sociologists like William James and George Herbert Mead, and political activists like his wife Alice Chipman, established the themes of his contribution to educational thought.

In education, Dewey recommended inter-disciplinary approaches to deepen understandings of democracy, sensory experience, pragmatism (in the sense of learning through doing), community, social learning and child-centredness. Knowledge for Dewey was not static or absolute, but open to interpretation, personal, provisional. He is seen by many as a founder of the 'Progressive Education' movement, though several of his later publications were written to counter the *laissez-faire* tendency of some progressive practitioners. Dewey sought balance between subject and experience, adult and child, society and individual, freedom and responsibility. He argued that children should be personally involved in creating knowledge through experience, problem-based learning (PBL) and experiment. He believed that individuals whose personal experience had been enlarged through education would enrich every community. Though personal reflection was important, he stressed the importance of the group:

> I believe that the only true education comes through the stimulation of the child's powers by the demands of the social situations in which he finds himself. Through these demands he is stimulated to act as a member of a unity, to emerge from his original narrowness of action and feeling, and to conceive of himself from the standpoint of the welfare of the group to which he belongs. Through the responses which others make to his own activities he comes to know what these mean in social terms.
>
> Dewey (1897: 77–80)

Rudolf Steiner (1861–1925)

Steiner was the son of Austrian gamekeeper. He was not a privileged child, moving home frequently as his station master father changed jobs and responsibilities. Steiner too had strong religious influences. He claimed at 9 years of age to have seen an apparition of a dead aunt no one knew had died. This experience and other profound religious encounters coloured the rest of his life and thought. Steiner was a polymath like Rousseau: an architect, literary critic, editor, political and social reformer, agricultural advisor and spiritual leader as well as an educationalist.

Steiner believed like Rousseau in the innate wisdom and goodness of human beings. In proposals for his 'Waldorf schools' (Steiner, 1919), he gave a detailed outline of a curriculum led by the physical and psychological development of the child. His work editing and critiquing the poet Goethe's writing on science led him to believe that reality could be experienced in many ways. Thought was just one means of understanding the world, observation, dance, music, art and drama were others. Thinking, he wrote, "is no more and no less an organ of perception than the eye or ear. Just as the eye perceives colours and the ear sounds, so thinking perceives ideas" (Steiner, 1908: 7).

Steiner's curriculum made connections. It was science-based, but like his architecture and literary interests, was strongly infused with artistic sensibility. His *Waldorf* curriculum (named after the cigarette factory where he first shared his philosophy) was rapidly taken up by progressive educationalists and Steiner schools appeared in England, Germany, the Netherlands and the USA during the early 20th century. There are now some 1200 schools and 2000 Early Years settings in 60 countries. Steiner's curriculum mirrored the child's unfolding consciousness, physical and sensory development, creativity and imagination. Its classical aims – "to cultivate responsibility for the earth and other people and prepare children for the challenges of the future" (Steiner, 1919: 2) – were designed to offer a personally engaging, spiritually conscious, experience within the physical world of nature.

CONCLUSION

The thinkers introduced in this chapter helped shape approaches to cross-curricular learning. The global communications revolution starting in the 19th century has meant that ideas quickly spread.

The educational thinkers who laid the foundations of 'progressive' education in the 20th and 21st centuries often had personal reasons for developing the approaches they took. Many were fostered, disadvantaged children; each drew universal values from the religious traditions they were nurtured within; each worked with other like-minded individuals and each had a global or at least international outlook. These philosophers, psychologists and pedagogues championed big values like freedom, equality, care, justice, sensitivity, co-responsibility, inter-relationship and the right to happiness, arguably because education had liberated them from personal poverty and powerlessness. The giants of education history were perhaps as influenced by their early childhood experiences as we are.

REFERENCES

Berger, J. (2016) *Confabulations,* London: Penguin.
Black, R. (2001) *Humanism and Education in Medieval and Renaissance Italy: Tradition and Innovation in Latin Schools From the Twelfth to the Fifteenth Century.* Cambridge: Cambridge University Press.
Blom, P. (2005) *Enlightening the World: Encyclopédie, the Book That Changed the Course of History.* New York: Palgrave Macmillan.

Csikszentmihalyi, M. (2002) *Flow: The Classic Work on How to Achieve Happiness*. New York: Harper Collins.

Dewey (1897) My pedagogic creed. *The School Journal*, Vol. 54, No. 3, pp. 77–80, available at: http://dewey.pragmatism.org/creed.htm (accessed 25.10.17).

Froebel (1826) *The education of man*, available at: www.froebelweb.org/web7000.html

Jardine, L. (1993) *Erasmus, Man of Letters: The Construction of Charisma in Print*. Princeton, NJ: Princeton University Press.

Man, J. (2010) *The Gutenberg Revolution*. London: Bantam.

Murphy, D. (1995) *Comenius: A Critical Re-appraisal of his Life and Work*. Dublin: Irish Academic Press.

Pestalozzi, J. (1801) *How Gertrude Teaches Her Children*, ed. E. Cooke, trans. L. E. Holland and F. C. Turner. Syracuse, NY, 1894, letter VII, p. 97.

Rogoff, B. (2003) *The Cultural Nature Human Development*. New York: Oxford.

Rousseau, J.-J. (1776) *Émile* (1911 ed.). London: Dent.

Steiner, R. (1908) Available in translation (2016) *The Way of Initiation: How to Attain Knowledge of the Higher Worlds*. Los Angeles, CA: Enhanced Media Publishing.

Steiner, R. (1919) *Education: An Introductory Reader*. London: Rudolf Steiner Press.

CHAPTER 4

THE CROSS-CURRICULUM IN THE 20TH AND 21ST CENTURIES

SUMMARY

This chapter considers the contribution of some 20th and 21st century educationalists with an interest in cross-curricular and creative approaches. A sample of the characters who influenced the constructivist educational philosophies are introduced. The views of some challengers of constructivism are represented, as are those that championed wider, more inclusive interpretations of intelligence, creativity and learning.

20TH CENTURY DEVELOPMENTS IN CROSS-CURRICULAR EDUCATION

Dewey's ideas carried powerfully over into the 20th century. They affected British education legislation via the UK's Hadow Report (UK Board of Education 1931). Hadow's famous claim that, "The curriculum is to be thought of in terms of activity and experience rather than knowledge to be acquired and facts to be stored" (Para. 75) influenced cross-curricular thinking throughout the century. Dewey's impact on primary education was particularly notable in the Plowden report (1967) published 15 years after his death. In this seminal and research-based report: discovery, exploration, child-centred approaches and the idea that the school was not 'a teaching shop' dominated and influenced teaching and the curriculum throughout the 1970s. Steiner's ideas were more cautiously implemented in the UK though along with Dewey's, they strongly influenced the more progressive thinkers like A. S. Neill and his Summerhill School founded in 1921.

Maria Montessori (1870–1952)

Montessori was unusual for a late 19th century woman. She ignored her parents' wishes and trained as a doctor in an age when doctoring was considered a man's occupation. She gave birth to a child outside marriage and refused to marry the child's father because she would have had to give up doctoring. Her commitment to hospital work meant that her child was temporarily fostered, though she reunited with him in his teenage years. Montessori developed an interest in children with mental disabilities in a time when it was much more common to lock them out of sight. Her detailed observations of children with major barriers to learning helped her develop what she called 'scientific pedagogy'. Eventually by 1907, Montessori was applying to mainstream children her successful methods of teaching children with difficulties.

Montessori's independence as a person shows itself in the independence she sought to develop in the young. She developed a distinctive style of Early Years practice: child-sized furniture, light airy rooms, special materials placed on labelled shelves where children could access them independently. Practical activity was encouraged, including cleaning, sweeping, washing, flower arranging, the care of animals and cookery. She developed early reading and writing materials using cut-out pictures, with captions to match, sandpaper letters to feel, and moveable words and letters. Her schools timetabled clay modelling, painting, designing and outdoor physical exercise for all. Each child had their own responsibilities, keeping their class areas tidy and organised, and was encouraged to move around themed areas as they wished.

The Montessori method was adopted throughout Italy and by 1913 was used in pre-schools in Switzerland, the UK and the USA, New Zealand, Australia, China, Japan, Argentina, Syria, Mexico, Sweden and India.

Susan Isaacs (1885–1948)

Isaacs was another influential educationalist who lost a parent early in life and lived an unhappy childhood with a stepmother. She was born in Lancashire to a religious family, and when she converted to atheism at 15, her father refused to speak to her for two years. After a successful university education, Isaacs trained as a psychotherapist within the Freudian tradition and set up a psychoanalytical practice in 1923. Perhaps due to her unhappy childhood she focused on the experience of children in the early years of life and studied Melanie Klein's approaches to psychoanalysis with the young. Her commitment to Early Years led her to accept the headship of a private and experimental nursery school in Cambridge, where she implemented Dewey's ideas and implemented a curriculum led by play and the development of independence, curiosity, exploration and fantasy. Isaacs confirmed the necessity of play as the foundation of all later learning and championed the development of independence in Early Years children. (Giardiello, 2013)

Jean Piaget (1896–1980)

Much modern education theory is underpinned by the work of Piaget, one of the most quoted of all psychologists (APA, 2002). From the 1920s onwards, he and co-workers suggested that children pass through predictable stages in their learning journeys (Piaget, 1954). Piaget observed (largely in his daughter and nephew) that children learned first through the application of basic *sensorimotor* and reflex actions. Piaget noticed that children between 0 and 2 years use sensory and physical exploration of their environment to experiment with often nameless but tangible things. When objects are hidden, to the infant's mind they cease to exist. Gradually after 2, Piaget suggested that children move towards a *preoperational* stage. Objects increasingly have names and exist in the child's mind even when not visible – they have permanence. Children between 2 and 7 years, however, find difficulty in understanding that objects continue to have the same properties when the viewpoint or shape changes. Thus, an amount of sand poured into a tall thin container will be judged as more than the same amount poured into a low flat one. In this period, the child begins to understand that others have different minds than theirs. This appreciation of other minds, a gradual understanding of the conservation of properties and the recognition of the self as unique are features of Piaget's third stage of development, *'concrete operations'*. Between 7 and 13 years, children were observed to develop a deeper theory of mind and become less self-centred. At this age, most find it challenging to apply logic or understand hypotheses. Children normally arrive at the final Piagetian state of *'formal operations'* in adolescence. In this stage the child uses deductive reasoning, understands that there are multiple solutions to problems, uses reason and imagination, and applies abstract thought.

At each of Piaget's developmental stages the child creates *'schemas'*. These are workable concepts that help make sense of the world – they involve not only the names of things but their general category so that by 2, a child may know that even a bad drawing of a cat is a 'cat' and not a dog. A schema changes in line with experience and uses the processes of *accommodation* and *assimilation* – essentially adding detail and variation to their initial concept (or example understanding that both Chihuahuas and St Bernards are dogs, but a fox isn't). Piaget stressed that the child's mind changes during their journey from stages 1–4. Today, many recognise that different types of activity – for example, physical, moral, interpersonal, intrapersonal, imaginative or creative behaviours – may follow the developmental sequence at different times in a child's life. Most psychologists agree that the stages from sensory and emotional experimentation to abstract or 'higher order thinking' usually need to be passed through in order for a new concept is to be fully internalised and put into practice. If the exploratory or imaginative play typical of Piaget's first two stages are missing from child's experience, it is very difficult for them to make mature, reasoned sense of the world.

Piaget's research sample was small. He once described the child as 'a lone scientist' (Piaget, 1954) but more often children learn together. They learn through play and observation, through someone modelling a new thought or action (Bandura, 1994). Lev Vygotsky was among the first in the 20th century to stress the social nature of learning.

Lev Vygotsky (1896–1934)

Vygotsky was from a Jewish family from what is now Belarus. Despite the anti-Semitic trends of the time, he was educated at Moscow University. An exceptionally intelligent child, he had interests and skills across the curriculum. At school he excelled in humanities, arts and social studies, but was encouraged to study medicine by his parents, later transferring to law and then psychology. His most influential work drew attention to social intercourse and interdependence as crucial parts of learning. His work on developmental psychology only became well known in the west after translation into English, German and French, 30 years after his death (Vygotsky, 1962, 1978). Vygotsky's scientific observations of children learning showed that practical activity and social interaction, signs, symbols and speech – particularly 'inner speech' were closely involved in their mental development. He proposed the existence of a *'Zone of Proximal Development'* (ZPD) that supports children's learning in groups. The ZPD was a combination of previous learning, instruction, interaction and activity with more capable others. Vygotsky noted that children achieved more than would be expected on a purely developmental level when they worked in groups to solve problems.

A. S. Neill (1883–1973)

Like many leaders of educational thought, Neill was brought up in a highly religious home. Like many earlier education reformers, he was also poor and suffered sadness in his childhood, losing five of his 13 siblings. The religious beliefs of his parents rested on a presumption of original sin; the authority of God, the Bible and adults; strong feelings of guilt and fear of damnation. In the subsequent development of his education ideas, all these beliefs were abandoned and contradicted. Neill thought that children were naturally good and would become thoughtful, moral adults if they were left without adult or authoritative coercion. He believed that the aim of life was, "to find happiness, which means to find interest." He considered that most students were not interested in the standard curriculum subjects, but that "learning should come after play" and "not deliberately seasoned with play to make it palatable."

> Most school work that adolescents do is simply a waste of time, of energy, of patience. It robs youth of its right to play and play and play It puts old heads on young shoulders.
>
> (Summerhill School website)

He founded Summerhill School in Suffolk in 1921, a democratic and self-governing community in which children learned what and when they wanted with teachers who were ready to build upon interests they had discovered through play. Summerhill continues to educate 5–17-year-olds who choose whether or not to go to lessons, are democratically consulted on all issues regarding their education and community, and are given free access to play throughout their time there. Students do take GCSEs and attend lessons, but these are constructed so that students can come and go as they wish. Neill's belief that schools, authority, religion and adult society corrupt the innocence and enthusiasm of the child follows Rousseau's philosophy.

> The function of the child is to live his own life, not the life that his anxious parents think he should live, nor a life according to the purpose of the educator who thinks he knows best. All this interference and guidance on the part of adults only produces a generation of robots.
>
> (Neill, 1960: 15)

Reducing the 'power differential' between adult and child members of the Summerhill community is a central part of its safeguarding policy, but adults remain responsible to protecting pupils from harm.

Traditional curriculum subjects are taught but the curriculum itself is seen as much broader – the truly cross-curricular journey towards the discovery of identity.

21ST CENTURY THOUGHTS ON A CURRICULUM THAT CONNECTS

Jerome Bruner (1915–2016)

Bruner was born blind, only regaining his sight after an operation at the age of 8. In his educational work, he postulated the centrality of the social in children's education and has had profound impacts upon schools and curricular organisation in both the USA and the UK. Bruner's active longevity has meant that he is one of the most quoted psychologists of the 20th century (Bruner, 1968, 1996). Bruner's championing of 'discovery' methods echoes many enlightenment ideas. Under his influence, many teachers introduced forms of 'scaffolded learning', where 'more knowledgeable others' support the concept-formation of the rest. Making sense, according to Bruner, "is a social process; it is an activity that is always situated in a cultural and historical context" (Bruner and Haste, 1987: 4). He claimed that children could understand almost any concept given the appropriate level of support and his 'spiral' curriculum showed that revisiting the same educational issue at progressively higher intellectual levels, consolidated and deepened learning

Bruner's curriculum *'Man: A Course of Study'* (1965) was truly cross-curricular in linking the insights, skills and language of each of the humanities disciplines within a questioning, exploratory and open-minded context.

Eric Hirsch (1928–present)

E. D. Hirsch Jr. is the son of businessman and Rabbi Eric Hirsch, Snr. and his wife Leah. Born in Tennessee, successful and academic at school, he was made a Fullbright scholar at 25, became a literary critic and academic specialising in the Romantic period and wrote on Wordsworth and William Blake during the 1960s. Hirsch taught at Yale University and was a professor by his thirties. By the 1970s, his teaching led him to become interested in the fact that many of his students – especially the poorer ones – lacked what he called 'cultural literacy': the background knowledge to help them make sense of the curriculum. His subsequent books focused on how to make a curriculum that provided the cultural knowledge he found missing in many, (Hirsch, 1987, 1996, 2006, 2016, 2017). In these volumes, Hirsch recommend a much greater emphasis, especially in the primary years, on knowledge than was suggested by the child-centred approaches of Piaget, Dewey and Bruner. The focus on what Hirsch calls 'core knowledge' attracted the attention of UK government ministers Nick Gibb and Michael Gove. Nick Gibb echoed Hirsch's thinking when he stated that schools should teach "not just any knowledge but that knowledge which constitutes the shared intellectual currency of the society." (BBC, 2012). The problem with the Hirsch approach is that it is only the powerful that define what knowledge is 'core'.

The core knowledge sequence for art suggests for instance that a 5–6-year-old should:

▨ Recognise as a portrait or self-portrait: Leonardo da Vinci, *Mona Lisa*; Francisco Goya; Don Manuel Osorio Manrique de Zuñiga; Vincent van Gogh, *Self-Portrait* [1889]
▨ Recognise as a still life: Vincent van Gogh, Irises, Paul Cézanne, studies with fruit, such as apples and oranges
▨ Recognise as a mural (a painting on a wall): Diego Rivera, The History of Medicine in Mexico (Core Knowledge Foundation, 2010)

For music they should:

▨ Know that a composer is someone who writes music
▨ Become familiar with Wolfgang Amadeus Mozart as a composer who wrote what is known as classical music, and listen to the Allegro (first movement) from "A Little Night Music" ("Eine kleine Nachtmusik")

- Become familiar with the families of instruments in the orchestra: strings, brass, woodwinds, percussion
- Know that the leader of the orchestra is called the conductor
- Listen to Sergei Prokofiev, Peter and the Wolf (Core Knowledge Foundation, 2010)

Nel Noddings (1929–present)

Noddings is a philosopher whose feminist stance has had profoundly influenced many educators. She writes and lectures on the 'ethics of care' applied to education. Her philosophical and educational thought has been deeply influenced by her own liberal education experience which consisted of "a great deal of art, music, drama and no homework". She was an elementary school teacher and secondary mathematics teacher for 17 years before becoming an academic. She states that her life was 'rescued' by her 10 children and grandchildren (Noddings Centre website).

Applying an 'ethic of care' in schools involves, Noddings (2003) argues, the teacher trying to do 'something right' and "relational with the children they work with rather than simply passing on knowledge". Care in education, she claims, requires first that the teacher know and understand the needs of the child, whether they are *inferred* needs *(i.e.* not expressed and therefore have to be identified by knowing each child as an individual), *expressed* needs (through behaviour or words, which they should treat positively for fear of causing the child to repress or hide them), *basic* needs (for food, water, shelter), or *overwhelming* needs (which require the teacher to become one part of a cross-disciplinary team supporting the social, health, psychological and parenting needs of the child).

She observes that children who are poor, disadvantaged, abused, traumatised, anxious or unhappy often have basic and overwhelming needs that make motivation towards school learning weak or entirely missing. For such children, education easily becomes unmotivating and irrelevant. Unhappy children, Noddings suggests, are not well served by teachers and systems that prize professional detachment and unemotional responses (1992). Since education, in Noddings' terms, should aim primarily at children's happiness, she says:

> We will not find the solution to problems of violence, alienation, ignorance, and unhappiness in increasing our security, imposing more tests, punishing schools for their failure to produce 100 percent proficiency, or demanding that teachers be knowledgeable in the subjects they teach. Instead, we must allow teachers and students to interact as whole persons, and we must develop policies that treat the school as a whole community.
>
> (Noddings, 2005: 13)

Noddings's approach has been particularly important for the education of children with additional or 'special' needs.

David Kolb (1939–present)

Kolb believes that authentic experience is the most effective motivator of learning (1984). He observes that meaningful and novel encounters such as those in fieldwork, experiments, construction or the examination of an unusual object, constitute the first stage of learning.

This experience he sees as being followed by the learner reflecting on the experience, asking, for example, what it meant to them, what was special about it or how it worked. After thinking, Kolb hypothesises that learners go through a process of 'abstract conceptualization' where they attempt to construct a theory that fits into preexisting models, knowledge or explanations. The last stage of learning involves the learner experimenting or testing their new understanding to see how far it transfers to new situations. These stages are not necessarily sequential and often require repetition

Kolb's learning theory posits four kinds of learning and learners:

■ Assimilators – who learn best when they are given theories to work within. They enjoy planning, research, theory, inductive reasoning and abstract ideas.
■ Convergers – who learn when asked to practically apply new ideas. Learners with this strength tend to have narrow and well-focused interests and do best when there is a single best solution to a problem.
■ Accommodators – who need to 'do' before fully understanding. These learners tend to like actively carrying our plans in the real world with real implications and are less happy with abstractions. They tend to be relaxed taking risks with ideas and responding intuitively.
■ Divergers – who learn better when they observe and collect ideas and influences and experiences from many sources. These learners have a broad range of interests are happy with creative and diverse inputs and bringing disparate elements into a 'bigger picture'. (McLeod, 2013)

Kolb's experiential learning theory unsurprisingly places experience first. In a primary school setting, such experiences need not be formal or closely related to a single subject, but may cross a number of subject boundaries. According to Kolb, experience creates knowledge and learning relates to the ability to respond thoughtfully to that experience with others. Taking an integrative, connecting, interactive approach to the physical, social and inner environments, he argues, promotes learning and healthy communities.

Howard Gardner (1943–present)

Gardner worked with Bruner in the 1960s as a developmental psychologist. He was the studious son of a Jewish German refugee family which greatly valued education. As a child, he loved learning and particularly enjoyed the piano – he taught piano for 10 years. Like many of the educationalists we have encountered earlier, his early life was not without sadness however, he observes: "the accidental death of my older brother and my family's losses in the Holocaust – came to dominate my childhood" (Gardner, 2006: 1). Gardner's academic drive and wide range of interests and abilities eventually resulted in research into the mind and most famously, intelligence.

His influential book *Frames of Mind: The Theory of Multiple Intelligences* (Gardner 1993) countered traditional Intelligence Quotient (IQ) based definitions. His research and scholarship provided evidence across the disciplines of neuroscience, medicine, psychology, history and anthropology. His observations across contrasting cultural realities demonstrated many different and largely autonomous ways of being intelligent. Gardner's research suggested at least eight independent ways of making sense of the world. He named them: linguistic, logical-mathematical, spatial, bodily-kinaesthetic, intrapersonal, interpersonal, musical, naturalistic and perhaps spiritual intelligences. It challenged the idea that intelligence could only be measured in tests of logic, language or arithmetic and widened its definition so that it was possible for teachers to see many non-verbal, non-logical responses as intelligent. Gardner's work on intelligence and curriculum (1993, 1999) has resulted in a resurgence of informed interest in cross-curricular approaches across the world. *Time*, *Prospect* and *Foreign Policy* Magazines each placed him amongst the 100 most influential academics of the 20th century.

Gardner's work and influence has been strongly criticised by the work of his contemporary E. D. Hirsch Jnr. (1998).

Gardner's later work on how the disciplines can be combined (1999) how minds change or can be changed (2004), how minds can shape a better future (2005), how to lead creatively and how to let values lead (1999, 2012) has profound implications for the curriculum and the understanding of creativity. His proposed curricula seek to enhance moral and creative behaviour through widening and deepening understanding in a context where all feel valued and empowered to contribute. One ought, as he says, "always to be thinking about ways in which one should use one's skills and sensibility for the broader welfare" (Gardner, 2013: 88).

Robert Sternberg (1949–present)

Sternberg was born to poor parents, neither of whom completed secondary education. His family needed financial aid to help him enter tertiary education. He suffered extreme test anxiety and even in his youth determined that intelligence tests did not accurately measure his or others' true intelligence. As a result of his negative experience of tests, Sternberg studied and researched intelligence from 1970 until the late 1990s. His triarchic model of intelligence is perhaps his most significant contribution to education. The triarchic theory (1997) posits three types of intelligence: practical, creative and analytical. Analytical intelligence is most like the kind that intelligence tests measure; it is logical, academic, solves well-defined problems and expects a single correct solution. Creative or 'synthetic' intelligence is strong at dealing with unusual situations, multiple answers that bring together contrasting modes of thinking. Those with a strong practical intelligence use their knowledge and skills to solve specific and practical problems. Many children formerly labelled as having special educational needs show these kinds of intelligence.

Combined with memory and 'general' intelligence, Sternberg's three types of intelligence suggest that there are different ways of knowing, different ways of learning. It follows, he suggests, that a curriculum to suit these different types of intelligence must offer practical, creative and analytical means of addressing problems and presenting solutions. His triarchic theory also suggests that there should be at least three different ways of presenting and assessing knowledge in addition to traditional intelligence tests. His work on creativity has identified nine different ways of being creative (Sternberg and Kaufman, 2010).

Sir Robin Alexander (1941–present)

Alexander was the son of a filmmaker and an artist. He has degrees in music as well as education. He was a teacher and lecturer before he became an academic and researcher. He has lived and worked internationally throughout Europe and in Bangladesh and India. Alexander's writing and research on primary education since the 1980s has been highly influential in areas of policy, pedagogy, classroom studies, teacher education, curriculum evaluation. Alexander's contribution to what became known as the *Three Wise Men Report* (Alexander et al. 1992) on primary curriculum and organisation, initially resulted in a return to single subject teaching and a move away from cross-curricular 'Topic' work. He and his colleagues reported that, "the progress of primary pupils has been hampered by the influence of highly questionable dogmas which have led to excessively complex classroom practices and devalued the place of subjects in the curriculum" (Alexander et al., 1992). The Report recommended:

■ An appropriate balance of subject and carefully focused topic work
■ The preservation of the integrity of each subject
■ An appropriate balance of the various cross-subject activities; for example, reading, writing, talk, collaborative activity, practical work

More recently Alexander's work on comparative and cross-cultural education and the importance of the dialogic approach has brought cross-curricular approaches once again to the fore.

The Cambridge Primary Review (Alexander, 2010) recommends balance of disciplinary skills and cross-curricular themes. It speaks of the 'pernicious dichotomy' (2010: 243) between a broad and balanced curriculum and high standards in the basics recommending that both are important. It combines *aims* of education and *domains* of learning to propose a curriculum flexible enough to serve a wide variety of communities and localities. The cross-curricular tone of Alexander's proposal is clear.

Domains like 'place and time' and 'arts and creativity' clearly expect connections between geography and history and art, music and drama. The domains of physical /emotional health, language, oracy and literacy, citizenship and ethics and science/technology imply approaches which cut across traditional subject boundaries.

Sir Ken Robinson (1950–present)

Robinson was born into a working class family of seven children. He knew hardship and pain from an early age – his father became a paraplegic after an injury in a work accident. Robinson contracted polio at the age of 4 which first paralysed him and later confined him to a wheelchair. Through his primary school years, he gradually regained the ability to walk with the aid of calipers. Despite this barrier he developed a strong interest in drama and theatre, including dance, and completed his PhD on theatre in education. He led the *Arts in Schools* project (Robinson 1989) which strongly influenced the first iterations of the National Curriculum in England and Wales by the National Curriculum Council. By 1998, Robinson had been commissioned by the Labour government to lead a National Advisory Committee for Creative and Cultural Education (NACCCE). It published its ground-breaking report, *All Our Futures*, in 1999, which argued for the parity of all curriculum subjects, a strong focus on creative teaching and teaching for creativity. It provided definitions of creativity and culture that drew attention to their democratic and inclusive nature and the need to reflect our rapidly changing society (Robinson, 1999). It made the important point that the creative industries were of major importance to the UK economy and that facing the complex issues of the 21st century would require a workforce and population ready to work in creative teams at all levels.

Since 2000, Robinson has championed creativity the arts and a broad and integrated approach to the curriculum in schools. The national Creative Partnerships project which the NACCCE report recommended placed creative practitioners in thousands of schools in deprived areas of England over a period of nine years from 2002. Their job was to find creativity and promote it across the whole curriculum in primary and secondary schools.

Robinson's belief in the value of diversity and the need for education to reflect not just cultural diversity, but the diversity within each one of us, has directed much of his educational thought. Education should be individualised and the palette of curriculum choices kept as wide as possible. It should be arranged practically and emotionally so that curiosity and deep interest are likely outcomes of teaching and it should focus on the discovery of what is creative in each individual (see also OECD, 2004).

His critique of current education systems in both the UK and USA is that they are too dominated by tests, by an unengaging 'learning factory' approach which has led to over-standardisation, rigid compliance and a conformity that has stifled creativity and individuality.

CONCLUSION

The educators and movements of the 20th and 21st centuries have emphasised the importance of developing a range of mindsets to fulfil the purposes of education. They have recognised that education works best when it is fitted within greater ideals and wider philosophies. Traditional systems similarly placed education within the broader requirements of lifestyle, community and society. The most resilient approaches – whether ancient, traditional, Renaissance or Enlightenment – acknowledged that children learn best in active, sensory, emotional, relevant, personal and social contexts, but also as Nietzsche reminds us, within an authentic and all-embracing value set (Cooper, 2012). These thoughts are not narrowly 'Western' educational approaches. Thinkers and activists like Paulo Friere in Brazil, Tsunesaburo Makiguchi in Japan and Mohindas Gandhi in India profoundly influenced education in their countries in similar values-based and cross-curricular ways, and deserve serious attention from western educationalists.

A 1985 report on Gandhian education for the United Nations Educational, Scientific and Cultural Organisation (UNESCO 1985: 1), for example, began with the following words:

> One of the main reasons for the growing popularity of multi-disciplinarity as an approach to learning and teaching in our times is the growing conviction that the conventional discipline-based approach is only of marginal significance to the great issues of the world in which the youth of today is to assume its citizenship responsibilities tomorrow. The discipline-based school curriculum does not take into consideration the child's present and future learning needs; nor does it pay sufficient regard to his interests and level of maturity. By failing to recognise that the child learns essentially through activity and experience it inevitably encouraged memorisation, forgetting that memorisation alone does not enable the learner to understand and apply the information he has memorised. Nor does such a curriculum serve to facilitate the acquisition by him of the skills and attitudes considered essential for his intellectual and moral development.

Gandhi expounded the virtues of cross-curricular approaches by describing the ways in which disciplined knowledge could be related to craft activities like pottery, leather work, spinning, gardening, fishing, school cleaning or bookbinding. His followers suggested that links between these activities and the curriculum disciplines (maths, mother tongue, special studies, general science, arts, Hindi, PE and games) should be "determined by the naturalness of the opportunities offered by the programme" and that school subjects "be integrally related to he central handicraft chosen with due regard to the environment of the child" (1985: 1).

Gandhi acknowledged the influence of Rousseau, Froebel and Pestalozzi. He also knew of the project-based approaches based on Dewey's work and being experimented with in 1930s Europe and America, but his *Basic Education* published in 1956 was founded – like Kolb's –upon the idea that had direct relevance to the daily lives of the children was paramount. Like Noddings, Gandhi saw the Western approaches of project work to be contrived and rarely related to real emotions, thoughts, needs, materials and activities that directly applied to children's lives.

REFERENCES

Alexander, R. (2010) *Children, Their World, Their Education: The Final Report of the Cambridge Primary Review*. Maidenhead: Routledge.

Alexander, R., Rose, J. and Woodhead, C. (1992) *Curriculum Organisation and Classroom Practice in Primary School: A Discussion Paper*. London: Department of Education and Science, available at: www.educationengland.org.uk/documents/threewisemen/three wisemen.html (accessed 25.10.17).

APA (2002) The 100 most eminent psychologists of the 20th century. *Review of General Psychology*, Vol. 6, No. 2, p. 139.

Bandura, A. (1994) Self-efficacy, in V. S. Ramachaudran (ed.) *Encyclopedia of Human Behaviour*, Vol. 4. New York: Academic Press, pp. 71–81.

BBC/Gibb, N. (2012) Available at: www.bbc.co.uk/news/education-20041597 (accessed 25.10.17).

Bruner (1965) *Man: A course of study*, available at: http://files.eric.ed.gov/fulltext/ED178390. pdf (accessed 24.10.17).

Bruner, J. (1968) *Towards a Theory of Instruction*. New York: Norton.

Bruner, J. (1996) *The Culture of Education*. Cambridge, MA: Harvard University Press.

Bruner, J. and Haste, H. (1987). *Making sense: the child's construction of the world*. London: Methuen.

Cooper, D. (2012) *Authenticity and Learning: Nietzsche's Educational Philosophy*. London: Routledge.

Core Knowledge Foundation (2010) Available at: www.coreknowledge.org/ (accessed 24.10.17).

Gandhi, M. (1956) *Basic Education*. Ahmedabad: Navajivan Publishing House.

Gardner, H. (1993) *Frames of Mind: The Theory of Multiple Intelligences* (2nd ed.). London: Fontana.

Gardner, H. (1999) *The Disciplined Mind: What All Students Should Understand*. New York: Simon and Schuster.

Gardner, H. (2004) *Changing Minds: The Art and Science of Changing Our Own and Other People's Minds*. Boston, MA: Harvard Business School.

Gardner, H. (2005) *Five Minds for the Future*. Boston, MA: Harvard Business Review Press.

Gardner, H. (2006) 'A Blessing of Influences' in Schaler, J. (2006) (ed.) *Howard Gardner Under Fire: The Rebel Psychologist*. Chicago: Open Court.

Gardner, H. (2012) *Changing Minds* (2nd ed.). New York: Basic Books.

Gardner, H. (2013) *Gardner, mind, work and life*, available at: www.pz.harvard.edu/sites/default/files/gardner%20mind,%20work,%20and%20life.pdf (accessed 25.10.17).

Giardiello, P. (2013) *Pioneers of Early Childhood Education*. Abingdon: Routledge.

Hirsch, E. D. (1987) *Cultural Literacy, What Every American Needs to Know*. New York: Random House.

Hirsch, E. D. (1996) *The Schools We Need and Why We Don't Have Them*. New York: Anchor Books.

Hirsch, E. D. (2006) *The Knowledge Deficit: Closing the Shocking Education Gap, for American Children*. Boston, MA: Horton Mifflin.

Hirsch, E. D. (2016) *Why Knowledge Matters: Rescuing Our Children From Failed Educational Theories*. Cambridge MA: Harvard Education.

Hirsch, E. D. (2017) *The Making of Americans: Democracy and Our Schools*. New Haven, CT: Yale University Press.

Kolb, D. (1984) *Experiential Learning: Experience as the Source of Learning and Development*. Englewood Cliffs, NJ: Prentice-Hall, Inc.

McLeod, S. (2013) *Kolb – Learning Styles*, available at: www.simplypsychology.org/learning-kolb.html (accessed 19.02.18).

Neill, A. S. (1960) *Summerhill School: A New View of Childhood*. New York: St.Martin's Press.

Noddings Centre website, available at: http://beckyreed.wixsite.com/nodding-center/about-nel-noddings (accessed 26.10.17).

Noddings, N. (1992) *The Challenge to Care in Schools*. New York: Teachers College Press:

Noddings, N. (2003) *Happiness and Education*. Cambridge: Cambridge University Press.

Noddings, N. (2005) *Educating Citizens for Global Awareness*. New York: Teachers College Press,

OECD (2004) *Starting strong: Curricula and pedagogies in early childhood education and care*, available at: www.oecd.org/edu/school/31672150.pdf

Piaget, J. (1954) *The Construction of Reality in the Child*, trans. M. Cook. New York: Basic Books.

Plowden, B. (1967) *Children and their primary schools*, available at: www.educationengland.org.uk/documents/plowden/plowden1967-1.html (accessed 24.10.17).

Robinson, K. (1989) *The Arts in Schools: Principles, Practice and Provision*. London: Gulbenkian.

Robinson, K. (ed.) (1999) *All Our Futures: The Report of the National Advisory Committee on Creative and Cultural Education*. London: DFE.

Sternberg, R. (1997) *Successful Intelligence*. New York: Plume.

Sternberg, R. and Kaufman, J. (eds.) (2010) *The Cambridge Handbook of Creativity*. New York: Cambridge University Press.

Summerhill School website, available at www.summerhillschool.co.uk (accessed 12.02.18)

UK Board of Education (1931) *The Primary School* (Hadow Report). London: HMSO.

United Nations Scientific and Cultural Organisation (UNESCO) (1985) *Ghandi's approach to interdisciplinary teaching*, available at: http://unesdoc.unesco.org/images/0006/000641/064126eb.pdf (accessed 25.10.17).

Vygotsky, L. (1962) *Thought and Language*. New York: Wiley.

Vygotsky, L. (1978) *Mind in Society: The Development of Higher Psychological Processes*. Cambridge, MA: Harvard University Press.

CHAPTER 5

CHOOSING CROSS-CURRICULAR THEMES

SUMMARY

This chapter will examine and illustrate themes for cross-curricular learning. It argues that themes arising from the lives of teachers and pupils most easily connect to the priorities, connections and attitudes important them. The overarching meta-theme suggested in this chapter is that of sustainability. Each suggested theme is illustrative and chosen to help generate the globally conscious, confident friendly, flexible, collaborative, secure and creative individuals needed to tackle the challenges of 21st century life now and an in the future. Two contrasting cross-curricular approaches will be introduced.

INTRODUCTION: THEMES FROM AUTOBIOGRAPHY

The events, preferences and responses that define us are a unique resource. When set within an inclusive, clear and agreed value set, I believe personal links are essential to sustaining fulfilling lives in education and building capacity in both teachers and students. Of course, every curriculum should reflect a world wider than individual lives, and care must be taken with all curriculum and pedagogical choices, but the motivating force of personal experience and enthusiasms should not be dismissed, underestimated or unexploited.

The incidents and environments that have influenced us do not remain in the past. Life's journey is punctuated by moments and relationships that affect its pace and direction. This chapter begins with two snapshots from my past. Each captured an occasion in a foreign landscape that profoundly influenced my thinking and teaching about sustainability.

Snapshots of the birth of a theme

My first teaching job was in 1974 in the highlands of Kenya, where I taught secondary history, geography and English for 30 months. Ten years and two UK schools later, I took my young family to Malaysia and taught English and art in another secondary school – we stayed for almost three years. There we lived in a stilted traditional house backing on to a tract of dense equatorial forest. As I examine two snapshots taken during these migrant experiences, I reflect on the genesis of themes constantly revisited throughout my subsequent teaching life.

Snapshot 1

Taken by my wife Cherry, this photo shows me walking with two pupils along the rocky floor of the Rift Valley in central Kenya. The east side of the valley rises steep, almost vertical, rutted and about a mile high. It grows gradually greener towards the top where you can just make out tall forest trees. We, however, are at the inhospitable bottom, near a shallow and acrid smelling soda lake, almost devoid of life and edged by concentric bands of crispy, white soda flakes on a cracked mud shore. To our right two moderate sized geysers puff steam and boiling water from the bowels of the earth, even nearer there are a few boiling mud pools. It is very hot, dry and dusty. I remember that our mouths felt like fine-grained sandpaper. Around us there is little life aside from anthills, thorn bushes and Acacia trees. Our car was stuck in mud and we were looking for help, lost, worried and thirsty – I had packed no water for our journey. The boys, trying to keep my spirits up, pointed out and dug up edible or water-holding plants or roots. In the snapshot, everything looks dry and dead, but each brittle stick or dusty root offered was indeed edible, watery just as the boys promised. We came across beautiful butterflies and a swarm of black bees – the boys smelt a python, though we don't see it. Two hours after this photo was taken we stumbled into an apparently deserted village where the only occupant gave us water, cooked us food and took us to bathe in a hot and sacred spring of soapy soda water bubbling up from deep underground.

Snapshot 2

This photo captures me in a section of equatorial forest just behind our wooden house. It is thick with a thousand different tree varieties – a fern filled, water-logged, spidery area and I stand on a shaky raised wooden walkway that eventually rises up to bridge a wide muddy river. The banks of the river are invisible, marked only by drowned reeds and stringy plastic rubbish collected around their stems. Birds, bugs, floppy fish, alarmingly loud frogs, insects and small reptiles, evidence themselves all around me. Long, bare and muddy islands appear as thick, chocolaty waters slide between buttressed tree trunks. To the left, nearer the sea, the river widens, spreads and shallows further, and dozens of new islands slow its flow – too shallow for fishing boats, too muddy to cross on foot, too polluted for fishing. To my right a little distant, a two-year-old oil palm plantation shows its sharp, bent, dark green leaves through the closer tangled roots, fallen trees, ferns, creepers, vines, broad leaves and epiphytes of the last remaining strip of virgin forest. If the photo had a sound button, you would hear the whine, crash and roar of loggers in the distance.

Powerful experiences like these leave a lifetime of questions and interests. That East African Rift Valley landscape gave me an abiding fascination in volcanicity, climate, extreme conditions, natural patterns but also an expectation of human kindness wherever I go. The rainforest fragment behind my Malaysian house heightened my consciousness of environmental degradation, bio-diversity, waterways and climate change, and confirmed in me a high sensitivity to sounds. I am motivated as strongly by such themes today as when I stood in these landscapes.

Personal memories do not have to be exotic to be woven expertly into stories that initiate and sustain enthusiastic teaching, principled curriculum choices and meaningful learning.

A story and a theme from your life

Subjective narratives underpin our teaching style and interactions. We use memories of key events to sustain us and explain the sources of our ideals and interests. This is why having conversations about your life stories with trusted colleagues should be an important part of your professional development. Find a photo of yourself sometime in the past, perhaps when you were a child or a teenager, in a setting that has become important to you. Look carefully at the photo, remembering what is just outside the frame and what sounds, sights, feelings and memories are awoken by it. Capture some of these memories in the text box below:

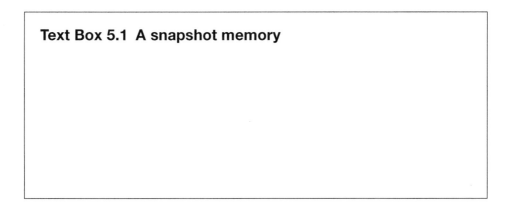

Text Box 5.1 A snapshot memory

In the following text box list some of the themes for teaching that might arise from the sensory and emotional memories aroused by the photo.

Text Box 5.2 Themes arising from reflecting on a photograph

SUSTAINABILITY A KEY THEME FOR THE 21ST CENTURY

An inclusive and connecting education takes us beyond self to bigger issues. Environmental, cultural, social and moral sustainability an example of such issues. We currently treat our environments, oceans, natural resources, bodies, minds and neighbours in unsustainable ways (Hicks, 2014; Bourn et al., 2016). In this context educationalists, like Scoffham and Owens (2017) stress the need to help children:

▪ Know what sustainability and unsustainability mean and involve
▪ Know how they can change things for a better present and future

The overarching theme of sustainability can generate a wide range of cross-curricular sub-themes applicable across the primary school. Table 5.1 is a sample of sub-themes noted down during a collaborative exercise in a small primary school staff meeting this year.

CHOOSING RELEVANT THEMES FOR CROSS-CURRICULAR LEARNING

It is not always easy for children to find relevance in school curricula. For many, curriculum choices have narrowed towards external definitions of essential or 'core knowledge' (Hirsch, 2010; Ainscow et al., 2016). As a result, curricula have often become less emotionally and locally focused, more centralised and standardised (Scoffham and Barnes, 2017). Though teachers tell us that children more easily relate to themes linked to daily life, home and playground, these are often pushed aside in favour of more measurable aspects of a performability and accountability culture (Ball, 1998; Hicks, 2014; Claxton and Lucas, 2015; Cremin, 2015).

Methods of *constructing* relevance vary with teacher and class. What is 'real' generally arises from social, sensory, physical and emotional interactions. Choosing meaningful themes also involves engaging with the views of children. Exciting-sounding topics like *Pokemon*, *Pirates* or *Titanic* may seem relevant, but they can be as uninspiring as my primary school essay on "The Life of a Penny". I recently observed a year group following a 'Land Ahoy!' theme – no child could tell me what 'ahoy' meant, or could link the title to what they had been learning (about the last journey of the Titanic). Although another class

---

▪ **Table 5.1** Some sub-themes related to sustainability

Some possible sub-themes related to sustainability

➤ Borders and boundaries	➤ Village life	➤ The air we breathe
➤ Gardening	➤ Getting to school	➤ Energy
➤ Caring for others	➤ A country study	➤ Water for all
➤ Knowing myself	➤ Recycling	➤ Our house
➤ Climate	➤ Oceans	➤ Green
➤ Bio-diversity	➤ Human relationships	➤ Through the microscope

was following an earthquakes theme just as as two well-reported and huge earthquakes occurred in New Zealand and in Japan, neither event was referred to in the teaching.

Greater relevance can be be generated for children by promoting:

a)   A single subject across a theme
b)   Current/local events or settings
c)   Connections to their emotional life, relationships and identity
d)   Modern technologies
e)   Specific values.
f)   Creative thinking and learning
g)   A shared culture

a) Applying a single subject across a theme

Consider using a single subject to promote learning across a range of other curriculum subjects (Figure 5.1). Mathematics is a good case in point. In geography, mathematical skills are used in scale, mapping and statistics. The chronological aspects of history use mathematical concepts and skills; in art and design, maths help scale images up or down or produce repeating or symmetrical patterns. Mathematics is used in PE, games and athletics for planning, scoring, averaging and measuring. Its role as a metaphor or symbol can be used in religious education, poetry or prose. In science mathematics is essential for weighing, measuring, volumes, classification and spotting patterns. Mathematics is present in the early days of language learning and essential to music notation and rhythm. A linking and overarching theme question might be: 'How does mathematics help us build a more sustainable world?' Answers might involve the ways that in geography, mathematics helps us understand pollution, drought or global warming and the fair distribution of resources. In design/technology, mathematics helps ensure products are safe, beautiful and eco-friendly; and in science, it helps identify foods are good for us and the soil.

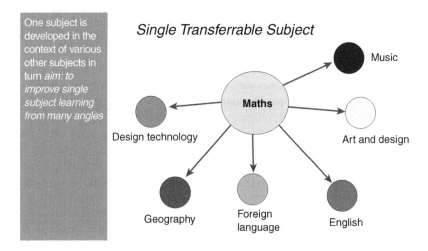

One subject is developed in the context of various other subjects in turn aim: to improve single subject learning from many angles

Single Transferrable Subject

Music

Maths

Design technology

Art and design

Geography

Foreign language

English

■ **Figure 5.1** Single transferrable cross-curricular learning

b) Using current international, national or local events

The news can be a powerful source of engagement. Some classes watch BBC's *Newsround* programme every week. Teachers might bring in newspapers and display 'current events' on the classroom wall or regularly consult children on themes from a news app.

Table 5.2 offers a sample of themes from local and international news in 2016–2017 that provided children and teachers opportunities to apply geographical, scientific and other subject understandings to authentic world issues:

▨ **Table 5.2** The news and themes for cross-curricular learning

Title	News item	Subject knowledge and cross-curricular skills to apply (English is strongly involved in each)
➤ *Earthquake*	New Zealand and Japan Earthquakes	Geography, science
➤ *The ice melts*	Reports of global warming causing the break-up of parts of Antarctica and impacting on weather and animal populations in northern Canada	Geography, science, art
➤ *Europe and Brexit*	Learning more about the 28 countries of the European Union and about the background to the UK leaving.	History, geography, SMSC, citizenship
➤ *The Great Barrier Reef*	The death of high percentages of corals and other life off the coast of eastern Australia	Science, geography, PSHE, SMSC
➤ *Beached whales*	Hundreds of whales came ashore in New Zealand, many were rescued by locals	Science, geography, mathematics
➤ *Eruption of Mount Etna in Sicily*	Eruption nearly killed a team of observers – they escaped but the images were scary	Geography, history (Pompeii), art, music science

Recently a group of Year 5 students chose *Syria to Calais* as their term's theme because of upsetting scenes seen on TV and social media. Group members quickly internalised facts and map-reading skills on Middle Eastern and European geography, modes and routes of transport, religions and the science of floating. They made personal and emotional responses in letters to refugees and authorities, produced paintings and sculptures and performed a dance-drama about care and kindness to parents. In another school a whole school 'Arts enrichment day' was mounted on a *Refugees* theme. Reception children drew and talked about things that made them feel safe, while Year 3 made abstract paintings using a range of creative techniques to express visually the journey from insecurity to safety. Year 6 made and photographed a series of 'mannequin challenge' or freeze-frame images describing the hot and dangerous land journey from Sudan to Libya and by sea to Lampadusa off the coast of Italy. The field notes below were written while observing this event. They capture some of the ways teachers tried to create relevance

Case Study 5.1 Syria to Calais whole school project

Syria to Calais project (the school is 25 miles from Calais). After presentation on journey from Syria to Lesbos, teacher asked children what they felt like on their first day in school. What were they frightened about? Who made them feel good? What made them feel bad? What things happened to make them feel relaxed, safe, comfortable and hopeful? Children were quickly able to transfer powerful memories of those feelings and fears to their assessment of what children on the Mediterranean dinghies or the reception centres in Lesbos might feel. Under the direction of an artist, Year 4 children went on to make tiny origami boats to represent the journey. They wrote messages to refugees on them. Some children collected the value-laden words their classmates had used in their messages and presented a graph showing that the most-used words were: 'friend(ship)', 'peace', 'safe(ty)', 'welcome', 'safe', 'love' and 'same'. Empathy for their asylum-seeking peers showed itself subsequently in an intense class focus on the geography of the refugee journey, eager questions showing deep interest in the background to the situations they were fleeing, a critical approach to newspaper coverage and a desire to help expressed in support for the School Bus Project. (www.schoolbusproject.org)

Relevance can also be found at a more local level. Traffic, redevelopments, shop closure, tree felling or the building of a by-pass, playground, supermarket or park may provide direct and local relevance. Through locally meaningful projects children can apply their understanding of broader concepts like beauty, community, consequences, collaboration, evidence, humanity, fairness or communication. Case Study 5.2 involved a Year five/six project thinking about the redevelopment of derelict land just beyond their school playground.

Case Study 5.2 The Tannery Project

The school lies just north of a derelict tannery. The site was overgrown with weeds and shrubs and scattered with empty industrial buildings, chimneys, rusting tanks and machinery. It had been empty for 20 years. When the council announced that it was to be redeveloped, teachers saw their chance to launch a themed and cross-curricular study – 'The Tannery Project'. The school governors included an architect, an archaeologist, a hospital administrator and a builder. Parent volunteers included photographers, shopkeepers, mathematicians and five reading mentors. These adults, plus three days of an English Heritage expert and a local council planning officer (for two days) supported the project. Teaching staff agreed to devote 2.5 days a week for 12 weeks to the theme that would involve the planned targets in history, geography, art and design/technology. Mathematics and English were heavily involved, and also taught separately throughout. Music, foreign language, science, and PE were taught as separate subjects.

Children met the adult supporters and enthusiastically became involved in making a series of inter-related surveys. They sought local residents' views about the redevelopment of the site, investigated its past through guided walks and photography sessions, mapped and recorded unique aspects of the character of the area. After collating and presenting these surveys, children worked with a local planner to decide how the site might be developed. They decided, for example, that the small river running through the site was under-used and could become a special feature in redevelopment plans. Later, children worked with archaeologists to make a historical survey. They discovered that there were records about the site going back to 1200 AD and evidence for Roman track and burials in the area. Groups of children were loaned a Surface Proton Magnetic Resonance Machine to help identify clues beneath the surface of their playground. A small dig was carried out and a human skeleton revealed. Assessment was continuous and formative and done by experts in planning, surveying, archaeology and photography, as well as teachers and governors.

After discussions about the future of the site, classes and architects introduced the processes involved in planning an environmentally sensitive redevelopment scheme, using Ordnance Survey maps, aerial photography and information available on the internet. Children learned model making from a student architect to present their proposed schemes in the most attractive way. They learned how to improve the river for wildlife to make it more attractive for visitors. The two year groups divided into teams of six (architect, planner, non-working citizen, worker, child and tourist), and decided on their proposals. Towards the end of the project, one group attended a real council planning meeting to see what happens to proposals for redevelopment. They reported back to their classes and guided decisions on an exhibition of their survey results, scale models and sustainable redevelopment plans. The city's mayor and planning committee, parents and former tannery owners came to choose the most acceptable proposal.

Case Studies 5.1 and 5.2 offer examples of *thematic* cross-curricular learning (Figure 5.2).

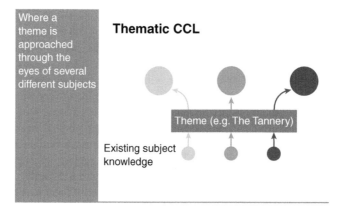

▪ **Figure 5.2** Thematic cross-curricular learning

Teachers working in these case study schools reported significant improvements in behaviour, achievement and motivation among children in their classes. They also stressed that they had plenty of time to ensure that the rest of the curriculum continued undisturbed. Children's positive attitudes and detailed knowledge about sustainability issues and the local community were remarked upon by many adults involved. Skills in surveying, model making, imagining the future and critical thinking were later transferred to other work throughout the following year.

Authentic projects in the locality often have a lasting effect on children's values and attitudes. Many UK and international studies (for example Wrigley, 2012; WHO, 2016; Fairclough, 2016) have confirmed the social and psychological importance of children's participation with adult experts in real-world, practical projects.

The United Nations (UN) Convention on the Rights of the Child (CRC) (1989) emphasises the need for the real-world activity illustrated in these case studies. Understanding and participating in local decision making is not only a right, but an important introduction to democracy (Potter, 2002; Wrigley, 2005; Ruddock and MacIntyre, 2007; Alexander, 2001, 2010). Along with the rights to play, practice their culture and speak their native language, signatory governments of the CRC confirmed every child's right to think and believe what they want and express views and feelings in any form so long as it does not harm others. CRC Article 12, for example, states that children should be consulted on *all* decisions affecting their lives (UNICEF, 1989). Such rights have major implications for teachers and curriculum.

The establishment of Children's Commissioners in England, Northern Ireland, Scotland and Wales (Children's Commissioner website) is another outcome of the CRC. These commissioners give children a voice to 'speak the truth to power', represent their rights, interests and concerns. Sadly however, in England over 65% of children and young people (compared to 33% in Norway and 25% in Columbia for example) *do not know* of the existence or content of their rights (Children's Society, 2016). The UNICEF *Rights Respecting Schools Programme* has shown that it is possible to address this lack of information and lead children toward significant and positive attitude change, related to disability, diversity, others and community responsibilities (Sebba and Robinson, 2010)

c) Using children's interest in emotions, identity and relationships

Studies of children's preoccupations (e.g. Hicks, 2006; Greenfield, 2010) indicate that identity and relationships deeply concern them. Children become increasingly aware of their uniqueness and interdependence as they grow older. Topics on influential individuals offer opportunities to examine such issues at a safe emotional distance. Historical characters like Mary Seacole, Thomas Equiano, Martin Luther King, Gandhi, Eleanor of Aquitaine, Emmiline Pankhurst and Churchill help children understand aspects of history, but their stories can also, for example, support work in citizenship, RE and Personal Social Health and Economic education (PSHE). Seeing how sustainable social change was achieved by small groups or individuals in the face of multiple barriers can inspire hope and new focus. Some schools in central and south Africa use the relationships-based concept of Ubuntu – "I am because we are; we are because I am" (Sellman et al., 2014: 56) to express the interdependence of all human beings and guide responsible, fair and caring action in the community (HM Government, 2018).

Being kind, humble, trustworthy, thoughtful, hard-working, faithful, hospitable, fair or generous may need unthreatening, un-embarrassing practice. What is good in relationships can be rehearsed through role play, drama, poetry and arts. Case Study 5.3 shows how a school in Malaysia tackled issues of identity and relationships.

Case Study 5.3 Being a friend in Malaysia

A Year 6 class in Malaysia chose 'Being a Good friend' for a six-week integrated learning topic. After discussing friendship and friends, children had to construct tableaux that exemplified friendship to others. Groups of four or five gathered to make freeze-frame representations of the qualities of friendship and captured them through titled photo frames: 'listening to each other', 'helping each other when we feel sad', 'sharing acts of kindness', 'spending time together', 'remembering birthdays,' 'praising achievements' and 'being dependable'.

Following this work on friendship, children became interested in developing design/technology expertise and social skills to build some useable play forts to promote friendship in younger pupils. Later in the same week, the class broke into pairs and held a 'speed chatting' afternoon in which children asked each other prepared questions about each other. Teachers then asked children what new information they had learned about each other. All were amazed at the wealth of new and fascinating detail.

d) Making full use of modern technologies

Technological connections dominate much of our lives. We are more technologically and globally linked and informed than at any time in history. About 97% of British households have an internet connection (Office of National Statistics [ONS] website). About 70% of children have a tablet through which they access the internet. Mobile phones are the most common means of sending and getting information, communicating, gaming, storing popular music, finding out, calculating and collecting images, sounds and notes. Mobiles are owned by 63% of British 5–15-year-olds, who view a screen (increasingly YouTube) for an average of 6.5 hours a day (BBC News, 2015, website). This technological world should be centrally represented in curricula, but many schools continue to ban mobile phones and underuse tablets and other mobile technology. There are often specific reasons for these bans, but teachers who commonly and confidently use mobile and digital technologies argue that they strongly engage children and deepen knowledge. Indeed, the concept of *learning* itself has changed in a world of digital technologies, as increasingly for students learning becomes "associated with the generation of partial and contingent knowledge – not to be stored or accumulated, but to be replaced once the context changes" (Andreotti, 2010: 7).

Mobile and digital technologies have changed our world. They are miracles of connectivity in themselves and link us rapidly together wherever we are. Cheap mobile phones now link the refugee, the stateless and the poor to an attractive world of excess and security, and beguile us all with the glamourous world of celebrity. The internet connects us to almost limitless funds of knowledge, stores our libraries, musical preferences, entertainment, plans and memories. Many of the focus exercises suggested in the Appendices use digital technologies to build and enhance motivation, but teachers can do more to experiment with tablets, drones, raspberry pi, mobile phones and other new technologies to engender more thoughtful questions, deeper engagement and creative solutions.

Familiar topics like 'Myself', Egyptians, Castles, Kings and Queens and Greek legends remain popular, but despite some use of technologies, tablets, interactive whiteboards and internet, they do not automatically reflect the child's world. The traditional view is that children 'ought' to know certain things. Schools are society's way of communicating 'worthwhile knowledge' or Bourdieu's (and Hirsch's) concept of 'cultural capital' (Hirsch 1996). This view was argued by education ministers and guided the revised national curriculum in England (DfE, 2014):

> Every child should have the chance to be introduced to the best that has been thought, and written. To deny children the opportunity to extend their knowledge so they can appreciate, enjoy, and become familiar with the best of our civilization is to perpetuate a very specific, and tragic, sort of deprivation.
>
> (Gove, 2009: 3)

Education has been slow to respond to the diverse world of children. Defining the 'best' or 'worthwhile' was once left to the powerful, but the internet has spread power more widely, and definitions of what constitutes 'core knowledge' are hotly contested. The young, connected digitally to social media, world news, (both fake and authentic) and instant knowledge, may understand, "the body of knowledge that makes up our intellectual inheritance" (Gove, 2009: 3) differently. Choosing what works of art, what experience and what knowledge *constitute*s that inheritance is more complex in today's more inclusive and multi-cultural society. Nonetheless, all children require critical thinking skills with which to differentiate between competing ideologies and need practice in applying apparently inborn human values like empathy, fairness and cooperation (Hart, 2017). Schools may be the only institutions that can offer such skills and the moral constants within which they can be applied.

e) Themes linked with values

Since 2014, the UK government has stressed the importance of what it calls the British values of:

- Democracy
- Respect and tolerance
- Free speech and individual liberty
- The rule of law

Other values might also be called 'British' – charitable giving, concern for the underdog, self-deprecating humour, kindness and politeness among them. Most societies and nations claim similar values. Taken seriously, however, the four UK government-approved values provide exciting opportunities for education.

Themes involving democracy

Schools must decide how far to apply democracy. Recent debates about lowering the voting age to 16 has shown that democratic rights can be highly meaningful to children. Inclusive definitions of democracy in school would affect participation in everything from financial and policy decisions, to the quality of interactions between adults and children. If children were truly consulted, behaviour policies, teaching styles, curriculum, playground activities and dress might be radically different.

Traditional curriculum themes may help children understand and critically explore democracy, for example:

■ Democracy in ancient Greece
■ Egyptian or Mayan hierarchies
■ 'Who Rules?'
■ 'People who help us'
■ Investigations into democracy in a particular country

Understanding democracy requires more than simple knowledge, however. Democracy should be experienced. School Councils claim to involve democratically elected representatives in decision making (School Councils, UK, website), but to be more than a token acknowledgement of children's voices, school councils should truly influence curriculum themes and pedagogical approaches – perhaps even address staff meetings (Barnes and Powell, 2008). Democratic Schools Like Summerhill in Suffolk (Summerhill School website), founded by A. S. Neill in 1921, take children's views very seriously, make lessons optional and play a right, and give children free and open access to arts, crafts, games and computers.

Most children show genuine concern for the environment. Growing numbers of Eco and Forest Schools have resulted in energetic campaigning to preserve tress, oppose car parks, build vegetable gardens and many other sustainable projects. One school followed these cross-curricular Eco themes for its curriculum in 2017:

■ A woodland walk
■ Design for a change
■ Planting on a sports theme
■ Home grown produce
■ Why do we need green spaces?
■ Nature photography (Ashley Primary School, website)

Ideas like *Room 13* (website) claim to support children's interests in identity, meaning and self-expression. In Room 13, children negotiate for extra lesson time with a resident artist or philosopher, earn money to support the extra staff and vote on how to use the profits. Elected children's parliaments (for example: Children's Parliament, website) generate inspiring examples of the influence of young voices. They meet regularly in India, Scotland, Bhutan, Bolivia, Namibia, France, Burkina Faso, the Democratic Republic of Congo and many more countries.

Respect and tolerance

Respect and tolerance of those with different faiths and beliefs is well-represented in many primary schools serving areas of 'superdiversity' like London, Birmingham, Leicester, Bradford, Liverpool, Manchester, Nottingham, Bristol and Glasgow (see HM Government, 2018). Rural areas often have less exposure to diversity. Consider with a colleague how you might promote respect (including for the natural world) in a cross-curricular context in Table 5.3

A Nottinghamshire primary school with a focus on respect for the earth chose these cross-curricular themes in 2017:

■ Conservation of the rainforest
■ How can we build community?
■ How can we create beauty together?
■ What does loving my neighbour mean?
■ Migrants and migration
■ Protecting our local environment
■ The earthquakes in Greece and Java
■ Fair trade
■ Poverty
■ Cleaning up our town
■ Our links with . . . [a school in the developing world]

The Social, Moral, Spiritual and Cultural (SMSC) aspects of education are now more evident in school curricula. Awareness of and good practice in SMSC can often make the difference between a good school and an outstanding one. The International Primary Curriculum (IPC, 2017), for example, offers units for 5–7-year-olds who can easily become vehicles for SMSC education:

■ Who Am I?
■ We are what we eat

■ **Table 5.3** Showing respect across the curriculum

Curriculum subject	What aspects of this subject can be used to demonstrate the value of respect?
Geography	
History	
Science	
Religious Education	
English	
Foreign language	
PSHEE	

- Live and let live
- What's it made of?

By 9–12 years, IPC topics include:

- Black Gold? (a study of the pros and cons of finite resources)
- Drugs education (good drugs/bad drugs)
- Going Global (our international dependence and links)
- Moving people (the story of past and present migrations of people)
- What price progress? (the benefits and problems of global and local economic development)
- Building a village (communities, technologies and infrastructures we depend on)
- Making the news (current events and their moral, geographical, social, historical context) (IPC, 2017)

Free speech and individual liberty

Interest in emotional literacy and child well-being (Noddings, 2003; Morris, 2005; Goleman, 2007; WHO, 2016; Children's Society, 2016) has encouraged teachers to listen more carefully to children. Whilst the UK Home Office places 'free speech' among its British Values (May, 2015), it does not feature in Department of Education guidance. However, it is difficult to separate individual liberty from freedom of expression, and schools – especially those serving diverse communities – use SMSC and PSHE to encourage children to speak openly about differences in an atmosphere of respect and friendship (Sebba and Robinson, 2010; Barnes, 2013; Casey, 2016).

Free speech involves dialogue and discussion. The examination of controversial issues is encouraged across the curricula of all four national education jurisdictions in the UK (Geographical Association, Historical Association and PSHE Association websites). Open debate, respectful attitudes, intercultural activities and a curriculum that represents our interconnected world are observable outcomes of free speech and individual liberty (HM Government, 2018). Genuine inclusion, friendly conversation and a welcoming atmosphere characterises schools that successfully prevent radicalization (Lancashire County Council, 2017). Themes that focus on individual liberty might also include studies on:

- Historical characters like Tsunesaburo Makiguchi, Nelson Mandela, the Suffragettes, William Wilberforce, Elizabeth Fry, Martin Luther King, Rosa Parks
- Events like the Peasant's Revolt, the Jarrow Marches of the 1930s or the signing of Magna Carta
- The story of Romeo and Juliet

The rule of law

Fairness, justice, boundaries, responsibilities, consequences, right and wrong are concepts familiar in every primary playground. They are the foundation of fair play in the child's world as well as the basis of adult law. The *rule* of law suggests the belief that there is no higher authority than that of the law. Taking these notions beyond assemblies, SMSC and PHSEE sessions might involve children participating in genuine local planning, environmental, educational or children's issues. A class following a project like the Tannery Project (Case Study 5.2) to its local authority committee stage is participating in democracy, the law, and (ideally) observing respect for others within authentic settings. Most local councillors and members of parliament (MPs) are keen to help facilitate such contacts, but be prepared for controversy – when children get to understand the implications of poor air quality, for example, they can act with determination (Evening Standard, 2017).

Other topics and themes involving fairness, justice, and respectful behaviour might include:

■ Visits to or from police and fire stations, local government centres, parliament, castles and law courts
■ How can we make living here better for everyone?
■ Why do we need clean air/water/beaches?
■ Being fair with resources
■ Keeping safe
■ Mapping our community
■ Boundaries, frames and laws
■ Rules and rulers
■ The law in . . . Rome, Egypt, Saxon times or a contrasting country

Other values

Many schools place values at the heart of their curriculum. Faith-based schools, Eco-Schools, internationalist and democratic schools (Democratic Schools website), values-creating schools and many more tie their whole curriculum to their overarching values. Take for example an Eco-school such as that in Case Study 5.4

Case Study 5.4: Rosetta Eco-school in Northern Ireland

Charities and Northern Ireland's Department of Agriculture, Environment and Rural Affairs supports Rosetta primary school. Eco sub-themes involve all subjects across the school; here are some examples:

■ Vegetable planting (Reception and Year 1)
■ Looking after the hens (Year 1)
■ Making, placing and observing bird feeders (Year 3)
■ Conserving water and informing others about water conservation (Year 4)
■ Recycling and litter bin projects (cross school)
■ Eco-friendly travel to school (Year 4 and 5)
■ Fairtrade (Year 6) (Rosetta Primary School website)

> The ethos of sustainability affects the life of this school. It was recognised in 2016 as a Fairtrade school with its own FairAware Award and in the same year became part of the UK wide Global Learning Programme (Rosetta Primary School website). The school also supported the Water Aid charity and held a Global Awareness Week and a 'Spring into Cycling' challenge to encourage more children to cycle and scoot.

f) Creative thinking and learning

Cross-curricularity promotes creativity. Creativity may be best generated, however, by *limiting the number of subject approaches* applied to a project. Most successful themes need only fuse the mindsets of two subjects to ensure creative outcomes and effective progression in subject learning. English is always present in speaking and listening, writing or reading, and is essential to all cross-curricular projects. The following themes arise from common childhood experiences, and each suggests interpretation through a different pair of subjects:

1   A game (PE and mathematics)
2   A well-told story (design & technology and English)
3   The visit of the community police officer (geography and citizenship)
4   A trip to relatives in Tyneside or Tanzania (geography and foreign language)
5   The death of a beloved hamster (science and RE)
6   A birthday trip to an adventure playground (history and music)

In the hands of a confident primary teacher, any two subjects can be applied to any theme – creativity comes in the imaginative and original fusion of these subjects. Experiment with this idea by swapping the suggested subjects for Theme 6 with those for Theme 1, so that a game would now have to be interpreted through the eyes of history and music. Linking a game to music and history is a real creative challenge, ideally engendering deeper involvement and provoking products of imagination and originality. Now discuss the implications of swapping the subjects suggested for Theme 2 with the those for Theme 5.

Creative thought can also be generated through the application of subject skills and knowledge to a visit or visitor. A drumming and rapping workshop was intended to spark ideas for creative writing, but a group of Year 5 children used their new-found skills to explain the water cycle to a Year 3 class. In a Scottish primary school, the visit of a mobile planetarium resulted in a series of complex animations about the solar system with an electronic soundtrack composed by a group of 8-year-olds. Energised by their email links, children in Northumberland and Gambia persuaded their teachers to let them mount a virtual art exhibition on the local environment of each school.

g) Building a shared culture

Values-led schools have a unique opportunity to construct a model of an ideal community. Cooperative schools (website) and academies, values-creating schools, internationalist,

Eco and Steiner, faith-based schools, 'Schools of Sanctuary' and many others try to make lived values a central to their ethos. Ledbury Primary school, for example takes its values from the Living Values Education (website). This school's chosen values influence all statements on its teaching and learning strategies, the generic skills it introduces, its behaviour policy, activities, SMSC, each curriculum subject and staff behaviour. Staff attempt to create and model a positive learning environment and the school prospectus claims that this:

> quickly liberates teachers and students from the stress of confrontational relationships, which frees up substantial teaching and learning time. It also provides social capacity to students, equipping them with social and relationship skills, intelligences and attitudes to succeed at school and throughout their lives.
>
> (Ledbury Primary School website)

CONCLUSION: THEMES DEFINING AN ETHOS

Thoughtfully chosen themes arise from and can define the aims and ethos of a school and the relationships within it. This chapter has suggested that meta-themes like sustainability, identity, humanity, environmental sensitivity, the arts, rights, faith, community, cooperative and inclusive values have the potential to engage children emotionally and socially in learning activity that stretches each child's mental and physical ability. Placing sensitively chosen themes within a cross-curricular context and addressing real issues and authentic problems through them creates the conditions for creative thinking and learning.

REFERENCES

Ainscow, M., Dyson, A., Goldrick, S. and West, M. (2016) Using collaborative inquiry to foster equity within school systems: Opportunities and barriers. *School Effectiveness and School Improvement*, Vol. 27, No. 1, pp. 7–23.

Alexander, R. (2001) *Culture and Pedagogy International Comparisons in Primary Education*. Oxford: Blackwell.

Alexander, R. (2010) *Children, Their World, Their Education*. Cambridge: Cambridge University Press.

Andreotti, V. (2010) Global education in the 21st century. *International Journal of Development Education and Global Learning*, Vol. 2, No. 2, pp. 5–21.

Ball, S. J. (1998) Performativity and fragmentation in 'Postmodern Schooling', in J. Carter (ed.) *Postmodernity and Fragmentation of Welfare*. Abingdon: Routledge, pp. 187–203.

Barnes, J. (2013) *What sustains a life in education?* Unpublished PhD thesis, Canterbury Christ Church University.

Barnes, J. and Powell, S. (2008) *Independent Evaluation of the TRACK Project Final Report*. Future Creative: Deal.

Bourn, D., Hunt, F, Blum, N and Lawson,H. (2016) *Primary Education for Global Learning and Sustainability: A Report for the Cambridge Primary Review Trust,* Cambridge: Cambridge Primary Review Trust.

BBC News (2015, March 27) Available at: Children's Parliament website www.childrenspar liament.org.uk/ (accessed 24.10.17).

Casey, L. (2016) *The Casey Review: A review into opportunity and integration,* London: Crown.

Childrens' Commissioner (England) website, available at: www.childrenscommissioner.gov.uk (accessed 24.10.17).

Children's Parliament website, available at: www.childrensparliament.org.uk/ (accessed 24.10.17).

Children's Society (2016) *Good childhood report 2016*, available at: www.childrenssociety.org.uk/sites/default/files/pcr090_summary_web.pdf (accessed 24.10.17).

Children's Society website, available at: www.childrenssociety.org.uk/sites/default/files/The GoodChildhoodReport2015.pdf (accessed 24.10.17).

Claxton, G. and Lucas, B. (2015) *Educating Ruby: What Our Children Really Need to Know.* Carmarthen: Crown House.

Cooperative Schools website, available at: www.co-operativeschools.coop/ (accessed 24.10.17).

Cremin, T. (2015) *Teaching English Creatively.* Abingdon: Routledge.

Democratic Schools website, available at: www.democraticeducation.co.uk/ (accessed 24.10.17).

Department for Education (2014) *National curriculum for England programmes of study*, available at: www.gov.uk/government/publications/national-curriculum-in-england-english-programmes-of-study (accessed 24.10.17).

Evening Standard (2017, May 8) Available at: www.standard.co.uk/news/london/lambeth-schoolchildren-in-pollution-hotspot-write-to-theresa-may-pleading-for-clean-air-a3533571.html (accessed 24.10.17).

Fairclough, M. (2016) *Playing With Fire: Embracing Risk and Danger in Schools.* Woodbridge: John Catt Educational.

Geographical Association website, available at: https://www.geography.org.uk/ (accessed 12.02.18).

Goleman, D. (2007) *Social Intelligence, the New Science of Human Relationships.* London: Arrow.

Gove, M. (2009) *Royal Society of arts speech*, available at: www.thersa.org/globalassets/pdfs/blogs/gove-speech-to-rsa.pdf (accessed 24.10.17).

Greenfield, S. (2010) *You and Me: The Neuroscience of Identity.* London: Notting Hill.

Historical Association website, available at: https://www.history.org.uk/ (accessed 12.02.18).

HM Government (2018) *Integrated Communities Strategy Green Paper,* available at: https://www.gov.uk/government/uploads/system/uploads/attachment_data/file/689944/Integrated_Communities_Strategy_Green_Paper.pdf (accessed 17.03.18).

Hart, S. (ed.) (2017) *Inclusion, Play and Empathy: Neuroaffective Development in Children's Groups.* London: Kingsley.

Hicks, D. (2006) *Lessons for the Future*: *The Missing Dimension in Education.* Abingdon: Routledge.

Hicks, D. (2014) *Educating for Hope in Troubled Times.* London: Institute of Education.

Hirsch, E. D. (1996) *The Schools We Need and Why We Don't Have Them.* New York: Doubleday.

Hirsch, E. D. (2010) *The Making of Americans: Democracy and Our Schools.* New York: Yale.

IPC (2017) website, available at: www.greatlearning.com/ipc/the-ipc/units-of-work (accessed 19.02.18).

Lancashire Local Authority (2017) *Prevent advice*, available at:www.preventforschools.org/index.php?category_id=38 (accessed 24.10.17).

Ledbury Primary School website, available at: www.ledbury.hereford.sch.uk/, (accessed 12.02.18).

Living Values Education website, available at: www.livingvalues.net/context.html (accessed 12.02.18).

May, T. (2015) *British values*, available at: www.gov.uk/government/speeches/a-stronger-britain-built-on-our-values (accessed 24.10.17).

Morris, E. (2005) *Developing Emotionally Literate Staff: A Practical Guide*. London: Paul Chapman Publishing.

Noddings, N. (2003) *Happiness and Education*. Cambridge: Cambridge University Press.

Office of National Statistics (2016) *Internet access: Households and individuals*, available at: www.ons.gov.uk/peoplepopulationandcommunity/householdcharacteristics/homeinternetandsocialmediausage/bulletins/internetaccesshouseholdsandindividuals/2016#activities-completed-on-the-internet,www.ofcom.org.uk/__data/assets/pdf_file/0027/76266/childrens_2014_report.pdf?lang=cym) (accessed 24.10.17).

Ofsted (2015) *Framework for inspection*, available at: www.gov.uk/government/publications/common-inspection-framework-education-skills-and-early-years-from-september-2015 (accessed 24.10.17).

PSHE Association website, available at: https://www.pshe-association.org.uk/ (accessed 12.02.18).

Potter, J. (2002) *Active Citizenship in Schools: A Good Practice Guide to Developing Whole School Policy*. London: Kogan Page.

Room 13 website, available at: http://room13international.org/

Rosetta Primary School website, available at: www.rosettaps.co.uk/

Ruddock, J. and MacIntyre, D. (2007) *Improving Learning Through Consulting Pupils*. Abingdon: Routledge.

Scoffham, S. and Barnes, J. (2017) Geography, education and the future, in S. Scoffham (ed.) *Teaching Geography Creatively* (2nd ed.). Abingdon: Routledge, pp. 222–231.

Scoffham, S. and Owens, P. (2017) *Teaching Primary Geography*. London: Bloomsbury.

School Councils website, available at: www.schoolcouncils.org/ (accessed 12.02.18).

Sebba, J. and Robinson, C. (2010) *Evaluation of UNICEF UK's Rights Respecting Schools Programme. Final Report*. Brighton: University of Sussex.

Sellman, E., Cremin, H. and McCluskey, G. (eds.) (2014) *Restorative Approaches to Conflict in Schools*. London: Routledge.

Summerhill School website, available at: www.summerhillschool.co.uk/

UNICEF (1989) *Rights respecting schools*, available at: www.unicef.org.uk/rights-respecting-schools/ (accessed 24.10.17).

United Nations (1989) *Convention on the rights of the child* (summary), available at: www.unicef.org/crc/files/Rights_overview.pdf (accessed 24.10.17).

World Health Organisation (WHO) (2016) *Growing Up Unequal*: *The Health Behaviour of School Aged Children Report*. Geneva: World Health Organisation.

Wrigley, T. (2005) *Schools of Hope: A New Agenda for School Improvement* (reprinted ed.). Stoke-on-Trent: Trentham.

Wrigley, T. (2012) *Changing Schools: Alternative Ways of Making a World of Difference*. Abingdon: Routledge.

CHAPTER 6

MIND-FULL APPROACHES
Living and learning in the present

SUMMARY

This chapter will help you focus on the importance of experience in the 'here and now' in learning. It starts with a personal attempt to describe a 'timeless' moment when body, mind and spirit were wholly engrossed in an experience that kept me fully in the present. Using stories of other people's experiences of total involvement, I will ask you to iden-tity and reflect on similar events in your own life and consider any implications for you and your teaching. Using outlines of psychological and neuroscientific research, I will examine these mindful occasions and discuss their importance. I suggest that education should re-establish a focus on the values-driven, meaningful, present-tense, personal and creative aspects of living. We will consider how far an educational diet rich in awesome, exciting, emotional and age-appropriate experiences would help develop more resilience, motivation, engagement and achievement in children. These approaches to creative and cross-curricular learning will be reviewed in the light of current research and scholarship.

INTRODUCTION: VALUING EXPERIENCE IN THE PRESENT

The following entry comes from my diary for 2 July 2003. I was writing after I had strug-gled to an abandoned temple at the top of an enormous granite batholith rising 500 metres above the centre of the busy city of Dindigul, south India.

> *Sitting alone drawing on the steps of the lofty Abirami temple. Looking down on Dindigul from the smooth orange/yellow granite rock was awe-inspiring – not for the beauty of the view – which is exceptional, but from the extraordinary cacophony rising from half a kilometre below. Beautifully, even musically capturing the com-plex, confusing, colourful, multicultural life of the city . . . its varied sounds gently caressing the smooth and shower-slippery rock slopes, passing through the encir-cling walls and gates of the fort, around and among the crumbling domes, between the granite posts and lintels of the decaying temple. Near me a regular and continu-ous ostinato of sweeping from a dozen coconut spine brushes, down in the distance*

*an imam calls to prayer, then another at a different pitch and with long – pregnant
– gaps and yet another call, slower, more mournful further north. These melodies
make counterpoint with the soundtracks of a dozen different Tamil movies with their
unison strings and pentatonic scales. More sounds . . . drums from a demon-chasing
ceremony, shop radios, old tape recorders from the market, loudspeakers on cars
announcing political meetings, wedding speeches, spluttering engines, screeching
singers, electronic drones from the new Hindu temple below and Pentecostal hymns
from the open-sided church – all these punctuated by the harsh call of brown crows,
the shrill cries from circling eagles and an occasional muffled blast from a distant
quarry . . . these muzzy sounds blend now with the warm cushion of rising air from
the dusty streets below. I feel elated among and part of this wonderful polyphony and
somehow sense a silence too.*

This verbatim diary entry was only intended for myself. It was an attempt on the spot to
capture something extraordinary – the sense of being so occupied in the moment that I was
transported to a zone outside the normal constraints of life. I look back upon this short
event as one of inexpressible happiness, though I was not trying to be happy at the time
or even conscious of it. It was a moment of heightened senses, deepened consciousness,
reflection, inner stillness and profound meaning for me.

INTRODUCING FLOW

Feelings like those related in the previous section are frequently remembered as happy
times. Such moments were the focus of an extended and international study by Hungarian
psychologist Csikszentmihalyi and his team. He named this common and apparently universal 'outside time' experience as 'flow' (Csikszentmihalyi, 2002). During his research,
Csikszentmihalyi discovered that these remembered moments of happiness were expressed
in remarkably similar ways regardless of income level, gender, culture, country or age
group. The features of flow or 'optimal experience' (2002: 3) usually involve a combination of the following perceptions: that . . .

■   Goals are clear
■   Feedback is quick
■   One's skills are up to the challenge
■   Action and awareness become merged
■   Distractions and current worries are ignored
■   There is little worry about losing control or failing
■   Self-consciousness disappears as concentration is enhanced
■   The sense of time is 'distorted'
■   The activity is done for its own sake (it is 'autotelic') (2002: 71)

My top-of-the-hill experience in India ticked each of Csikszentmihalyi's nine boxes. As
I think of other personal flow experiences, for example when I paint or sing in a choir,
I recognise that at the best of times my skills are often "stretched to [their] limits in a voluntary effort to accomplish something difficult or worthwhile" (Csikszentmihalyi, 2002:
3). In such times, many – if not all – of the features of flow are present. Flow occurs in an
endless variety of contexts. Reading is reported to be the most common flow activity the

world over, but running, climbing, walking, hunting, knitting, playing with one's children, drawing, constructing, discussing, dancing, singing, playing chess, fishing, yoga, prayer and any other activity that engages body, mind and spirit is likely to generate flow.

Another way of describing intense involvement in the present is 'mind-full-ness'. The practice of concentrating fully on the internal and external experiences in the 'now' is well-known to Buddhists and other contemplative religious and secular approaches. Mindfulness is often understood to require practice and training in meditative techniques, but a mind full of interest and engagement in the present moment is also a common feature of childhood. I therefore want to interpret mindfulness broadly, extending it to the unrehearsed, often daily and ordinary experience of children – those moments when they are completely absorbed. In these situations, children's minds are so filled with the happenings and feelings of the present that little can distract them. These are precious times, often held long in the memory, and they can be planned into our curricula. Well-thought-out, cross-curricular and creative activity can be a powerful route towards such episodes (Barnes and Scoffham, 2009).

Over past decades, many psychologists and physiologists have researched into mindful states. Bishop et al. (2004) captured two important commonalities arising from descriptions of mindfulness:

> The first component involves the self-regulation of attention so that it is maintained on immediate experience, thereby allowing for increased recognition of mental events in the present moment. The second component involves adopting a particular orientation toward one's experiences in the present moment, an orientation that is characterized by curiosity, openness, and acceptance.
>
> (Bishop et al., 2004: 232)

Although describing a perhaps desirable adult mind-state, this condition does not only arise in adults or necessarily arise from training or a specific religious or cultural context. 'Mind-full-ness' captures my unexpected 'top of the hill moment', but also the experience of children during play or fascination.

Flow and you

Descriptions of the state of flow overlap strongly with Kabat-Zinn's definition of 'mindfulness'- the state that brings 'being and doing together' (2016). When teachers and others are asked what *flow* feels like, they offer a wide range of descriptions that involve feelings of fulfilment, calm, quiet, involvement, wrapped attention or being in the 'right' place. Year 5 children involved in a school-based mindfulness course called *Breathing Space* recently made the following comments:

> I think it's unique, because we do different things that not many other children would get to do, like the three minute breathing space, because no one else would think of doing it in school.
>
> Its not a subject so you don't get worried that you've got the wrong answer, you just do different meditations to keep you calm and relaxed.
>
> Its about focusing on something you're doing rather than having your mind in one place and your body somewhere else.

. . . Forget about the past and don't think about the future, just think about what's happening now.

(Children from Sandwich Junior School, Kent)

A primary head teacher captures a moment during a school day packed with examples of flow amongst children and adults alike. Children and teachers had been involved in a 'Spirit of the Marsh' event in the wetlands near their urban school, and learned some of the craft skills practised by the Bronze Age inhabitants of the marsh 3,000 years ago:

I had just spent an hour pulling a trailer load of wood for the fire from the main school site to the roundhouse and then splitting the logs with an axe whilst a group of children were making the fire and erecting shelters. It was wet, windy and very muddy but already the children had a kettle of water boiling over the flames. Groups of children were foraging for food whilst others were busy flint knapping or tending the earth furnace with bellows. One particular child came over to me as I warmed myself against the fire and offered me a cup of hot coffee. He was covered head to toe in mud and had a small cut on his finger which he had received whilst flint knapping. He asked me how I was doing and then looked at me and said "this is the best day of my life."

(Fairclough, 2016: 87)

In this fragment of story, quick feedback, the absence of normal worries or self-consciousness, total engagement and the sense of timelessness and satisfaction, typical of flow are all evident. The child summarised his experience as a time of complete happiness.

Where or when have you experienced flow in everyday life?

Reflect and identify an occasion when you experienced high degrees of engagement in some valued and stretching activity that was so all-consuming that there seemed little mental space left for considerations of time, embarrassment, mistakes or worries. Describe the activity and its accompanying feelings to a friend or colleague or record them privately in the box below.

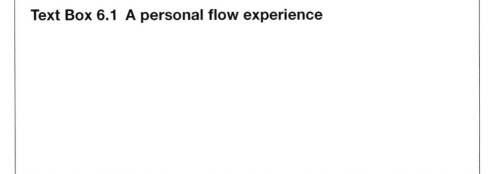

Text Box 6.1 A personal flow experience

Flow or mind-full-ness in school

Csikszentmihalyi (2002) noted that flow was rarely a feature of school work, though children often credit particular teachers with inspiring it. When asked to list typical settings for mind-full states in children, ITE students frequently cite involvement in practical science, art, music, creative writing, design/technology, computing and PE sessions. Currently primary schools may be tempted to avoid the hands-on, practical and outdoor activity that often leads to fully involved responses (e.g., Barnes and Scoffham, 2017; Fairclough, 2016; Carter, 2015; Ofsted, 2011; Alexander, 2010), despite the evidence of their effectiveness in generating deep and lasting learning. What might lead teachers to avoid such practical activity?

Look out for examples of complete engagement in school. Observe a sample of five or six children over a week, identify some of the causes of mind-full-ness in Table 3.1:

▨ **Table 6.1** Observing mind-full-ness or flow at school

Questions about children's full involvement	What did you observe?
What prompted this moment of deep engagement?	
How was initial interest sustained?	
What stopped the period of intense engagement?	
How might I build similar times of flow into my planning?	

Perhaps some observations will demonstrate *no* moments of profound involvement. In that circumstance more pertinent questions may be:

- ▨ Is this child engaged in ways that I have not noticed?
- ▨ Why am I providing nothing that engages this child?
- ▨ What barriers are there to this child's engagement?
- ▨ What can I do about it?

Mindfulness is often linked with physical and mental well-being. It has been defined as the "awareness that arises through paying attention on purpose in the present moment, non-judgmentally" (Kabat-Zinn, 2016). In medicine, it is increasingly used to support those suffering anxiety, stress, pain and illness (for example Davidson and Kabat-Zinn, 2003). In these times of high levels of child mental illness (Public Health England, 2016; HM Gov., 2017), it is crucial that schools provide a curriculum and pedagogy that promote feelings of resilience, full involvement and success. States that could be defined as mindfulness are also connected in research to self-reported feelings of inner happiness, imagination, originality and creativity (Fredrickson, 2009; Kabat-Zinn, 2016; Huppert et al., 2007). If mindful or flow states provoke the wide range of positive emotions their advocates claim, they probably also offer the foundations of the transferrable, lasting, meaningful, creative learning most educationalists seek.

Flow and our non-meditative form of mindfulness can be experienced in both moral and immoral contexts. One imagines bank robbers feel it during a robbery, as do conquerors, raiders, dictators and torturers. Sex and violence, drug taking, eating and hunting are cross-culturally reported as flow inducers, reflecting perhaps that our minds and bodies have evolved to take pleasure in these things. Teachers, and other caring professionals, therefore must take care to place the pedagogical and curriculum decisions they make within a moral context. The values context of school and society discussed in Chapters 1 and 2 is therefore crucial and needs constant revisiting.

The flow state does not describe just pleasant experience in the moment. More lasting positive physical and psychological changes appear to be associated with it. In conditions of flow, our blood pressure and sugar levels tend to fall, our bodily organs operate more efficiently, we breathe and digest better, think better, relate better and feel more relaxed and content (Davidson and Saron, 1997; Csikszentmihalyi, 2002; Huppert et al., 2007: Critchley, 2015). Optimal conditions like flow are associated with important psychological strengths like the sense of hope, (Seligman, 2005), resilience (Fredrickson and Tugard, 2004) and feelings of meaning and purpose.

FLOW AND CREATIVITY

Creativity is observable in the actions of primates, other mammals and birds, but it holds a very special place in our own species (Kaufman and Kaufman, 2015). In animals, it seems confined to the actions associated with finding food, mates, status or shelter, but perhaps self-awareness and the knowledge of our own mortality gives creativity a greater importance for human beings. It has become associated with meaning (Csikszentmihalyi, 1997; Mithen, 2005; Harari, 2011). While this is not the place to examine claims about creative animals, the place of creativity in schools and education is the focus of this book and series. Creativity based in present-tense engagement may be examined under the following headings:

■ Creativity, positivity and teaching
■ Threats to creativity
■ Spending more time in the present

Creativity, positivity and teaching

A 'positive psychology' movement has emerged over the last 20 years. Positive psychologists argue for a research and practice focus on the healthy mind, looking at the positive aspects of selfhood and brain and not just its illness. Psychologists like Csikszentmihalyi, Diener (2008) Fredrickson, Peterson (2006) and Seligman (2005) concern themselves with aspects that *enrich* and enable the satisfactory life. Fredrickson and colleagues (Fredrickson and Levinson, 1998; Fredrickson and Branigan, 2005; Fredrickson and Tugard, 2004; Fredrickson, 2009), for example, suggest major differences in psychological, social and physical health between those with positive and negative outlooks. They argue that remembered states of 'positive emotion' contribute to a mental bank of positive scenarios which can be recalled and used to generate resilient responses in times of difficulty. Fredrickson's *'Broaden and Build'* theory of positive emotions (Fredrickson, 2004; 2009) sets out the argument that the full range of positive emotions – reflection, calm, mild, moderate or intense interest, contentment, security, amusement, fascination, joy, elation, love, ecstasy – contribute to the development of a positive and thus resilient 'thought-action repertoire'.

Positive states make us 'feel good' and more ready and able to build new links, explore new ideas, places or materials, and broaden our existing knowledge, physical abilities, attitudes and relationships. They also give us the resources to face life's inevitable trials and tragedies. Fredrickson, like Kabat-Zinn (2013), has claimed that positive emotions generate enhanced abilities to be creative, imaginative and to integrate past knowledge and present circumstances. Many 'common sense' understandings of the links between body mind and action are confirmed by science, but in somewhat counterintuitive ways. From cognitive neuroscience we now know that the mind constantly assesses the condition of the body and its organs and responds with appropriate mental and physical feelings. Even a false expression of happiness or enquiry can 'fool' the brain into responding with a chemistry that provokes connecting, confident and collegiate behaviour (Damasio, 2003). Slowing the rate of our heartbeat (through peaceful visualisations or even counting slowly, for example) diminishes feelings of fear and insecurity. Physiologists and neuroscientists observe that we empathise with others literally viscerally before we mentally recognise the feelings of sympathy and concern (Critchley, 2009; Garfinkel and Critchley, 2016). We know also from Fredrickson's research (2009) that the damaging effects of prolonged negative feelings often show in poor resilience, deteriorating relationships, avoidance of risk taking, limited ideation or creativity and a range of well-known negative physiological changes in blood pressure, inflammation, immune system and digestion (Fredrickson, 2009). Such observations offer important guidance for teachers and the taught.

Common *and highly necessary* emotions like fear, anger, sadness, embarrassment or envy provoke a brain chemistry that seems to cause us to be *less* able to trust, relax, connect, think expansively, or have new ideas. Humans rely upon such narrowed, highly focused, risk-averse, self-preserving mindsets in times of danger, dearth, disease and disaster. When negative emotions are prolonged, however, and particularly when they are unrelated to direct life-threats, our health, relationships, thinking, creating and even our lifespans can be damagingly affected (Fraser-Smith et al., 1994; Frasure-Smith et al., 1995; Seligman, 2005; Fredrickson, 2009). Even mild negative feelings like disinterest, boredom or discomfort tend to have narrowing effects on thought and action (Fredrickson, 2009). Encouragingly, it appears that experience of positive emotion not only engenders improved mental, physical and social health, but according to Fredrickson it also *'undoes'* many of the negative physical health effects of negative emotions:

> Experiments have [] documented that positive emotions can undo the cardiovascular reactivity that lingers following a negative emotion and that this undoing effect is both reliable and generalizable. . . . Importantly, the evidence suggests that two different positive emotions – contentment and amusement – although distinct in their phenomenology, share the ability to undo negative emotional arousal. Moreover, correlational evidence suggests that the undoing effect may extend beyond speeding physiological recovery. Positive emotions may also undo the psychological or cognitive narrowing engendered by negative emotions.
>
> (Fredrickson, 2009: 9)

A positive mindset is also associated with a sense of 'self-efficacy' – the confidence to believe we are capable of reaching our goals (Bandura, 1994; Baron and Byrne, 2004). Belief in our ability to succeed is not evenly spread across a population, however (Isen, 2009; WHO, 2016). Self-efficacy tends to arise from those that have already experienced feelings of success, satisfaction and security. Teachers may be the only professionals in a position to spread such positivity more fairly across a population. The curriculum is their vehicle.

The curriculum and pedagogical approaches in schools can significantly benefit from the findings of positive psychology. Teachers are well aware that the signs of fulfilment are commonly apparent in contexts where both they and their children experience the state of flow. We have seen above that sports, social play, exploration, discovery, experimentation and creativity provoke a sense of flourishing. The school playground is the most likely place to observe flow, but playful, challenging, exploratory and experimental conditions are possible (and desirable) across the curriculum, too. These are also places where children are led to *think*.

If, as Perkins suggests, "learning is a consequence of thinking" (1992; Richhart and Perkins, 2008), then our curriculum and teaching should be angled towards provoking situations where children *have* to think (see also Robinson and Aronica, 2015). Watch children at play. Where do you observe creative responses to problems? Spend time observing the ways they sort out arguments, deal with disputes within games, make and mend friendships, invent new games, improvise tools, construct new environments, adapt to new situations, make and use language, experiment with sticks, stones, leaves and mud, or support a sick or worried friend. Both Fredrickson and Csikszentmihalyi connect the positive states of mind that generate or support such actions with the ability to think of creative solutions. Indeed, Csikszentmihalyi suggests that happiness itself is sometimes a result of creativity:

> Creativity involves the production of novelty. The process of discovery involved in creating something new appears to be one of the most enjoyable activities any human can be involved in.
>
> (1997: 113)

Perhaps conversely, Fredrickson claims that creativity results from happiness. Whatever the prime mover, the suggested connections between happiness and creativity offer an important lead to teachers. Creativity can be placed in a virtuous cycle where feelings of well-being generate creative thought and action and creativity generates feelings of well-being (Hope et al., 2008).

Throughout the Routledge creativity series, educationalists have argued that creativity is so important to the spirit that it cannot be confined to particular subjects or settings. Creativity is essential to the vitality of every school subject. Creativity is a contested concept however. Csikszentmihalyi's definition of creativity, for example, asserts that children cannot be creative (1997: 156). He defines a creative person as someone "whose thoughts or actions change a domain . . . or transforms an existing domain into a new one" (1997: 28), and children are not usually in a position to make such a major impact. Fredrickson (2009), on the other hand, sees creativity as far more ubiquitous and involving new, unusual and imaginative connection making at all levels. The 'democratic' definition of creativity (NACCCE, 1999; Robinson and Aronica, 2015) used throughout this book presents it as part of the birthright of every human being; a defining attribute of the *Sapiens* genus (Harari, 2011: 183). Craft offers a compromise by recognising two types of creativity – *big C* (paradigm-shifting) creativity and *little c* (everyday) creativity (Craft, 2001).

Creativity for Robinson is "the process of having original ideas that have value" (Robinson and Aronica, 2015: 118). Imagination – the ability in the moment to conceive of things beyond everyday experience – is crucial to creativity. If creativity is indeed the driver of human progress, then teachers should become experts at understanding, promoting and using it. Teachers identified as 'creative' by their colleagues appear skilled at promoting creative thinking in others, in touch with their own creativities, keen to share creativity and, significantly, also consistently report high degrees of job satisfaction (Grainger et al., 2009; Barnes, 2014). Creativity is also often linked with fulfilment and flourishing, but in many educational contexts, especially those in England, it has a low priority (Alexander, 2010, 2014). Asked about the curriculum in her English primary school, one head recently replied, "We are too busy being judged on maths and English, we're dominated by English and maths. . . . Ofsted otherwise just make a general judgment on the whole curriculum" (Barnes and Scoffham, 2017. Many teachers suggest that creativity along with arts, humanities and the other 'non-core' subjects is in danger of being edged out of the primary curriculum.

Threats to creativity

Educationalists have long expressed concerns about the decline of creativity in British and American schools (Alexander, 2010). In the UK, this was addressed by the government-sponsored Creative Partnerships programme between 2001 and 2011 (Creative and Cultural Education, 2012) and its benefits addressed by a number of reports (Roberts, 2006; Thomson et al., 2012). Since 2012, many have observed a rapid decline in creative opportunities in primary schools, particularly in England. Its National Curriculum of 2014 (DfE, 2014) maintained a trend towards closed, fact-led, rather than *thinking*-led, definitions of learning and didactic teaching approaches (Beetlestone, 1998, NACCCE, 1999; Craft, 2001, 2005; Jeffries and Woods, 2003; Abbs, 2003; Grainger et al., 2009; Robinson, 2010, 2017; Alexander, 2010; Claxton and Lucas, 2015). The current uncreative emphasis is explicit in curriculum documents by the lavish use of command words. In English national curriculum history and geography, for example, every section on subject content begins with the words "pupils should be taught to (or taught about)." In geography, pupils are required to 'name', 'locate', 'identify' and 'use'. The term 'understand' is only used once in Key Stage 1 and twice at Key Stage 2. Current geographical issues such as resource shortages, fair trade, globalisation, sustainability and climate change are absent. In history, the strong focus on British history before 1066 offers little opportunity for primary school children to consider local or recent history, international perspectives, global movements or non-European points of view. The Scottish 'Curriculum for Excellence', by contrast, commonly uses terms like 'discuss', 'consider', 'explore', 'appreciate' and 'explain', and takes a more global and internationalist view.

Csikszentmihalyi observed similar anti-creative trends in school experience in the USA twenty years ago:

They make serious tasks seem dull and hard. And frivolous ones exciting and easy. Schools generally fail to teach how exciting, how mesmerizingly beautiful science or mathematics can be; they teach the routine of literature or history rather than the adventure.

(1997: 125)

Despite the threats, there remain many opportunities within current curricula for creativity to regain a central position. Many successful schools have shown that creativity can thrive without endangering their league table position, standardised testing results, health and safety record, inspection reports or children's 11+ chances – indeed the schools with best records and reputations are very often those with the broadest, most balanced, risk-taking and integrative curriculum (Alexander, 2010; Fairclough, 2016).

Spending more time in the present

Csikszentmihayi's mention of the 'mesmerizing' qualities of science or mathematics returns us to the theme of now. Gardner, a 20th and 21st centuries psychologist and neuro-scientist, sees real-world and present-tense experience as fundamental to deep and lasting learning:

[T]he brain learns best and retains most when the organism is actively involved in exploring physical sites and materials and asking questions to which it actually craves the answers. Merely passive experiences . . . have little lasting impact.

(Gardner, 1999: 82)

Since Rousseau, experiential education has been argued to be an effective, inclusive and moral route toward deep learning. Engagement in the present is essential to an education relevant to our fast-changing and digital technology-dominated times (Claxton and Lucas, 2015). Arguing for engagement is not simply a philosophical position – real-world, sensory, emotional, heuristic, social, investigative and connective interactions mirror the way our brains appear to work best. We now know that the child's brain does not mature evenly; different abilities mature at different rates. Crudely caricatured, the connectivity within the brain matures from its back and core (areas controlling the senses, emotions and physical abilities) to its front (the parts associated with thinking, planning, synthesising and analysing). Between birth and early teenage years, we are therefore largely sensorally, emotionally and physically driven creatures. From mid-teenage years to our early twenties, under the influence of culture as well as brain maturation, we become increasingly more thoughtful, able to plan and be aware of consequences (Thompson et al., 2005). Brain imaging techniques and longitudinal neuroscientific research have repeatedly confirmed the central role of authentic and sensory experience in promoting lasting learning especially among children in the primary school (Goleman, 1996; Damasio, 1995, 2003; Le Doux, 1999; Pangsepp, 1998; Gogtay et al., 2004; Damasio and Immordino-Yang, 2007; Greenfield, 2010; McGilchrist, 2010).

Outside nursery education, many primary curricula disregard most of the senses much of the time. Listening and seeing are well-exercised, but making fine distinctions of vision, hearing, touch, smell, taste and emotional response can be completely absent from a child's experience in school. Compare the education Alex Ntung described in Chapter 3 (pp. 32–35) with the current experience of children in UK primary schools, and consider which system exercises and builds most efficiently on the maturing strengths of the child's brain and mind.

INVOLVEMENT AND TEACHER/PUPIL WELL-BEING

Teachers are essentially involved in changing children's minds (Gardner, 2004). They are schools' most costly and essential resource. Their well-being is central to the success of any educational venture – yet increasing numbers of teachers report depression, stress and unhappiness. There are multiple reasons for the loss of well-being among so many teachers, but one cause is the perception of diminishing opportunities to express and develop their own creative strengths (NUT, 2001; PCAH, 2010). Encouragingly, many studies (for example Bacon, et al., 2010) have shown that well-being can be improved even without changing other aspects of policy. Though there is likely to be a genetic influence on well-being and individuals move around a 'set point' of personal happiness, *average* set points tend to be higher in settings where policies support individual and collective well-being. In their report on happiness and public policy, Bacon et al. (2010: 43–45) suggest these policies should include the following:

▪ Lessons that build up children's resilience
▪ Building connections with local neighbourhoods and communities
▪ Providing environments "based on principles of consideration for others, self-understanding and the cultivation of of constructive interests" (p. 45)
▪ Supporting strong family bonds, social networks and friendships
▪ School policies that encourage more exercise

For adults including teachers:

▪ Health provision that gives equal weight to well-being and clinical outcomes
▪ Lower commuting times
▪ Apprenticeships and other programmes that strengthen psychological fitness
▪ Community policies that encourage neighbours to get to know each other

In 2009, the agency then known as the Department for Children Schools and Families (DCSF) – now the Department for Education – picked up some of these themes and claimed that well-being would be a focus of education policy:

> Every pupil will go to a school that promotes their health and wellbeing, where they have the chance to express their views and where they and their families are welcomed and valued. Every school should be a healthy school, and every child should receive personal, social, health and economic education (PSHE) as part of their curriculum entitlement.
>
> (DCSF, 2009: 5)

However, scrutiny of primary schools and their curricula eight years later reveals significantly less than 5 hours per week of physical education, less emphasis on child and teacher well-being, and less policy and curricular attention given to community, family and resilience (Alexander, 2016). Each of Bacon's factors mentioned previously are primarily experienced *in the moment* and on emotional, sensory and/or physical levels. For adults, especially teachers, while health, relationships, environment, economic, security, religious/spiritual life, friendships and work fulfilment are key factors influencing personal happiness (BBC, 2006), staff development programmes rarely focus on these ephemeral things (see also Barnes, 2014). The rapid rise of digital technologies and children's easy access to them has meant fundamental changes in family and child behaviour over the last 25 years. Most children now have TV monitors in their bedrooms, many spend hours alone playing virtual reality games, TV programmes have been replaced by YouTube and other videos, and even the concept of knowledge has changed for many in an age when communications technology makes it instantly possible to find out answers and connections which 30 years ago would have taken hours of searching in a library (Andreotti, 2010).

CONCLUSION

In education, we do not spend enough time in the present. We do not reflect enough or put children (or ourselves) in situations where awe and wonder are normal responses. True involvement, deep engagement in a subject or an activity, often takes us out of ourselves into a zone where time does not matter so much and distractions or current worries lessen. As teachers, we need to seek out more opportunities for ourselves and for our children to experience these degrees of immersion. If we do we should expect deeper learning, better relationships and a happier learning community.

REFERENCES

Abbs, P. (2003) *Against the Flow*. Abingdon: Routledge.

Alexander, R. J. (2010) *Children, Their World, Their Education: The Final Report of the Cambridge Primary Review*. Maidenhead: Routledge.

Alexander, R. J. (2014) The best that has been through and said? *FORUM*, Vol. 56, No. 1, pp. 157–165.

Alexander, R. J. (2016) *What Is Education For? Submission to the House of Commons Education Committee Inquiry Into the Quality and Purpose of Education in England*. York: Cambridge Primary Review Trust.

Andreotti, V. (2010) Global education in the 21st century: Two different perspectives on the 'post' of postmodernism. *International Journal of Development Education and Global Learning*, Vol. 2, No. 2, pp. 5–22.

Bacon, N., Brophy, M., Mguni, N., Mulgan, G. and Shandro, A. (2010) *The State of Happiness: Can Public Policy Shape People's Wellbeing and Resilience*. London: Young Foundation.

Bandura, A. (1994) Self-efficacy, in V. S. Ramachaudran (ed.) *Encyclopedia of Human Behaviour*, Vol. 4. New York: Academic Press, pp. 71–81.

Barnes, J. (2014) *The Haringey Lullabies Project: Music Enhancing Health and Education Outcomes in an Early Years Setting*. Canterbury: Canterbury Christ Church University.

Barnes, J. and Scoffham, S. (2009) Transformational experiences and deep learning: The impact of an intercultural study visit on UK initial teacher education students. *Journal of Education for Teaching*, Vol. 35, No. 3.

Barnes, J. and Scoffham, S. (2017) The humanities in English primary schools: Struggling to survive. *Education 3–13*, Vol. 45, No. 3.

Baron, R. and Byrne, D. (2004) *Social Psychology* (10th ed.). London: Allyn and Bacon.

Beetlestone, F. (1998) *Creative Children: Imaginative Teaching*. Milton Keynes: Open University Press.

Bishop, S., Lau, M., Shapiro, S., Calson, L., Anderson, N., Carmody, J., Segal, V., Abbey, S., Speca, M., Velting, D. and Devins, G. (2004) Mindfulness: A proposed operations definition. *Clinical Psychology: Science and Practice*, Vol. 11, No. 3, pp. 230–241, doi:10.1093/clipsy.bph077.

British Broadcasting Corporation (BBC) (2006) *Happiness*, available at: http://news.bbc.co.uk/1/hi/programmes/happiness_formula/4771908.stm (accessed 24.10.17).

Carter, Sir A. (2015) *The carter review of initial teacher training*, available at: www.gov.uk/government/publications/carter-review-of-initial-teacher-training (accessed 24.10.17).

Claxton, G. and Lucas, B. (2015) *Educating Ruby: What Our Children Really Need to Learn*. London: Crown.

Craft, A. (2001) *Creativity in Primary Schools*. London: Routledge.

Craft, A. (2005) *Creativity in Schools Tensions and Dilemmas*. London: Routledge.

Creativity, Culture and Education (2012) *Changing Young Lives*. Newcastle: CCE.

Critchley, H. (2009) Psychophysiology of neural, cognitive and affective integration: fMRI and autonomic indicants. *International Journal of Psychophysiology*, Vol. 73, No. 2, pp. 88–94.

Critchley, H. (2015) The predictive brain: Consciousness, decision and embodied action. *The British Journal of Psychiatry*, Vol. 206, No. 6, pp. 524–524.

Csikszentmihalyi, M. (1997) *Creativity: Flow and the Psychology of Discovery and Invention*. New York: Harper Collins.

Csikszentmihalyi, M. (2002) *Flow: The Classic Work on How to Achieve Happiness*. New York: Ebury Press.

Damasio, A. (1995) *Descartes' Error*. London: Harper Collins.

Damasio, A. (2003) *Looking for Spinoza: Joy, Sorrow and the Feeling Brain*. Orlando, FL: Harcourt.

Damasio, A. and Immordino-Yang, M. (2007) We feel, therefore we learn: The relevance of affective and social neuroscience to education. *Mind Brain and Education*, Vol. 1, No. 1, pp. 3–10, available at: http://onlinelibrary.wiley.com/doi/10.1111/mbe.2007.1.issue-1/issuetoc (accessed 24.10.17).

Davidson, R. and Saron, M. (1997) 'The Brain and Emotions,' in Goleman, D. (ed.) *Healing Emotions*. Boston, MA: Shambhala.

Davidson, R. and Kabat-Zinn, J. (2003) Alterations in brain and immune function produced by mindfulness meditation. *Psychosomatic Medicine*, Vol. 65, No. 4, pp. 564–570.

Department for Children, Schools and Families (DCSF) (2009) *Your Child, Your Schools Our Future: Building a 21st Century Schools System*. London: DCSF.

Diener, E. and Biswas-Diener, B. (2008) *Happiness: Unlocking the Mysteries of Psycholgical Wealth*. Hoboken NJ: Wiley Blackwell.

Fairclough, M. (2016) *Playing With Fire: Embracing Risk and Danger in Schools*. Woodbridge: John Catt Educational.

Frasure-Smith, N., Lespérance, F. and Talajic, M. (1995) The impact of negative emotions on prognosis following myocardial infarction: Is it more than depression? *Health Psychology*, Vol. 14, No. 5, pp. 388–398.

Fredrickson, B. (2004) The broaden and build theory of positive emotions. *Philosophical Transactions of the Royal Society: Biological Sciences*, Vol. 359, No. 1449, pp. 1367–1377.

Frederickson, B. (2009) *Positivity: Groundbreaking Research Reveals How to Embrace the Hidden Strength of Positive Emotions, Overcome Negativity and Thrive*. New York: Crown.

Fredrickson, B. and Branigan, C. (2005) Positive emotions broaden the scope of attention and thought – action repertoires. *Cognition and Emotion*, Vol. 19, No. 3, pp. 313–332.

Fredrickson, B. and Tugard, M. M. (2004) Resilient individuals use positive emotions to bounce back from negative experiences. *Journal of Personality and Social Psychology*, Vol. 80, No. 2, pp. 326–333.

Gardner, H. (1999) *The Disciplined Mind: What All Students Should Understand*. New York: Simon and Schuster.

Gardner, H. (2004) *Changing Minds: The Art and Science of Changing Our Own and Other People's Minds*. Boston, MA: Harvard Business School.

Garfinkel, S. and Critchley, H. (2016) Threat and the body: How the heart supports fear processing. *Trends in Cognitive Science*, Vol. 20, No. 1, pp. 34–46.

Gogtay, N., Giedd, J., Hayaski, K., Greenstein, D., Vaituzis, C., Hugent, T., Herman, D., Clasen, L., Toga, A., Rapoport, J. and Thompson, P. (2004) Dynamic mapping of human cortical development during childhood through early adulthood. *Proceedings of the National Academy of Sciences of the USA*, Vol. 101, No. 21, pp. 8174–8179.

Goleman, D. (1996) *Emotional Intelligence*. London: Bloomsbury.

Grainger, T., Barnes, J. and Scoffham, S. (2010) *Creativity for Tomorrow*. Deal: Future Creative.

Greenfield, S. (2010) *Your and Me: The Neurology of Identity*. London: Notting Hill.

Harari, Y. (2011) *Sapiens: A Brief History of Humankind*. London: Vintage.

HM Gov. (2017) *Children and young people's mental health – the role of education*, available at: https://publications.parliament.uk/pa/cm201617/cmselect/cmhealth/849/849.pdf (accessed 26.10.17).

Hope, G., Barnes, J. and Scoffham, S. (2008) A conversation about creative teaching and learning, in A. Craft, T. Cremin and P. Burnard (eds.) *Creative Learning 3 11 and How We Document It*. Stoke on Trent: Trentham.

Huppert, F., Baylis, N. and Keverne, B. (2007) *The Science of Well-Being*. Cambridge: Cambridge University Press.

Isen, A. (2009) A role for neuropsychology in understanding the facilitating influence of positive affect on social behaviour and cognitive processes, in C. Snyder and S. Lopez (eds.) *Oxford Handbook of Positive Psychology* (2nd ed.). Oxford: Oxford University Press.

Jeffries, B. and Woods, P. (2003) *The Creative School*. Abingdon: Routledge.

Kabat-Zinn, J. (2013) *Full Catastrophe Living: Using the Wisdom of Your Body and Mind to Face Stress, Pain, and Illness*. New York: Bantam Dell. ISBN: 978-0-345-53972-4.

Kabat-Zinn, J. (2016) *Mindfulness for Beginners: Reclaiming the Present Moment in Your Life*. Louisville: Sounds True.

Kaufman, A. and Kaufman, J. (2015) *Animal Creativity and Innovation*. New York: Academic Press.

Le Doux, J. (1999) *The Emotional Brain: The Mysterious Underpinnings of Emotional Life*. London: Phoenix.

McGilchrist, I. (2010) *The Master and His Emissary: The Divided Brain and the Making of the Western World*. London: Yale.

Mithen, S. (2005) *The Singing Neanderthals: The Origins of Music Language Mind and Body*. London: W&N.

National Advisory Council on Creative and Cultural Education (NACCCE) (1999) *All Our Futures: Creativity, Culture and Education*. London: DfEE.

National Union of Teachers (NUT) (2001) *Teachers leaving*, available at: www.teachertoolkit.co.uk/wp-content/uploads/2017/07/teachers_leaving-1.pdf (accessed 24.10.17).

Ofsted (2011) *Geography: Learning to make a world of difference*, available at: www.gov.uk/government/publications/geography-learning-to-make-a-world-of-difference (accessed 24.10.17).

Pangsepp, J. (1998) *Affective Neuroscience: The Origins of Animal & Human Emotions*. New York: Oxford University Press.

Perkins, D. (1992) *Smart Schools*. New York: Free Press.

Peterson, C. (2006, July 27) *A Primer in Positive Psychology*. London: Oxford University Press.

President's Committee on Arts and Humanities (PCAH) (2010) *Reinvesting in arts education: Winning America's future through creative schools*, available at: www.gov.uk/govern ment/uploads/system/uploads/attachment_data/file/575632/ (accessed 24.10.17).

Public Health England (2016) *The mental health of children and young people in England*, available at: www.gov.uk/government/uploads/system/uploads/attachment_data/file/575632/ (accessed 24.10.17).

Richhart, R. and Perkins, D. (2008) *Making thinking visible*, available at: www.visiblethinkingpz. org/VisibleThinking_html_files/06_AdditionalResources/maki (accessed 24.10.17).

Roberts, P. (2006) *Nurturing creativity in young People: A report to government to inform policy*, available at: www.creativetallis.com/uploads/2/2/8/7/2287089/nurturing-1.pdf (accessed 24.10.17).

Robinson, K. (2010) *The Element: How Finding Your Passion Changes Everything*. London: Penguin.

Robinson, K. (2017) *Out of Our Minds: The Power of Being Creative*. Chicjester: Wiley.

Robinson, K. and Aronica, L. (2015) *Creative Schools: Revolutionising Education From the Ground Up*. New York: Penguin.

Seligman, M. (2005) *Authentic Happiness: Using the New Positive Psychology to Realise Your Potential for Lasting Fulfilment*. New York: Free Press.

Thompson, P., Giedd, J., Woods, R., MacDonald, D., Evans, A. and Toga, A. (2005) Growth patterns in the developing brain detected by using continuum mechanical tensor maps. *Nature*, Vol. 404, pp. 190–193.

Thomson, P., Hall, C., Jones, K. and Sefton-Green, J. (2012) *The Signature Pedagogies Project: Final Report*. Newcastle: CCE, available at: www.creativitycultureeducation.org/ wp-content/uploads/Signature_Pedagogies_Final_Report_April_2012.pdf (accessed 24.10.17)

World Health Organisation (WHO) (2016) *Growing Up Unequal: The Health Behaviour of School Aged Children Report*. Geneva: World Health Organisation.

CHAPTER 7

PLANNING FOR AND CREATING CREATIVITY

SUMMARY

This chapter concerns provoking and nurturing creativity in yourself and children. Starting with a personal encounter with creativity, it will lead you to use your own experience to plan the conditions for creativity in school. The chapter poses provocative questions and opportunities to plan creative and connected learning for your classes. It will discuss making physical changes like seating arrangements, wall displays and outdoor learning as well how to recognise, nurture, celebrate and develop creativity in every child. Inter-disciplinary cross-curricular learning, an approach designed to stimulate creativity, will be introduced and explained. Case studies will provide examples of inter-disciplinary methods and interactive tables will help you define, recognise and plan for creativity.

INTRODUCTION

If you want to define and recognise creativity and understand the conditions most conducive to it, it may be useful to understand and value the creativity in ourselves.

Creativity and me

Creativity has long been important to me. It arose from many sources but was often recognised only in retrospect. The discovery of my personal creative strengths is part of the life's narrative I have constructed. It continues to motivate and guide my actions. In the following autobiographical extract, I relate an early experience of creativity. It involves a moment in a single music lesson that took place 56 years ago:

> *I am sitting with a class of 35 others in a bright, tall windowed, cool tiled, school hall. It smells of floor polish and sick. The upright piano stands dark and heavy to the left and Mr Maynard with his floppy white hair and rectangular metal glasses plays gently. . . .*

> *Earlier I had sat cross-legged in the same hall in assembly, listening to an introduction to our 'Composer of the Week', Benjamin Britten. His black and white photograph portrait, sitting in a fishing boat on a stony Aldeburgh beach, was framed in*

pinkish sugar paper directly in front of me. I remember realising that Britten was only composer not represented by a painted portrait. I was impressed that he was still alive. . . .

British folksongs were a major feature of music lessons at the time and that day we were introduced to a 17th century Scottish song of love called 'Oh Waly Waly'. We learned words and tune quickly by heart. Mr Maynard then introduced a 'special' accompaniment that added meaning to the words. It had been written just 12 years before by Britten himself.

He accompanied the first verse with a slow, tender rocking movement: da daaa daa – da daaa da – da daaa daa – which gave the feel of a gently bobbing boat.

The water is wide, I cannot get o'er
And neither have I wings to fly
Give me a boat that will carry two
And both shall row, my love and I.

Subsequent verses told a sad story of trust and disappointment accompanied with the same rocking theme but with occasional hints of tension. The final verse summarised the whole story:

O, love is handsome and love is fine,
And love's a jewel while it is new,
But when it is old, it groweth cold,
And fades away like morning dew.

Something (to me) extraordinary happened as we sang this verse. The piano music slowed on the words, 'But when it is old . . .' and then with, '. . . it growth cold,' . . . I felt three chilling dissonances played to the same sad rhythm – and the hairs on my neck stood up at this tiny change in the music.

This five or six second event, remains clear in my memory. It was the first time I realised that words and music could make me feel something, I experienced a fusion of sound and language that created a deep and unforgettable emotional experience that still affects me. At that point I began to recognise (without knowing the word) what creativity might be, that someone had invented something that could sensitise and make meaning for me . . . a good and valuable feeling.

The impact of those few seconds could not have been planned for. It is unlikely creativity was 'a target' in Mr Maynard's lesson plan. The intention of the lesson would surely have been for us to have learned the folksong accurately and musically. But he may have had a deeper plan, for he was clearly passionate about music and perhaps wanted us to love it too. For me, at that time, in that place, the conditions for learning about creativity were right. Analysing memories of those conditions I can identify the following generative features:

■ A highly motivated class of calm, comfortable, undistracted peers
■ A larger cultural context to the lesson
■ A passionate, talented, knowledgeable, likeable teacher
■ A caring and sensitive school staff, clearly friends and committed to a coherent, culturally-framed curriculum
■ A comprehensive, well-organised and practical introduction to music and musical personalities
■ A song about emotionally significant feelings like love, loss and sadness
■ My own participation in recreating what we were encouraged to think of as a work of art

Creativity in your childhood

Consider your own childhood and youth. Do you remember an event in school or elsewhere where you understood something to do with your or someone else's creativity? Perhaps you made, did, experienced, observed or heard something *new* and *valuable* which used *imagination* in some striking way. Maybe someone recognised something special in what you had done or made, and said so. You needn't have generated a product – you might have been playing, acting, singing, arranging, planning, forming, talking or involved in any other activity. Try to remember any details of that moment. Discuss with others what 'doing something creative' or what 'creativity' itself might mean in your early experience.

Thinking or talking about areas of personal creativity may awaken dormant connections and memories. Remember that creativity does not apply just to the arts, but might have occurred in a game; a mathematics, computing or technology lesson; a run round the school field (or inventing a brilliant excuse for not running); or in sorting out an interpersonal problem in the playground. If you can identify such a memory, summarise it in Table 7.1.

■ **Table 7.1** Memories of creativity in a school setting

I remember . . .

In the context of this memory of young creativity, ask yourself the following questions:

■ Was it planned as such by a teacher or other adult?
■ Was this event or thought named as 'creative', or were other words used?
■ What conditions applied at that moment?

Consider the questions in Table 7.2 and write any answers in the box alongside.

Many of the conditions for discovering creativity will have been unplanned and dependent on a particular but incidental moment. The question therefore arises: How is it possible to plan creativity in a school setting? – I believe it *is* possible.

▨ **Table 7.2** The impact of school environment on my creative thought and action

Building an environment for creativity	Your answers
What do you think your teacher/parent/ mentor planned for you to learn in this lesson?	
Describe the place where your creative moment happened.	
Describe the people you were with and/or place you were.	
Outline the task you were involved in.	
Describe anything special about the atmosphere in the place/room/lesson.	
Describe the teacher/adult/other person/people working with you at the time.	
Describe your feelings when you were involved in something you now would call creative.	
Add here any further points that might throw light on the sources of creative thought and action.	

PLANNING AN ETHOS FOR CREATIVITY

Values underpin the arguments for creativity and cross-curricularity made in this book. Values that engender creativity tend to be positive, inclusive, social and sensitising. They focus on present-tense structures, relationships and attitudes that influence the ethos of a community. These values might involve:

▨ Democratic structures
▨ Invitations to participation
▨ An atmosphere of support
▨ An interest in current and controversial issues (e.g. sustainability)
▨ A celebration of diversity
▨ Shifting leadership roles
▨ An interest in knowledge and skills
▨ A relaxed attitude to challenge and difficulty
▨ An openness to powerful personal experiences
▨ A tendency towards affirmation
▨ Safe, secure, comfortable and stimulating environments

Children occupy many environments. Their cultural environment incorporates the beliefs, attitudes, practices, customs, language(s) and behaviours that surround them. Their economic, physical and social environments are often a product of socio-economic status, community, locality and accommodation. Spiritual, intellectual and emotional environments include dominant religious beliefs, attitudes to education, confidence, extraversion or introversion, and the values of the family.

Educators everywhere witness the effects of these multiple environments on a daily basis. Some environments (spiritual, social, moral/values, intellectual, cultural or emotional) vary from family to family, even individual to individual. Economic and physical environments may be shared across a community. Pinker's (2002) concept of the 'unique environment', however, reminds us that each of us occupies a slightly different web of environments that makes us who we are, and probably the degree of creativity we exhibit.

Use Table 7.3 to help you think about how you might generate the conditions for creativity in your classroom. You may believe, for example, that celebrating diverse heritages and role models through displays and visitors will provide some children the confidence to make creative connections. Others might need a more comprehensive and accessible choice of classroom resources to equalise their chances of developing creative strengths. Still others will respond better to opportunities to connect with their inner selves in a quiet, reflective, mindful period at the start of each day. The experiences that drew you towards education will influence your views, but be prepared to share them. Collect some of the thoughts of your group in the chart below:

■ **Table 7.3** Planning an ethos for creativity

Some environments affecting children's learning	How can we construct an environment that allows all children to develop creative thinking and learning?
Cultural – shared beliefs, behaviours and attitudes	➣ *Respecting different cultural understandings* ➣ *Accepting diverse answers to problems* ➣ *Tolerating ambiguity* ➣ *Talking about what values we share* ➣ *Establishing class values*
Economic – relative wealth or poverty	
Emotional – state of mental well-being or ill-health	
Intellectual – ability to think, plan, remember, decide, critique	
Moral/values – understanding of right and wrong/good and bad	
Physical – comfort, security, space, quality and resources	
Social – friends, family, the degree of respect and support	
Spiritual – beliefs about meaning and purpose of life	

Physical changes

After discussion, you may agree on some changes to the classroom to support an ethos of creativity. These might include:

- Choosing tables and chairs that can be moved frequently and quickly
- Arranging seating for group practical work and conversation
- Changing the timetable to allow time for reflection
- Making wall displays that encourage creative interaction
- Bringing the outside into the class or accessing it more easily
- Ensuring accessible links to digital technologies
- Providing easier access to resources
- Constructing mini environments and play areas
- Using ceilings, windows, views and other spaces

Wall displays should change often. Avoid displays for decoration but encourage child participation and collaboration in mounting them. Use challenging vocabulary, highlight newly-learned Key Words and refer to them frequently while teaching, ask questions to which there are many answers. Plan interaction in the following ways:

- Children place 'Post-its' on a display with questions for internet investigation
- Design big and open-ended questions into display
- Place aspects of display behind 'doors' with extra information
- Link two-dimensional display to real objects placed on a table in front
- Ask children to write captions for an artefact display
- Use micro recording pads to capture children's comments or provide a soundtrack
- Place strings on a map or display to allow children to position responses
- Include a 'letter box' for questions and answers related to a display
- Include smells, music or sound-effect pads
- Link Closed Circuit Television (CCTV) (for example, to a nesting box) or a related website to a display
- Attach whiteboards and pens for children to make lists of ideas arising from a display

Bringing the outside in will include plans for practical, independent work outside the classroom. Work outdoors is quickly understood by children as involving their 'real' world and tends to stimulate better questioning, connections, imagination and new collaborations. Such responses are the seeds of creativity. Opportunities to take learning outside (Table 7.4) will give children learning experience that contrasts with linear models dependent upon the process of fact-teaching, related tasks and an assessment. Owens (2017) has argued for a 'wildthink' approach, characterised by authentic and diverse interactions with the outdoors, genuine questions and difficulties, deviations from the straight path, encounters with uncharted territory and emotionally significant experiences. These experiences she argues provoke deeper learning and more creative connections. Consider the following table based on Owens's work and discuss how it can apply to the environment nearest you:

GENERATING CREATIVITY

Most current definitions recognise creative thought as possible and preferable in all disciplines. For every subject, creativity involves a product, novelty, usefulness and a social context (e.g., Plucker, 2017). The idea that such thinking and learning is shared by most humans is now commonly expressed (NACCCE, 1999; Plucker et al., 2004; Scoffham and Barnes,

■ **Table 7.4** Outdoor learning and creativity

Outdoor learning experience	Your example from the urban or rural landscape nearest you
Informal, interactive assessment opportunity	
Conversation focus	
Opportunity for imagination	
Barrier to negotiate	
Productive detour	
Risk to heighten perception/ concentration	
Possibility of an emotional encounter	
Chance for awe and wonder	
Chance for critical thinking	

2007). While honey badgers, bonobos, birds and many other animals may be creative in particular directions, humans are defined by their ability to imagine useful, novel, valued products and solutions across every aspect of life. Creative thought involves the bringing together or 'bisociation' of two unrelated ideas, objects or thought processes to produce unexpected and valued results (Koestler, 1964). It frequently involves collective and social responses (John-Steiner, 2001; Boden, 2004), and few would disagree with Csikszentmihalyi's claim that "for better or for worse our future is now closely tied to human creativity" (2015). Creativity can be either exercised or extinguished by personal experience, particularly in schools (Csikszentmihalyi, 2002; Craft, 2010; Sternberg, 1997; Sternberg and Kaufman, 2010; Gardner, 2010).

More than 90 years ago, Graham Wallas identified creativity as valuable way of thinking, involving a process of *preparation, incubation, intimation, inspiration* and *verification* (Wallas, 1926).

Wallas's model of creative thinking

In Wallas's model, *preparation* might involve a teacher defining an issue or problem and asking children to gather relevant information to solve it. An *incubation* period would occur when children stand back, reflect or do something unrelated. Wallas described the incubation period as "voluntary abstention from conscious thought on any problem" and remarked that it may:

> take two forms: the period of abstention may be spent either in conscious mental work on other problems, or in a relaxation from all conscious mental work.
>
> (Wallas, 1926: 86)

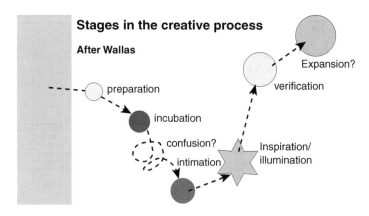

▩ **Figure 7.1** Stages of creative thinking, after Wallas

Wallas noted that the human psyche often used intuition to anticipate the arrival of new and valuable ideas – the *intimation* stage of creativity. This sub-conscious aspect of creativity is captured in Sondheim's words from *West Side Story*:

> *Could it be? Yes, it could.*
> *Something's coming, something good,*
> *If I can wait!*
> *Something's coming, I don't know what it is,*
> *But it is*
> *Gonna be great!* (Sondheim, 1957)

The psychological aspects expressed in Wallas's incubation and intimation stages remind of the importance of allowing time for the playful, relaxed, secure and dreamy in schools. Such difficult-to-measure activities are increasingly absent from school but may be essential to healthy and productive minds (Claxton, 1998; Kabat-Zinn, 2013).

When an intuited thought or solution bursts into consciousness, Wallas described it as the *illumination* or *inspiration* stage of creativity. This phase is evident when children become deeply involved in an activity and share and develop their own ideas. Finally, for creativity to be of value, a stage of *verification* that tests for usefulness, appropriateness or value is required and possibly leads to expansion of an idea (Figure 7.1).

Case Study 7.1 illustrates Wallas's processes of creativity in the context of education.

Case Study 7.1 A Year 3 walk along the school lane

A class of 7-year-olds in a Gandhian school in south India went for a 400-metre walk along the street near their school. They took five parents and their class teacher with them. Each group of five or six had a different task and one adult supporter. Their tasks were related to either geography or religious education. They were to:

- Plot the position of trees and bushes on their map of the street
- Identify and plot buildings on their prepared map
- Make lists of structures, posters, street names, signs and symbols associated with Hinduism, Christianity and Islam
- Conduct a traffic survey
- Photograph key religious buildings and sites along their route

The children returned to class with maps, photographs and collections and rejoined timetabled classes in English, Tamil and mathematics. Two days later, their teacher reminded them of their short walk and showed them images of themselves at work in the street. She asked questions like: "How can we tell the children in our sister school in the UK what life is like in this town? What can we use to show them? What would give a true impression of what its like here?"

The children were initially puzzled – they wanted to provide a glossy impression of their town and avoid portraying its complex, multi-layered nature. Their teacher insisted responses to her question must be true and unvarnished, and asked the class what impression their walk with its different foci had given them. The children were allowed to discuss their responses in groups and eventually gave their teacher a list of what they had seen and questions about them. For example:

- Religion is everywhere
- We couldn't walk even two metres without seeing some religious sign or other
- There were lots of posters for religious meetings
- Should we call the cycle repairers under the trees 'shops'?
- We found loads of trees and bushes we didn't notice before
- There are so many Hindu shrines and offerings all along the street – and in the taxis and auto-rickshaws
- There are not so many Christian and Muslim signs but we saw two churches and a mosque
- Lots of traffic
- More bicycles and motorbikes than cars, only two bullock carts
- We saw a funeral procession with drums and singers on the way to the cremation site

The class teacher asked each group to use these observations to assemble a five-slide presentation using information gathered from their walk. There was much talk and argument at first and some children did not know what to do. Some were worried and confused, and needed help from others. Eventually the groups quietened, eyes began to brighten and sparkle, and one or two members started to hatch an idea which the others joined. At this point, minds seemed generally to focus on the task. Different jobs (editing, writing, making a 'storyline', assembling) were shared out amongst the group and they worked quickly to complete their mini project. The teacher moved between groups encouraging children to combine ideas in imaginative and captivating ways. Each group shared their presentation with the class who offered feedback by giving two points of focussed praise and asking one formative question. Groups adapted their presentations after getting feedback. The PowerPoints were emailed to the sister school the next day and received in the UK with great enthusiasm.

▨ **Table 7.5** Stages in the creative process (after Wallas, 1926)

Wallas' Stages in the creative process applied to a problem/question/issue. e.g. Tell a school in another country what life is like in the locality of our school	*Problem*: *Example from case Study 7.1*
preparation	A.
incubation	B.
intimation	C.
inspiration	D.
verification	E.

Use Table 7.5 to identify the five stages of creativity by completing boxes A – E using examples from the Case Study 7.1.

Promoting creativity

Consider some of the following recommendations made by educationalists over the last 90 years:

▨ Plan *experiences* for children rather than just lessons (Dewey, 1938)
▨ Establish a positive, *secure*, predictable and comfortable atmosphere in which to learn (Bowlby, 1988)
▨ Provide a *range* of practical, creative and analytical activities within each unit of work (Sternberg, 1997)
▨ Encourage *'flow'* in the classroom, by progressively introducing skills and providing engaging challenges pitched just a little above current ability (Csikszentmihalyi, 2002)
▨ Establish authentic *group work* amongst peers (Vygotsky, 1978; Damon, 1984)
▨ Use just *two or three subjects* to throw cross-curricular light on a theme (Barnes, 2015)
▨ Build *emotionally significant* links to the life of each child, engaging all the senses (Damasio, 2003)
▨ Involve a *developmentally appropriate* progression in skills, knowledge and under-standing in all planned learning (Piaget, 1954)
▨ Emphasise *cooperative* thinking (John-Steiner, 2001, John-Steiner and Moran, 2003)
▨ Promote *thinking* itself as the key route to learning (Perkins, 1992)

■ Provide *formative assessments* to foster security and progress in learning (Blythe, 1998; Wiliam, 2006)

■ Plan a wide range of opportunities to discover interest, engagement, enjoyment and other *positive* emotions (Fredrickson, 2011)

While the atmosphere and physical changes you make in your classroom may promote creativity, the way you teach will probably have the greatest impact.

CREATIVITY AND TEACHING

A pedagogy of creativity involves (a) teaching creatively, (b) teaching for creativity, (c) creative ways of learning and (d) identifying creativity.

Teaching creatively

Creative teaching uses imaginative, useful and original methods to make learning more interesting and effective (Figure 7.2). All teachers should be knowledgeable and have a genuine commitment to children but a *creative* teacher is characterised by combinations of enthusiasm, flexibility, originality, curiosity, humour, imagination and risk taking. The pedagogical skills required include the ability to make connections, provoke questioning, encourage independence and to find multiple entry points for learning (Cremin et al., 2009).

Teaching creatively offers no guarantee that children will *learn* to be creative. Teachers can be so good at presenting things creatively that their students perceive creativity as an exclusive and rare capacity. Creative teachers help children make connections. They encourage relationships, illustrations, subject choices and approaches that promote motivation and curiosity and lead children confidently to use their knowledge and skills in

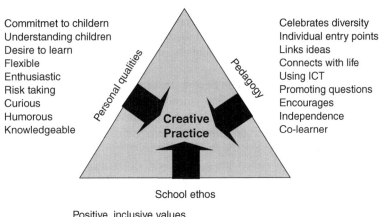

■ **Figure 7.2** The school and teacher qualities that promote creative practice

creative ways. Such creativity is recognised as "a necessary part of all good teaching" (NACCCE, 1999: 102; NCSL, 2011). For teachers, creativity requires an extra quality: that of a speedy, almost reflex response. They often have to react sensitively, quickly and inventively to unexpected problems, questions and answers presented by children. Quick, values-consistent, bespoke or surprising responses are part of a teacher's toolkit. In some contexts, creativity becomes a professional and personal survival skill, but survival is not the aim of education – there are higher justifications.

Creativity is good for teachers' well-being and builds capacity to give more (Barnes, 2015). Teachers finding new ways of bringing novelty, usefulness and imagination to their job often report heightened job satisfaction and a greater willingness to give (Cremin et al., 2009; Barnes, 2016). Similar positives are found in many job and life settings where creativity is encouraged (Csikszentmihalyi, 2002; Seligman, 2004; Pangsepp, 2004). Children show similar joy and confidence in creative situations (Thomson et al., 2012; Runco, 2014), and this positively impacts on teachers. If creativity can generate happiness, flourishing, fulfilment and "promote quality and coherence in education" (NACCCE, 1999: 103), then units on creative teaching and teaching for creativity *should* be heavily present in the curriculum, education and development of teachers. This is not generally the case in ITE in England. There is barely a mention of creativity in the English primary national curriculum of 2014 (Department for Education, 2014), while the *Curriculum for Wales* uses the word over 30 times in its curriculum for 3–7-year-olds (Welsh Government, 2015) and Scotland's *Curriculum for Excellence* (Scottish Government, 2016) makes more than 45 references to creativity. Creativity, however, is increasingly sidelined in inspection regimes throughout the UK in favour of more easily-tallied knowledge and skills.

Teaching for creativity

Creativity can be taught and measured. Emerging understandings of how the brain works suggest that creativity, like intelligence, is not fixed, but can be enhanced through teaching, training (Gruzelier, 2003) and experience (Perkins, 2009). On the other hand, over-structured, highly controlling, teacher-centred methods impede originality, questioning and alternative viewpoints. If challenge, ambiguity, speculation and exploration are discouraged, creativity cannot thrive.

To be creative, children need to feel secure with 'safe' risk taking. The leadership and ethos of school must therefore construct that security and arrange opportunities for risk taking if teaching for creativity is to be sustainable. Teaching for creativity is best supported by head teachers and senior managers who:

▨ Help staff to develop and sustain creativity in themselves
▨ Promote the qualities inherent in creative teachers
▨ Establish a curriculum and resources that encourage creativity across all subjects (Cremin et al., 2009)

Use the checklist in Table 7.6 to reflect on the character attributes you might boost in order to teach for creativity.

Creative people can also be awkward, discomforting and critical. They make unusual connections, challenge, speculate, imagine, explore, envisage, avoid 'certainty' and reflect critically on assumptions, processes and products (Thomson et al.,

---

■ **Table 7.6** Becoming a teacher for creativity

Are you a teacher who:	Give yourself a score out of 10
tolerates ambiguity and diverse alternatives?	
promotes mutual support among children?	
encourages confidence, imagination and thinking 'outside the box'?	
keeps options open?	
works with other (non-teacher) adults?	
demonstrates flexibility?	
praises effort?	
encourages criticality and reflection?	
recasts 'failures' as opportunities?	
applies knowledge to a genuine problem?	
gives children the scope to complete a full response?	
encourages two or more minds to work together?	
applies the thought processes of two or more subjects to a problem?	

2012). Such features remind us that creativity must exist within a values context comprehensible by all.

I suggest that the curriculum structure most effective in promoting creativity in children is inter-disciplinary cross-curricular learning.

Inter-disciplinary cross-curricular learning and creativity

Inter-disciplinary learning (Figure 7.3) capitalises on the plurality of knowledge, its complexity and the idea of keeping options open (Andreotti, 2010). The Latin prefix *inter-* indicates linkages between two or more entities. Inter-disciplinary teaching and learning methods connect the unique thinking approaches of several subject-disciplines together in response to a question or challenge. We saw in Chapter 3 how combining disparate approaches, cultures or skill sets oftentimes in history led to creative advances in culture, art and science. Similarly today, only cross-disciplinary, multi-cultural teams working creatively together can bring solutions to complex global issues like climate change, resource inequity, terrorism, pollution and war (Rogoff, 2003). On a humbler scale, inter-disciplinary work in schools encourages social and personal connections that result in deeper, transferrable learning among many participants (Barnes, 2016).

Inter-disciplinarity involves combining two or more disciplines to solve a problem or address an issue. The intention is to make creative connections across the disciplines and a more 'rounded' view.

In Case Study 7.1, teacher and children used *inter-disciplinary* cross-curricular learning to:

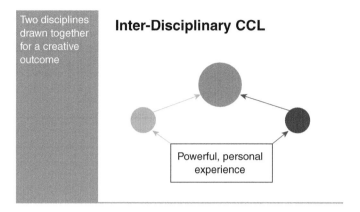

Figure 7.3 A Inter-disciplinary cross-curricular learning

■ Share an authentic, powerful and personal experience
■ Learn and apply relevant skills and knowledge from two subjects in a context
■ Apply existing skills in English to an authentic task
■ Pool, use and develop new knowledge, skills and experience in discussions and plans
■ Tackle further challenges connected with improving their product
■ Understand the contribution of two different subjects to understanding their world
■ Combine knowledge and skills in three subjects to produce an original, imaginative and useful product

IDENTIFYING CREATIVITY

Creativity shows itself in many ways. It need not be astonishing or wacky; it is often evident in everyday problem-solving. Its attributes of originality, imagination, use and value can be recognised in the activities and products of children as much as adults. Sternberg identified eight models of creativity that capture its variety and range. Several models are particularly applicable to children's creative thought and action. Creativity can involve: *replication, redefinition, forward movement, redirection* and *integration* (Sternberg and Kaufman, 2010). Though these models describe adult creativity, I have applied them to the learning of children of 3–11 years. The descriptions may help teachers and children (Powell and Barnes, 2008) identify 'small c' creativity in their daily lives.

Replication

Replication is the simplest form of creativity. Replication happens when the creative act of another is imitated. In schools, it is seen as children learn nursery rhymes, or make copies of Van Gogh's or Monet's paintings. School choirs and orchestras reproducing the music of others or classes copying maps, diagrams, theorems and algorithms invented by someone else are replicating creativity.

Redefinition

Redefining a problem involves looking at an action, creation or artefact from a different point of view. A group of 7-year-olds may, for example, have been given a simple poem or passage and asked to represent it as a series of freeze-frame tableaux. One class recently observed used paintings by the artist Miro as a musical score to make musical compositions using classroom percussion instruments.

Forward movement

Sternberg sees Forward Movement as the kind of creativity where an individual or group takes an idea further than expected. This I noticed happening as a group of 8-year-old children in a Rwandan primary school searched their school grounds for examples of how they could survive in Stone Age times. I expected them to identify branches, leaves, roots, stones and clay as the elements with which they could build shelters, tools and weapons. One group gathered round two children who had found a banana leaf with a strong indented spine running down its centre. They argued that if they put several leaves in a little hollow in the earth the morning dew would run down the spines to collect in another cupped leaf at the bottom to provide water to drink. This was a creative response in the direction I expected, but far in advance of what I anticipated.

Redirection

Some children take an idea in a totally different direction to that expected. This can be a creative act. Gill Hope describes a session when a child responded unexpectedly to a teacher's expectation of simple forward movement creativity:

> [W]hen Zara was in year 3 her class had a Design and Technology lesson (linked to their work in Literacy) in which they were asked to make a model maze to help Theseus escape from the Minotaur. Zara quickly made a building with a single dividing wall and a Minotaur drawn on the floor and then spent the rest of the lesson making a river with a crocodile and a ship for Theseus to escape the crocodile.
>
> (Hope, 2005: 37)

Zara's creative response was to ignore most of the brief and go outside expectations to deal with the bigger issue that preoccupied her – how Theseus was going to escape once he had got out of the maze.

Integration

Integrative creativity occurs when two or more ways of thinking are combined, or bisociated, in tackling a problem. Integration is close to the inter-disciplinary cross-curricular approach outlined previously. Bisociation frequently happens when children work in groups and becomes creative when it leads to something new and useful. I observed this among children involved in making a den in a wooded area as part of a 'forest school' activity. One child thought technologically about the structure as another contributed geographically-inspired ideas about the best position to site the den and another suggested making enough room to invite a second group to have their packed lunches there. The combination of all three suggestions in practice integrated the thinking of three participants.

Sternberg's models are not necessarily self-contained. Children might operate several models in a single lesson, or different models overlap. These models can, however, help you recognise and celebrate the signs of creative development in children. In so doing, you help build an ethos in which children become confident to take the risks involved in creative practice.

Lucas, Claxton and Spencer's creative *'Habits of Mind'* (Collard, 2014) are helpful in assessing creative thought and action. Inquisitive, persistent, imaginative, disciplined and collaborative thoughts, words and actions are indicators of creative thinking. Use Table 7.7 to help describe the detail of each mindset.

UNIT PLANNING FOR CREATIVITY

Inter-disciplinary cross-curricular learning needs careful planning. You may have designed a stimulating learning environment and adapted your pedagogy to promote creativity. Perhaps you have considered working on your personal characteristics like flexibility, curiosity, imagination, humour or risk taking. Now you should consider the big issues that you *most* want your class to understand during your year together. These year-long goals can

■ **Table 7.7** Planning the development of Creative Habits of Mind

Habit of Mind	Evidence	Typical activities in subject areas
Inquisitive	Wondering and questioning Exploring and investigating Challenging assumptions	Geography: how our town is changing/ linked to the rest of the world Science: what plants and animals we can find in the wild area History: what the evidence tells us about Roman technologies
Persistent	Tolerating uncertainty Sticking with difficulty Daring to be different	Design/Technology: investigating different ways of joining materials PE: successfully learning a gym exercise or new game Music: making individual contribution to a class composition
Imaginative	Playing with possibilities Making connections Using intuition	Maths English Art
Disciplined	Crafting and improving Developing techniques Reflecting critically	Foreign language Art and design English
Collaborative	Cooperating appropriately Giving and receiving feedback Sharing or presenting the 'product'	RE Computing Music

unite your teaching across the curriculum and influence attitudes, interactions and responses far beyond it. Such goals will be few, but involve big themes like relationships, nature, sustainability, love, truth or beauty.

Choosing year-long goals

The goals you articulated when you entered education are important. They have the power to motivate and sustain you, so you should fight to express them in your teaching and curriculum choices. Similar goals may also be significant to the members of your class, but they may have other learning goals. Year-long goals might be expressed in a sentence that begins: "After a year in my class children will understand (or appreciate) that. . . . " Translating such major ambitions into the curriculum necessitates crossing subject-discipline boundaries. Year-long goals will differ for each teacher and arise from the narratives you have constructed about your life. Such goals should be negotiable and responsive if they are to represent and be supported by the community you serve. Enriching our super-diverse communities should involve values that have universal appeal like those listed in Table 7.8, but add goals of you own too.

Year-long goals will also suggest specific shorter term targets for teaching and learning. Each major issue also has its opposite which could also be part of any unit of work. Take, for example, three overarching goals from the list in Table 7.8: *beauty*, *self (or identity)* and *sustainability*. Questions arising from these themes might be: What is beauty or ugliness? Can efficiency be the opposite of beauty? How am I special or unique/what do I share with others? or How can we sustain the best (and identify and minimise the worst)

■ **Table 7.8** Planning overarching learning goals

Learning goal	After a year in my class, children will understand/appreciate:
Anti-racism	that human diversity is a valuable part of our lives, bringing interest and new ideas and understandings across the curriculum.
Beauty	that beauty can be discussed, defined, appreciated and shared in all curriculum contexts.
Belonging	the unique characteristics of their locality and express their pride and belonging to it.
Citizenship	their rights as a citizen and their role in being a good citizen.
Helping others	cross-curricular examples of how people help and have helped each other and how we should act.
Identity	what is unique about themselves and how to contribute to the community through it.
Peace	what peace is, why it is important and how it can be expressed in different curriculum subjects.
Respect	what respect looks like in different curricular contexts and how it is shown to others, things and places.
Sustainability	how we can live in ways that do not harm the future.
Truth	the different ways the subject-disciplines help us discover what truth is.

Table 7.9 Medium term planning for creativity

Age of class	Big issue	Overarching learning goal	Subjects involved	Shorter term goal in the form of a question	New knowledge and understanding in two or three curriculum subjects	Typical activities
4 years	Self or identity	Children will know and value their own unique strengths and characteristics and appreciate those of others.	Personal, social and emotional development (PSED); language	How can I learn more about myself in the free play areas?	Children will know that they: can develop new skills, can operate independently, can make contributions to others' lives, are members of different communities, can connect different parts of their life, and their learning is valued and supported by teacher.	Choosing construction materials. Entering and using their choice of role play areas. Interacting with specific areas of interest set up by practitioners. Talking about their 'Heritage Bags' (Small bags containing photos, and objects that relate to their life outside school). Listening to others talk about them.
7 years	Beauty	Children will think, share ideas and make decisions about beauty. They will learn about the beauty of the natural world and be able to respond to what they see as beautiful by making drawings, paintings and models of natural things.	Art and design, science, philosophy	What does beauty look like in nature? How can I use nature to make something beautiful?	Children will be able to: see, scientifically describe and appreciate the beauty of patterns, shapes and structures in nature; understand how to create art objects that capture beauty in natural forms; and understand beauty from others' point of view.	Woodland walk and collection resulting in detailed examination of leaves, flowers through microscopes, magnifiers and drawing. Group choices of classification categories. Paintings, drawings and prints based on patterns and structures found in nature. Discussion on beauty using the art of painters who depicted nature.
11 years	Sustainability	Children will understand that resources, lifestyles and environments are fragile and certain changes in thinking, attitude and behaviour can contribute to sustainable development.	Geography, citizenship, PSHEE, Learning for sustainability (Scotland), Sustainable development and Global Citizenship (Wales)	How can the school farm help me learn about sustainability and global citizenship?	Children will know that: decisions about consumption and waste can be changed in response to knowledge and engagement in sustainable development goals, human and animal life is inter-related and inter-dependent, and sustainable development is an important global issue.	School allotments cared for and maintained by staff, friends and pupils. Children involved in decisions about growing and cooking fruit and vegetables, keeping chickens safe and comfortable, and collecting and selling chickens' eggs. They look after and milk goats in the school grounds, make cheese and market milk to a local dairy. They compare their husbandry activities with those of a linked school in Sierra Leone.

in our world? Such questions occupy politicians, community leaders, practitioners and academics in all fields. The same issues can be just as important to a primary school child.

Table 7.9 offers examples of how overarching goals can link to two or three curriculum areas to specific aims in the primary school. Make a similar table to explore how you might work toward meeting an overarching goal of your choice.

CONCLUSION

Creativity keeps us moving forward. Steiner and Dewey, and later Herbert Read (1943), saw it as a liberating and humanising force. For Csikszentmihalyi (1997), it is a 'central source of meaning'. Despite its 'tensions and dilemmas', many educationalists agree on the educational and personal value of helping children discover their creative strengths (Craft, 2005; Robinson, 2015; Claxton and Lucas, 2015; Runco, 2012). Similar philosophies have inspired global exhortations, for example by UNESCO:

> [E]very child, is said to be a potential neurotic capable of being saved from this prospect, if early, largely inborn, creative abilities were not repressed by conventional Education. Everyone is an artist of some kind whose special abilities, even if almost insignificant, must be encouraged as contributing to an infinite richness of collective life.
>
> (Thistlewood, 2002: 07)

REFERENCES

Andreotti, V. (2010) Global education in the 21st century: Two different perspectives on the 'post' of postmodernism, *International Journal of Development Education and Global Learning*, Vol. 2, No. 2, pp. 5–22.

Barnes, J. (2015) Towards a creativity rich curriculum for the well-being of children 3–7 years, in T. David, S. Powell and K. Goouch (eds.) *The Routledge Handbook of Philosophies and Theories of Early Years Education and Care*. Abingdon: Routledge.

Barnes, J. (2016) Creativity and promoting wellbeing in children and young people in school settings, in S. Clift and P. Camic (eds.) *Oxford Textbook of Creative Arts Health and Wellbeing; International Perspectives in Practice, Policy and Research*. Oxford: Oxford University Press.

Blythe, T. (1998) *The Teaching for Understanding Guide*. San Francisco, CA: Jossey Bass.

Boden, M. (2004) *The Creative Mind, Myths and Mechanisms*. Abingdon: Routledge.

Bowlby, J. (1988) *A Secure Base: Clinical Applications of Attachment Theory*. Abingdon: Routledge.

Claxton, G. (1998) *Hare Brain, Tortoise Mind*. London: Fourth Estate.

Claxton, G. and Lucas, B. (2015) *Educating Ruby: What Our Children Really Need to Learn*. Carmarthen: Crown.

Collard, P. (2014) *Creativity, culture and education*: *Assessing creativity in education*, available at: www.wise-qatar.org/measuring-creativity-education-paul-collard#_ftn1

Craft, A. (2005) *Creativity in Schools Tensions and Dilemmas*. Abingdon: Routledge.

Craft, A. (2010) *Creativity and Education Futures: Leaning in a Digital Age*. Stoke on Trent: Trentham.

Cremin, T., Barnes, J. and Scoffham, S. (2009) *Creative Teaching for Tomorrow: Fostering a Creative State of Mind*. Deal: Future Creative.

Csikszentmihalyi, M. (1997) *Creativity: Flow and the Psychology of Discovery and Invention*. New York: Harper Collins.

Csikszentmihalyi, M. (2002) *Flow: The Classic Work on How to Achieve Happiness*. New York: Ebury Press.

Czikszentmihalyi, M. (2015) *The Systems Model of Creativity: The Collected Works of Mihalyi Csikszentmihalyi*. New York: Springer.

Damasio, A. (2003) *Looking for Spinoza: Joy, Sorrow and the Feeling Brain*. Orlando, FL: Harcourt.

Damon, W. (1984) *Peer education- the untapped potential*, available at: www.researchgate.net/profile/William_Damon2/publication/223299779_Peer_Education_The_Untapped_Potential/links/563a44cb08ae337ef29841e3/Peer-Education-The-Untapped-Potential.pdf (accessed 24.10.17).

Department for Education (2014) 'The National Curriculum for England framework for Key Stages 1–4,' available at: https://www.gov.uk/government/publications/national-curriculum-in-england-framework-for-key-stages-1-to-4 (accessed 16.02.18).

Dewey, J. (1938) *Experience and Education*. New York: Collier Books.

Fredrickson, B. (2011) *Positivity: Groundbreaking Research to Release Your Inner Optimist and Thrive*. New York: Crown.

Gardner, H. (2010) *Leading Minds: An Anatomy of Leadership*. New York: Harper Collins.

Gruzelier, J. (2003, October) Enhancing music performance through brain rhythm training. *Music Forum* (Journal of the Music Council of Australia), pp. 34–35.

Hope, G. (2005) *Teaching Design and Technology 3–11, the Essential Guide for Teachers*. London: Continuum.

John-Steiner, V. (2001) *Collaborative Creativity*. Oxford: Oxford University Press.

John-Steiner, V. and Moran, S. (2003) Creativity in the making, in R. Sternberg (ed.) *Creativity and Development*. Oxford: Oxford University Press.

Kabat-Zinn, J. (2013) *Full Catastrophe Living: Using the Wisdom of Your Body and Mind to Face Stress, Pain, and Illness*. New York: Bantam Dell.

Koestler, A. (1964) *The Act of Creation*. New York: Penguin.

NACCCE (1999) *All our futures: Creativity, culture and education*, available at: http://sirkenrobinson.com/pdf/allourfutures.pdf (accessed 24.10.17).

NCSL (2011) *Creating the conditions for positive behaviour to help every child succeed*, available at: http://dera.ioe.ac.uk/12538/1/download%3Fid%3D158591%26filename%3D promoting-the-conditions-for-positive-behaviour-to-help-every-child-succeed.pdf (accessed 24.10.17).

Owens, P. (2017) Wildthink: A framework for creative and critical learning, in S. Scoffham (ed.) *Teaching Geography Creatively*. Abingdon: Routledge.

Pangsepp, J. (2004) *Affective Neuroscience: The Origins of Animal & Human Emotions*. New York: Oxford University Press.

Perkins, D. (1992) *Smart Schools*. New York: Free Press.

Perkins, D. (2009) *Making Learning Whole: How Seven Principles of Teaching Can Transform Education*. San Francisco, CA: Jossey Bass.

Piaget, J. (1954) *The Construction of Reality in the Child*, trans. M. Cook. New York: Basic Books.

Pinker, S. (2002) *The Blank Slate*. London: Penguin.

Plucker, J. Beghetto, R. and Dow, G. (2004) 'Why Isn't Creativity More Important to Educational Psychologists? Potentials, Pitfalls and Future Directions in Creativity Research,' in *Educational Psychologist,* Vol. 39, No 2, pp 83–96.

Plucker, J. (2017) *Creativity and Innovation: Theory, Research, and Practice*. Wako, TX: Prufrock.

Powell, S. and Barnes, J. (2008, May) *Independent Evaluation of the TRACK Project, Final Report for Future Creative, (Formerly Creative Partnerships Kent)*. Canterbury: Canterbury Christ Church University.

Read, Sir H. (1943) *Education Through Art*. London: Faber and Faber.

Robinson, K. (2015) *Creative Schools: Revolutionising Education Form the Ground Up*. London: Penguin.

Rogoff, B. (2003) *The Cultural Nature of Human Development*. Oxford: Oxford University Press.

Runco, M. A. (2014) *Creativity Theories and Themes: Research Development and Practice*. London: Elsevier.

Runco, M. A. (2012) *Theory of personal creativity*, available at: www.markrunco.com/articles/the-theory-of-personal-creativity-and-implications-for-the-fulfillment-of-childrens-potentials-book-chapter (accessed 24.10.17).

Scoffham, S. and Barnes, J. (2007) *Uncorrected evidence: Memorandum to parliament*, available at: https://publications.parliament.uk/pa/cm200607/cmselect/cmeduski/memo/creativepartnerships/uc2002.htm (accessed 24.10.17).

Scottish Government (2016) *Curriculum for excellence*, available at: www.gov.scot/Topics/Education/Schools/curriculum (accessed 16.02.18).

Seligman, M. (2004) *Authentic Happiness*. New York: Basic Books.

Sondheim, S. (1957) 'Something's Coming' from Act 1, *West Side Story,* available at: https://www.allmusicals.com/lyrics/westsidestory/somethingscoming.htm (accessed 16.02.18)

Sternberg, R. (1997) *Successful Intelligence*. New York: Plume.

Sternberg, R. and Kaufman, J. (eds.) (2010) *The Cambridge Handbook of Creativity*. New York: Cambridge University Press.

Thistlewood, D. (2002) *Herbert read*, UNESCO, available at www.ibe.unesco.org/sites/default/files/reade.pdf (accessed 24.10.17).

Thomson, P., Hall, C., Jones, K. and Sefton-Green, J. (2012) *The Signature Pedagogies Project: Final Report*. Newcastle: CCE, available at: www.creativitycultureeducation.org/wp-content/uploads/Signature_Pedagogies_Final_Report_April_2012.pdf (accessed 24,10.17).

Vygotsky, L. (1978) *Mind in Society: The Development of Higher Psychological Pocesses*. Cambridge, MA: Harvard University Press.

Wallas (1926) *The Art of Thought*, Now available as a reprint by, Tunbridge Wells: Sollis Press (2014).

Welsh Government (2015) *Curriculum for wales: Foundation phase framework*, available at: http://gov.wales/docs/dcells/publications/150803-fp-framework-en.pdf (accessed 24.10.17).

Wiliam, D. (2006) *Excellence in assessment*, available at: www.assessnet.org.uk/e-learning/file.php/1/Resources/Excellence_in_Assessment/Excellence_in_Assessment_-_Issue_1.pdf (accessed 24.10.17).

CHAPTER

8

CHILD AND TEACHER-LED LEARNING

Opportunistic approaches

SUMMARY

This chapter asks you to consider your experience of child-initiated learning. It discusses the essence of child-centred philosophies and research, provides case studies from four contrasting settings and tables of provocative questions to help you consider the pros and cons of child-centred approaches. This theme provides opportunity to outline some significant and recent findings from affective and cognitive neuroscience with a discussion on their implications for the classroom. Introducing opportunistic cross-curricular learning, I make a distinction between the whole class methods common in Early Years settings and the individual or group approaches more commonly used with 7–11-year-olds. The chapter offers practical guidance on how to set up and maintain child-focussed approaches, and notes their disadvantages.

INTRODUCTION

My life in education has moved backward through the age ranges. Returning to England after teaching in Kenya, I taught art, art history, geography and history to 12–18-year-olds by day, art for three evenings a week with some of their older brothers in the local prison, and architectural history to their grandparents in the Worker's Education Association (WEA). After teaching secondary English in Malaysia, I returned to the UK as an all-subjects junior school teacher, and later a primary head working with 4–11-year-olds. I often covered reception and infant classes when staff were ill. Lecturing in Initial Teacher Education involved all primary age groups, but my research interests increasingly led me towards the education of babies and nursery-aged and children and their adult carers. I made the following notes last year as I participated in a session with 2–3-year-olds:

> *Victorian church hall in NE London, . . . echo-ey, high and up a longish flight of steps. 19 two and three year-olds, . . . 12 languages, . . . one nursery leader, . . . three support workers. Dave the dancer was already moving, making broad welcome movements, silently and smilingly as the children entered – full of bustle, noise and agitation. He indicated silently that they should join him on the hall floor strewn with soft mats. Dave lay down motionless for a minute saying nothing and a few children*

copied him . . . Raised his arm and gently waved, some children responded. He slowly rolled, crawled, curled up, relaxed and eventually sat in the middle of the hall, by which time many children were copying his slow, deliberate movements. Next he began to improvise a song about the rain (outside it was raining) accompanied by measured and quiet movements that gradually involved all children and adults: pitter patter (gentle 'pitter patter' on each other's faces), rain pouring down (gentle sweeping movements from top of the head down centre of back) splashy puddles (slow motion splashes with feet and arms,). After some other warm-ups using quiet repetitive music, Dave wordlessly gathered children around him and began telling a story continually illustrated with big expressions, touch, wordless sounds and improvised gestures shared around the group.

. . . later some children took over and Dave became just another member of the group responding to child-initiated movements round the room to quiet repetitive music, but intervened quietly when he saw potential problems . . . at one point of the story, children decided to climb over each other and the adult helpers and Dave showed them silently and with many smiles, how to balance and move safely, keeping their hands free. Dave called this, "developing their core stability and strength", to me it seemed they were developing motor control in a creative context, rehearsing responsibility for their own movements, respect for each other, graceful actions and peaceful, reflective, generous communication. . . . When he saw attention was flagging or no one was offering new shapes or actions Dave surreptitiously led new movements until a child took over again and he quickly released the role of leader . . . children moved and interacted meaningfully and gently with less and less talking . . . no instructions given, very few words used by adults . . . who moved and responded to the children's lead, ended the session visibly happier . . . children smiling, relaxed and more at peace with one another than when they entered.

Reflecting on this session, I noted the strengths of its child-led aspects. Here the 2–3-year-olds were neither instructed or controlled, but their decisions were central, respected and acted upon. They appeared to own the situation and like it. They showed their pleasure in high levels of engagement. The adults working with them were continually alert to their health, safety and security, and learning intentions were achieved, but control was largely trusted to these very young children. I wondered had the prisoners I'd taught in the 1970s experienced such enabling, empowering experience, if their confidence and sense of self-worth would have made their false turns less likely.

There are difficulties in allowing children to lead. Outside nursery education teachers are often suspicious of child-led methods and may feel safer with pure subject learning and progression, partly because they were trained that way (Westbrook et al., 2013). It is harder to ensure progression when a class responds in divergent ways.

In my previous example, some followed the implicit instructions but others seemed bemused. The unpredictability of responses made anything but the most general planning impossible. Assessment was given too little time and more observation was needed to spot misconceptions and influence the next steps in learning. To be successful in sustaining useful learning through child-focused methods, teachers have to be strong in subject knowledge and the philosophy and practice of child-led education – some were not. Teachers also needed to understand the expectations and values dominant in the children's cultures, and the mental and physical development expected of the age group.

Child-initiated methods are common in settings where play is accepted as the major source and motivator of learning. If a session is truly child-led, it is almost bound to cross the curriculum.

Have you observed or participated in child-led sessions? Write your thoughts on the session in Table 8.1:

Table 8.1 Observing child-led learning in practice

The educational setting	Your description
Age of children involved	
Setting	
What did the teacher do/say/model? (a) at first (b) later	
Theme of activity (if any)	
List the things children did	
Behavioural issues	
Learning Issues	
Was it cross-curricular? How was it cross-curricular?	

EXPLORING KEY TERMS

The word *teacher* in this chapter includes all those that support learning: teachers, carers, parents, assistants, key-workers, helpers and sometimes peers.

This chapter uses three overlapping terms to describe teaching and learning: child-centred, child-led/initiated and opportunistic. Although they are related, I have tried to indicate distinctions between them.

Child-centred education is a broad concept where the child's interests, development, care and world are central to educational decisions. There are many ways to place the child at the centre – not all require the child to make decisions or lead the process. As educated, principled and sensitive adults, we may feel we *know* the child's world and what they need, and conclude that a *mix* of styles, approaches or foci is most appropriate.

Child-led/initiated learning means that children lead learning decisions. The teacher prepares spaces and materials but after that generally observes, takes notes and photographs, encourages, perhaps joins in or facilitates. Child-led approaches allow the child to define what, how much and where they learn. These methods characterise much Early Years and play-based education.

Opportunistic approaches can apply across the primary age range and beyond. They rely on chance engagements by a child or group, though sometimes a class might deliberately be granted the opportunity to take learning where they wish (Barnes and Shirley, 2007). Opportunistic methods respond to the random engagements that occur alongside the planned learning activities. Opportunistic cross-curricular teaching and learning can happen in a matter of moments or characterise a whole day's engagement.

CHILD-CENTRED APPROACHES

Child-centred education is rooted in enlightenment and democratic ideologies, and has been a political 'football' since the 1960s (e.g., Telegraph, 2014). Child-centred-ness extends the idea of democracy into school curricula and pedagogies. This liberal or 'lefty' ideology has been accused of 'damaging' generations of young people (see Hirsch's books), but similar methods are also hailed as powerful motivators of disaffected children (Roberts, 2006; Thomson et al., 2012).

Children are naturally inquisitive. They quickly become social learners, taking cues from older or more proficient peers. Bruner in his seminal lecture *The Processes of Cognitive Growth*: *Infancy* (1968: 9) summarised their typical behaviour as, "intelligent, adaptive and flexible right from birth." The affirmative attitudes, secure environments, sustained attention, inclusion, and well-focused feedback that facilitate the deeper, transferrable, useful learning build both flexibility and intelligence (Westbrook et al., 2013), but current trends towards competition, testing, greater accountability and conformity can cut across such positive experience.

Rousseau, Froebel and Steiner's child-centred philosophies argued that the *child's* interests and choices should be paramount. Child-centred methods became popular (at least with certain elites) in relatively liberal and open-minded times. As Alexander (2010) noted however, its pedagogies have been a minority interest and even at the post Plowden peak of child-led philosophies, very few primary schools wholeheartedly adopted its practices. The fact that Cambridge Primary Review (CPR) evidence argues the 'time has come' for child-centred education to be mainstream, is therefore significant.

The relationship between *involvement* and effective learning is highlighted by research across the disciplines over the last 30 years. Research for the World Health Organisation (WHO, 2016) and UNICEF (2016), for example, finds strong correlations between children's engagement in education and high life satisfaction scores, health and well-being. Education authorities around the world have begun to recognise the efficacy of student-centred educational methods (Fielding, 2006; Krechevsky and Mardell., 2016) but in these neo-liberal times, the justificatory emphasis has shifted from beliefs that child-initiated methods secure child well-being, towards claims they are good for the *economy* (Shuayb and O'Donnell, 2010). Claims are even made that child-led and social learning bolsters democracy:

> When children grow up in a culture and begin their schooling with support for thinking, feeling, and acting in groups, they are more likely to participate in and practice democracy as informed and caring citizens.
>
> (Krechevsky and Mardell, 2016: 13)

The CPR argues that placing subject learning and child-centred approaches at opposite ends of a spectrum of philosophies is a 'destructive discourse' (Alexander, 2010: 41). Both subject-led *and* child-centred approaches are necessary for progress in learning. The

CPR stresses throughout its 600 pages that children who feel empowered are likely to be better and happier learners. Such views are common in schools and universities and are represented in the introduction to the CPR:

> [P]ower relations in many schools are beginning to shift, but the picture is still mixed and children are far from uniformly regarded as young citizens with important and insightful things to say about their education. The Review says that the 'children's voice' movement is not a fad, but a trend that needs to become the way of school.
>
> (Alexander, 2010: 12)

What constitutes 'empowerment' and whether 'happiness' is a legitimate educational aim, remain subjects of intense media debate (e.g., Facer, 2011).

The CPR cites both international research and global conventions to recommend that primary schooling should:

> Respect children's experiences, voices and rights, and adopt the UN Convention on the Rights of the Child (CRC) as the framework for policy.
>
> (Alexander, 2010: 8)

Authorities in several jurisdictions have taken note of this advice. The Curriculum for Wales for example reminds us that the child should be "at the heart of any planned curriculum" (Welsh Government, 2015: 4) and highlights their right to be "listened to and treated with respect" (2015: 2). In its orders for 3–7-year-olds, the *Curriculum for Wales* paraphrases Plowden:

> At the centre of the statutory curriculum framework lies the holistic development of children and their skills, building on their previous learning experiences and knowledge.
>
> (Welsh Government, 2015: 3)

After referring to the importance of equality of opportunity and diversity, the Welsh curriculum describes its approach in terms familiar to 18th century enlightenment educationalists and 20th century progressivists alike:

> Children learn through first-hand experiential activities with the serious business of 'play' providing the vehicle. Through their play, children practise and consolidate their learning, play with ideas, experiment, take risks, solve problems, and make decisions individually, in small and in large groups. First-hand experiences allow children to develop an understanding of themselves and the world in which they live. The development of children's self-image and feelings of self-worth and self-esteem are at the core.
>
> (Welsh Government, 2015: 3)

The philosophies of Rousseau, Pestalozzi, Froebel, Dewey, Read, Plowden and the UN are similarly evident in Scotland's *Curriculum for Excellence* (Scottish Government, 2016), which refers to "taking account of [children's] views and experiences" (p. 10), children being enabled to "express themselves in different ways" (p. 55), and for their voices "to be heard and involved in decisions that affect them" (p. 73).

That guidance links well-being to curriculum and pedagogical models that place the child "at the heart of the educational process" (Plowden, 1967), but if pedagogy is genuinely child-centred, care for each child must also be characterised by variety and flexibility. Dogmatic adherence to single styles ignores the uniqueness of every child.

NEUROSCIENTIFIC EVIDENCE AND CHILD-CENTRED APPROACHES

Science leads us away from dogmatism. The possibility of examining the living brain through functional Magnetic Resonance Imaging (fMRI) and Positron Emission Tomography (PET) has resulted in increasing numbers of neurostudies on children's learning (Table 8.2). A recent literature review on children's cognitive development (Goswami, 2015) aligns itself with child-centred philosophies. Taken alongside Damasio's work (2003; Immordino-Yang and Damasio, 2007) on the emotional drivers of learning, Goswami's review confirms the strong influence of environment – even within the womb – on children's learning. Since environment plays a significant part in brain development, the quality of the child's physical, social and psychological surroundings should be a central concern of education.

Goswami also confirms the social nature of learning, the huge variability in types of learning and levels of ability in young children and the similarity between child and adult brains. The main differences between them is experience, and "largely a matter of neural enrichment" (Goswami, 2015: 4). Neuroscience applied to education confidently makes the following assertions:

These conclusions do not necessarily endorse child-centred approaches, but reinforce arguments for experiential, sensory and positive curricula. The strong evidence on

---

■ **Table 8.2** Some educationally significant conclusions from neuroscientific study

---

Joy is the optimal condition for learning, memory, reasoning, language and the other 'grand functions of the human mind. (Damasio, 2003: 299)

States of real or imagined threat evoke 'escape' behaviour and impede thinking. (Le Doux, 2003)

Learning in young children is 'socially mediated'. (Goswami, 2015: 24)

Learning by the brain depends on the development of 'multi-sensory networks of neurons distributed across the entire brain'. (Ibid.: 25)

Knowledge gained through 'active experience, language, pretend play and teaching' are each important for the development of children's 'causal explanatory systems'. (Ibid.: 25)

Imaginative or pretend play helps thinking, reasoning and understanding but scaffolding by a teacher is required if these are to be effective. (Ibid.: 25)

Individual differences in the ability to benefit from instruction and individual differences between children are large in the primary years hence any class of children must be treated as individuals. (Ibid.: 25)

Humans and other animals behave in flexible and creative ways during play. (Panksepp, 1998: 297)

---

the social aspects of learning suggests that visions of extensive electronic-learning for children are unlikely to be successful.

The recognition of neurodiversity suggests the need for a variety of educational approaches to provide access to learning to all. The 'whole brain', 'multi-sensory' characteristics of thinking argue that cross-disciplinary experiences *must* be among our collection of educational strategies. If learning is multi-sensory and distributed across the brain, then theories of 'left brain' and 'right brain' learning are unhelpful over-simplifications. Though Visual, Auditory and Kinesthetic (VAK) 'styles' of learning helpfully led teachers towards a wider range of approaches, the theory limits expectations and inaccurately explains the complex, individual nature of learning. Research continually reaffirms the *differences* between human brains, each shaped by unique experiences. It would indeed be surprising if these brains responded in the same way to one particular teaching style.

Learning in all mammals is strongly associated with emotions (Le Doux, 1999; Damasio, 2003, 2012; Panksepp, 2004). Emotions in humans appear to be controllable and physically identifiable in fMRI scans (Gruzelier, 2003; Kassam et al., 2013). Positive emotional states support memory (Trevarthan and Panksepp, 2016), while traumatic emotional experiences impact negatively upon memory and learning (Quidé et al., 2016). Positive emotion is a major motivator (and result) of learning itself (Immordino-Yang and Damasio, 2007). Psychology research claims similar relationships between emotional competence and effective learning (Curby et al., 2015) in infants and young children. This triangulation between practitioner knowledge and scientific research suggests that teachers should strive to involve young children at personal/emotional levels, practically, socially and through the senses.

Vygotsky's research resulted in the promotion of group work and became part of Western educational practice through the work of Bruner and more recently Wass and Golding (2014). Today neuroscience also suggests that the *attitudes* with which teachers use language are important, too. For example, positive, elaborative, conversational language oriented towards tenacity has been shown in studies to extend learning possibilities, (Reece et al., 1993; Karpov, 2005; Dweck, 2017).

Neuroscientific research confirms that within an emotionally secure, physically and socially enriched, multi-sensory environment, children will achieve more. Positive teacher support remains crucial too and may involve:

▨ Providing further examples of a concept
▨ Focussed praise
▨ Making explicit the learning that happened
▨ Encouraging metacognition
▨ Pointing out connections
▨ Helping memories to become more positive
▨ Creating playful scenarios that provoke learning
▨ Highlighting creative thinking or action

By contrast, neurostudies suggest that negative expectations and attitudes transfer easily to children, hampering development and diminishing potential (Goswami, 2015).

WHAT DO CHILD-CENTRED APPROACHES LOOK LIKE?

Case Study 8.1 Child-centred learning with 9-year-olds in a Kent primary school

A class of 9-year-olds walk down the street in which their Victorian school stands. At one end, there is a T-junction onto a busy main road. At the other end, the lane meets a churchyard and becomes a footpath. The street includes a medieval hall house, three eighteenth-century farmworkers cottages, two terraces of 19th-century town houses, a range of 1930s bungalows and a few late 20th century houses with large front gardens. Outside the normal health and safety guidance, children have been given only one instruction – to 'capture the essence' of their street to communicate to others. Children are divided into groups of six, each with an electronic tablet, sketchbook and a small recording device. After an hour walking, taking photos, recording, drawing and talking, the groups return to class with ideas formed during the walk. Brainstorming under the guidance of the teacher produce a wide range of ideas and in groups the children decide on projects to follow during the rest of the week:

- Compose and perform a musical journey from the main road to the churchyard – *using a collection of different sounds from each part of the street.*
- Make a 3D map of the street with models of all houses – *one member of the group had a dad who was an architect who could build models of houses – he agreed to come and show the group how to do it.*
- Interview five people about living in the street – *an old man had given a group photographs of the street in World War II; he had lived there for 80 years.*
- Mount an exhibition of 20 enlarged photographs of unusual views of the street – *one group was particularly excited at the contrasting building styles and materials; one member suggested 'unusual angles' because she'd seen it in a book.*
- Make up, write and illustrate a play about something that could *only* have happened in this street – *members of the group had done an exercise like this in a castle last term. An author had helped children find places in the castle where something dramatic could have happened. They improvised the pretended scene in three freeze-frames and decided what bits of the castle would be represented in scenery if they were to stage the same story back at school.*

The teacher and teaching assistant helped each group fulfil its plans during the week. Children recorded their final products in a filmed presentation. (records from school experience observations, June 2009)

CHILDREN LEADING

Teachers decided on the contexts for learning in the previous case study. The centrality of children's decisions remains evident in the following case study, where cross-curricular and creative responses dominate.

Forest schools

'Forest Schools' have been established across the UK in recent years. They claim to help children develop a sensitivity and care for the natural environment that will ensure its sustainability. These outdoor spaces, supervised by trained educators are based on an educational approach developed in Wisconsin, USA during the 1920s and taken up by the preschools and primary schools of Sweden and Denmark from the 1950s onward. Suitably dressed and sustained but with little formal structure, children play and explore these environments under the careful eye of their leaders and experts in woodland crafts. Leaders generally follow the interests of the children as they work to extend the spiritual, social, communication, physical, environmental and construction learning stimulated by their interaction with the woodland environment. This practice was observed in action by British teachers and brought to a number of UK schools during the 1990s. There are now well over 200 registered Forest School providers. In 2012, the Forest Schools Association was formed to ensure consistent quality learning experience in the natural world and train and licence providers (Forest Schools Association website).

One school expresses its contact with Forest School in the following words:

> Forest School is different from Outdoor Education as most people know it. Where Outdoor Education is task led, based around an issue or a problem to be solved, Forest School is led by the learners' interest within a loosely structured framework of intended outcomes that builds on the interests and curiosity of the learner. Forest Schools differ from other forms of learning in that they focus on the whole person in an environment outside the formal educational setting of classrooms.
>
> A woodland creates its own learning environment framed by safety routines and established boundaries. Children experience active learning, in a less structured manner which suits the individual learning styles of many children. (Staplehurst Primary School, Kent).

Case Study 8.2 A morning in a Forest School in Wales

A class of 6-year-olds line up and climb into the coach that waits outside the school gates every Wednesday morning. The journey to 'the woods' takes about 30 minutes. Two children strapped into the front seats are telling the driver (who already knows) when to turn left, when to go straight on and when to turn right (after three trips, many children knew the journey by heart and had also learned their left and right). As they arrive at the wooded area outside their town, children were reminded of the safety rules – always wearing their bright caps and fluorescent tabards, staying with their group, looking after each other and following instructions the first time. They a start their activities with a stone passing game, each child selecting a favourite rounded stone from the pebbly soil and singing a song in which 'their' stone is passed around the circle to the beat. When everyone's stone is returned, the song suddenly stops. The children play another rhythmic game as they sit in a circle and call out the names of things they can see around theme to a 1, 2, 3, 4 beat: *x x x x daffodil x x x x tree – x x x x branches x x x x lots of new leaves x x x x*, etc.

Today's walk takes them down a small valley toward a stream running on clay, and the groups talk animatedly as they go. Each prepared adult responds to questions and exclamations along the route. When they arrive at the shallow stream, some children want to make a new bridge, others are keen to construct a shelter and a third group wants to make a rival den on the other side of the stream. A fourth group remembers last week's game of making pictures out of branches and leaves, and wants to make another one and photograph it. The last group makes collections of colours on strips of card with double-sided tape. In each case the attendant adult helps and supports, and adds ideas or questions to conversations. The word 'we' dominates interactions. Social skills like: taking turns, listening carefully, taking majority decisions, and appreciating another are much in evidence.

Seeing two groups making shelters, the others want to build their own. Soon all five groups are making them, improvising tools, asking adults for help and improvising levers, braces, and hole-makers or roofing their constructions. Highly motivated to build a structure big enough for the group, the sense of focus and energy is strong and children are working hard and very cooperatively. One child suggests having their health snacks and drinks inside the new dens, and the teacher agrees (observation by author April, 2016).

Some children may be resistant to – even upset by – the lack of structure inherent in child-initiated methods (OECD, 2004). Experienced teachers will provide a supportive framework to support such children. A sample learning frame is illustrated in Table 8.3.

■ **Table 8.3** A simple frame to support creative and cross-curricular learning from objects, places, people and ideas

DRAW your object carefully (or draw a very detailed picture – every spot, bristle, shadow and dent – of the person, place, idea or thing you are looking at).	What do you KNOW (about an object, place, person, idea you are directed towards)? List 10 verifiable and obvious details you are quite sure about: size, colour, dimensions, shape, texture, joins, temperature, known materials, etc.
What do you GUESS (about the object, idea, person, place etc.)? List things you don't know but *think* might be true: materials, functions, strength, age, value to another person or a museum, value to you.	What questions would you ask your object, place, idea or person if they could talk to you? Ask five really searching questions.

Reggio Emilia

Reggio Emilia is a small, relatively wealthy province in Northern Italy. For the last 60 years, it has spent about 40% of its income on education – focusing on Early Years and primary education. The city and province recognised the health, social and economic benefits of generously resourcing pre-school education shortly after the end of World War II. Founded in 1945 and based upon the writings of Loris Malaguzzi (1920–1994), the Reggio method places the physical, social, health and psychological needs of the child *within community* centrally in its decisions on pedagogy, curriculum and environments. Malaguzzi [translated] puts it this way:

> Both children and adults need to feel active and important – to be rewarded by their own efforts, their own intelligences, their own activity and energy. When a child feels these things are valued, they become a fountain of strength for him. He feels the joy of working with adults who value his work and this is one of the bases for learning. Over-activity on the part of the adult is a risk factor. The adult does too much because he cares about the child; but this creates a passive role for the child in her own learning.
>
> (Malaguzzi, 1993: 4)

Reggio pre-school and primary buildings and resources are designed around the size and interests of the child and serve all formal subject-disciplines. School buildings maximise natural light, giving an airy feel to interiors. The use of mirrors and light boxes generates unusual views, deepens interest and enhances visual displays of children's work and stimulus materials. Spacious group work and well equipped '*atelier*' (workshop) areas and centralised '*plazas*' with role-play resources characterise the learning spaces. Generous spaces allow for free choice of activity, and teachers make lengthy and finely focused observations of children relating to each other, environments and objects. Such record keeping is a central role of the adults. Food preparation and communal eating is represented in the way that school kitchens are often placed at the centre of these buildings. Kitchen windows are placed at child level so that they can see in (and sometimes help) food preparation. Low windows also encourage the idea that the external environment is an important part of learning.

International visitors to Reggio schools see children working outdoors in the town, nearby villages and the fields and forests of the area. Children are prompted to make personal connections between the world beyond school or nursery and their learning. Parents are often part of daily activities. The preschools and primary schools aim to consult them regularly, recognising their role as first educators of the child (Hewett, 2001). The curriculum is thematic, based on open-ended questions, responsive to children's and teachers' interests, decidedly cross-curricular and aims to provide broad opportunities for the expression of what Malaguzzi called 'the hundred languages of children' – their many ways of expressing themselves, practically, socially, artistically, culturally and verbally. Creativity appears to abound in these schools (Reggio Emilia website).

OPPORTUNISTIC CROSS-CURRICULAR LEARNING

Teachers can be opportunistic in any context. Opportunistic cross-curricular learning (Figure 8.1) involves teachers bringing flexible, open and deliberately 'stretching' responses to *children's* engagement with real-life experience. Its methods are not confined to a particular age group or learning theory. In opportunistic mode, teachers encourage and facilitate, but also scaffold children's knowledge and understanding in an area of their choosing.

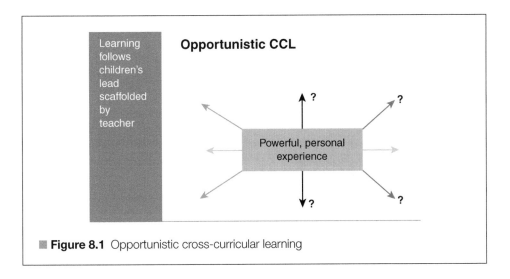

Opportunistic teachers *teach* enthusiastically, but only after the child or group has indicated interest. That interest may be completely unconnected to a lesson plan, but opportunistic teachers will allow themselves to be diverted by children's distractions, questions and comments. You might for example, follow up a group's interest in a molehill during a field trip, your highly planned geography lesson on volcanoes may be hijacked by a child's question about Pompeii or you may decide to abandon a well prepared science session on the parts of a flower because of an enthralling question about God. While unpredictable, these moments of opportunity hold a strong likelihood of engagement for children.

Children are captivated by different things. They make unexpected choices, especially in playful settings and experienced teachers will be ready to build on 'outside the box' responses. Children's interest shows in hundreds of ways. Life-changing enchantment can arrive in an instant – a professional clarinettist I know traces his love of the instrument to a moment of fascination as floodlights flashed on the silver keys of the instrument when his mum took him to a concert at 5 years of age.

Teachers seeking opportunistic contexts need to plan atmospheres and situations where the chances of authentic and autotelic engagement are more likely. Planning for unplanned opportunities might sound like an oxymoron, but it is possible throughout the year to arrange a background of provocative experiences for children to share. In these days of tests, targets, setting, streaming, profiles, strategies and spreadsheets, it is not easy to expect the unexpected, but some studies highlight the importance of a balance of approaches. Thomson et al. (2012), for example (Table 8.4), has shown how artists in schools offer free-ranging, creative, open-ended, confident and playful experiences that present opportunities for prolonged and personal engagement.

Austere times have reduced the number of creative practitioners engaged by schools, but pupil premium money is still spent by many primary schools on artists and scientists to enrich experience. Visits, visitors, stimulus displays, changed furniture arrangements, a play or song by another class, a concert, technique, exhibition, game, themed day or special event can each become opportunities. Such experiences can be shared *and* personal and the teacher's role is often simply to encourage children to enter into learning. Try the following ways of supporting children's learning (Table 8.5).

■ **Table 8.4** Artists provoking opportunities for deep and creative engagement (based on Thomson et al., 2012)

Types of approach used by artists in schools	Elaboration: artists in schools . . .
Hybrid	bring their life and priorities into the work of the school – they are not governed by the usual priorities of schools.
Collaborative and cooperative	rely on collaboration and cooperation (see also Roberts, (2006).
Mobile	move around the school, in and out of classes, around the community.
Time-flexible	have a relaxed attitude to time, timetables working through breaks and lunch, after school and before school, etc.
Permeable	let the outside world in, through using parents, experts, governors and other stakeholders.
Inclusive	take an approach to inclusion that expects all – no matter how many barriers to learning – to be capable of making contributions and bringing ideas.
Choice/agency dominant	listen to the child's voice and offer plenty of opportunities for improvisation, making meaningful choices and developing a sense of group or personal control over projects.
Large scale/ambitious	invent ambitious and relevant products and processes (Perkins, 2010).
Playful/absurd	use humour, unusual insights, and the voluntary suspension of belief.
Present-tense/lived experience	work on meaningful projects.

Some children may not be captivated, however. They may be culturally, temperamentally, neurologically or psychologically unable or unwilling to show interest. This does not stop the teacher from being child-centred, but reminds us that opportunistic methods are not appropriate for all children and settings. If our overriding aim is a 'pedagogy of care' (Noddings, 1992), the opportunistic styles are but one way of showing it.

Opportunistic cross-curricular learning is diagrammed in Figure 8.1.

If you are thinking of adopting child-centred approaches, consider the following critiques in Table 8.6 (Langford, 2010).

CONCLUSION

Child-centred approaches respond positively to the fact that young children appear genetically predisposed to learn opportunistically from the world around them. Learning from the immediate environment is inevitably cross-curricular, but in group settings it can lead

Table 8.5 Supporting children in opportunistic learning

- Joining in and becoming a co-learner
- Approving/encouraging
- Observing for assessment or to facilitate later learning
- Supporting deeper or extended interaction through questions and comments
- Prompting connections with previous learning
- Teaching a related skill or new knowledge where necessary
- Involving others to promote social learning
- Finding further examples of the same object of interest
- Making links to everyday life/class, school or home values
- Providing guidance or a framework to those who do not know what to do
- Leading those who find nothing of interest toward something that may capture them or others who will involve them in their interest
- Inventing challenges 10–15% higher than the child's or groups' current ability (Csikszentmihalyi, 2002)

Table 8.6 Critiques of child-centred and opportunistic approaches

Child-centred and opportunistic approaches may:

- Favour confident, articulate, children
- Favour male children and perpetuate assigned gender differences
- Ignore observations that children learn in different ways and thus discourage the use of alternative methods
- Take the teacher *away* from children since they 'observe' and 'facilitate' more than teach
- Cause some children to feel oppressed or threatened by the observations typical of child-centred approaches
- Be thought to be diametrically opposite to teacher-centred approaches – such a dichotomy is unhelpful (children can be empowered in either and many other contexts)
- Generate an illusion of child choice rather than reality – the child may still be manipulated to choose things the teacher wants them to choose
- Disadvantage children who feel constrained, unwilling or unable to make choices
- Represent a philosophical choice rather than a scientific one
- Too 'reified' and 'revered' (Langford, 2010: 113) as an education concept
- Too complex and difficult to thrust upon novice teachers or students in Initial Teacher Education

children in diverse and contradictory directions. Confident and knowledgeable teachers can handle and positively exploit this multiplicity of responses through opportunistic approaches. Confident and articulate children appear to benefit from such approaches and successfully develop creative and collaborative thinking through them. Less confident, less articulate students and those for whom the methods are culturally unfamiliar are less likely to thrive in child-initiated and opportunistic contexts. Curriculum, inspection and assessment expectations lead teachers to avoid child-led and opportunistic methods as children progress through primary education.

REFERENCES

Alexander, R. (ed.) (2010) *Children, Their World, Their Education: Final Report and Recommendations of the Cambridge Primary Review*. Abingdon: Routledge.

Barnes, J. and Shirley, I. (2007) Strangely familiar: Cross curricular and creative thinking. *Improving Schools*, Vol. 10, No. 2, pp. 162–179.

Bruner, J. (1968) *The Processes of Cognitive Growth: Infancy*. Heinz Werner Lectures. 20. Available at:

https://commons.clarku.edu/heinz-werner-lectures/20 (accessed 16.02.18).

Csikszentmihalyi, M. (2002) *Flow: The Classic Work on How to Achieve Happiness*. New York: Ebury Press.

Curby, T., Brown, C., Hamada-Barrett, H. and Denham, S. (2015) Associations between pre-schoolers' social emotional competence and pre-literacy skills. *Infant and Child Development*, Vol. 24, No. 5.

Damasio, A. (2003) *Looking for Spinoza: Joy, Sorrow and the Feeling Brain*. Orlando, FL: Harcourt.

Dweck, C. (2017) *Mindset – Updated Edition: Changing the Way You think to Fulfil Your Potential*. New York: Ballentine.

Facer, K. (2011) *Learning Futures: Education, Technology and Socio-Technical Change*. London: Routledge.

Fielding, M. (2006) Leaderships, radical student engagement and the necessity of person-centred education. *International Journal of Leadership in Education*, Vol. 9, No. 4, pp. 249–313.

Forest Schools Association website, available at: www.forestschoolassociation.org/membership-options-page/

Goswami, U. (2015) Children's cognitive development and learning. *CPRT Research Survey 3* (new series). York: Cambridge Primary Review Trust, available at http://cprtrust.org.uk/wp-content/uploads/2015/02/COMPLETE-REPORT-Goswami-Childrens-Cognitive-Development-and-Learning.pdf (accessed 24.10.17).

Gruzelier, J. (2003, October) Enhancing music performance through brain rhythm training. *Music Forum* (Journal of the Music Council of Australia), pp. 34–35.

Hewett, V. (2001) Examining the Reggio Emilia approach to early childhood education. *Early Childhood Education Journal*, Vol. 29, pp. 95–100.

Immordino-Yang, M. and Damasio, A. (2007, March) We feel, therefore we learn: The relevance of affective and social neuroscience to education. *Mind Brain and Education*, Vol. 1, No. 1, pp. 3–10.

Karpov, Y. (2005) *The Neo-Vygotskian Approach to Child Development*. Cambridge: Cambridge University Press.

Kassam, K., Markey, A., Cherkassky, V., Loewenstein, G. and Just, M. (2013) *Identifying emotions on the basis of neural activation*, available at: http://journals.plos.org/plosone/article?id=10.1371/journal.pone.0066032 (accessed 24.10.17).

Krechevsky, M. and Mardell, B. (2016, December) Innovations in early education: The international. *Reggio Emilia Exchange*, Vol. 23, No. 4.

Langford, R. (2010) Critiquing child-centred pedagogy to bring children and early childhood educators into the centre of a democratic pedagogy. *Contemporary Issues un Early Childhood*, Vol. 11, No. 1, pp. 113–127.

Le Doux, J. (1999) *The Emotional Brain: The Mysterious Underpinnings of Emotional Life*. London: Phoenix.

Le Doux, J. (2003) *The Synaptic Self: How Our Brain Became Who We Are*. London: Penguin.

Malaguzzi, L. (1993) *Your image of the child: Where teaching begins*, available at: https://reggioalliance.org/downloads/malaguzzi:ccie:1994.pdf (accessed 24.10.17).

Noddings, N. (1992) *The Challenge to Care in Schools*. New York: Teachers College Press.

OECD (2004) *Starting strong: Curricula and pedagogies in early childhood education and care*, available at: www.oecd.org/edu/school/31672150.pdf (accessed 24.10.17).

Panksepp, J. (2004) *Affective Neuroscience: The Foundations of Human and Animal Emotions*. New York: Oxford.

Perkins, D. (2010) *Making Learning Whole: How Seven Principles of Teaching Can Transform Education*. San Francisco, CA: Jossey Bass.

Plowden, B. (1967) *Children and their primary schools*, available at: www.educationengland.org.uk/documents/plowden/plowden1967-1.html (accessed 24.10.17).

Quidé, Y., O'Reilly, N., Rowland, J., Carr, V., Elzinga, B. and Green, M. (2016) Effects of childhood trauma on working memory in affective and non-affective psychotic disorders. *Brain Imaging and Behavior*. Vol 11, No 3, pp 722–735. doi:10.1007/s11682–016–9548-z.

Reece, E., Hayden, C. and Fivush, R. (1993) Mother-child conversations about the past. *Cognitive Development*, Vol. 8, pp. 403–430.

Reggio Emilia website, available at: www.reggiochildren.it/?lang=en

Roberts, P. (2006) *Nurturing creativity in young people: A report to government to inform future policy*, available at: www.creativetallis.com/uploads/2/2/8/7/2287089/nurturing-1.pdf (accessed 24.10.17).

Scottish Government (2016) *Curriculum for excellence*, available at: www.education.gov.scot/Documents/all-experiences-and-outcomes.pdf (accessed 24.10.17).

Shuayb, M. and O'Donnell, S. (2010) Aims and values of primary education, England and other countries, in R. Alexander (ed.) *The Cambridge Primary Review Research Surveys*. Abingdon: Routledge.

Telegraph (2014, March 21) We don't want lefty child-centred teaching. *Daily Telegraph*, available at: www.telegraph.co.uk/education/educationnews/10714820/Ofsted-chief-we-dont-want-lefty-child-centred-teaching.html (accessed 24.10.17).

Thomson, P., Hall, C., Jones, K. and Sefton-Green, J. (2012) *The Signature Pedagogies Project: Final Report*. Newcastle: CCE, available at: www.creativitycultureeducation.org/wp-content/uploads/Signature_Pedagogies_Final_Report_April_2012.pdf (accessed 24.10.17).

Trevarthan, C. and Panksepp, J. (2016) In Tine with feeling, in S. Hart (ed.) *Inclusion, Play and Empathy: Neuroaffective Development in Children's Groups*. London: Jessica Kingsley, pp. 29–48.

UNICEF (2016) *Fairness for Children A League Table of Inequality in Child Well-Being in Rich Countries*. Florence: UNICEF.

Wass, R. and Golding, C. (2014) Sharpening a tool fore teaching the zone of proximal development. *Teaching in Higher Education*, Vol. 19, No. 6, pp. 671–684.

Welsh Government (2015) *Curriculum for Wales: Foundation Phase Framework*, Cardiff: Welsh Government. Available at: http://learning.gov.wales/docs/learningwales/publications/150803-fp-framework-en.pdf (accessed 16.02.18).

Westbrook, J., Durrent, N., Brown, R., Orr, D. Pryor, J., Boddy, J. and Salvi, F. (2013) *Pedagogy, Curriculum, Teaching Practice and Teacher Education in Developing Countries*. London: DEFRA.

World Health Organisation (2016) *Growing up unequal: The health behaviour of school aged children report*, available at: www.euro.who.int/en/health-topics/Life-stages/child-and-adolescent-health/health-behaviour-in-school-aged-children-hbsc/growing-up-unequal.-hbsc-2016-study-20132014-survey (accessed 24.10.17).

CHAPTER 9

MAKING MEANING
Assessing creative and integrated learning

SUMMARY

This chapter concerns the meaning of education and life and how assessment can help us find answers to such big questions. I will introduce ideas about formative assessment – seeking to measure the connections between children's experience of education and their present and future lives beyond it. The chapter specifically focuses on assessing creativity and cross-curricular approaches. It asks why affirmation, authentic experience, transferability, connectivity, collaboration and shared human values should be important factors in such assessments. In presenting a 'performance' approach to assessment, it offers practical advice linking assessment with the planning and delivery of a connecting, relevant and meaningful curriculum.

INTRODUCTION

26 April 2017

On this day in 2011 my son Jacob died at the age of 21. He had leukaemia. He was one of the best pianists of his generation, studying at the Royal Academy of Music under an inspiring and empowering professor of piano. His greatest love was playing chamber music with friends. Throughout 18 months of the unrelenting, painful, horrific progress of his cancer, he continued to practice, play and give concerts with his friends. Just 9 days before he died he played a final concert to a packed hall, disabled and disfigured by his disease. Regardless of the cumulatively negative effects of chemo and radiotherapy and a gastric tube he accompanied an energetic sextet by Poulenc and a trio by Beethoven. For his final and solo encore he chose the slow movement from Beethoven's 11th piano sonata – we, his family still daren't listen to it.

I sat with Jacob as he played. I remember so vividly his trembling hands hovering over the keyboard as he prepared. The sonata starts with a simple hushed, restrained, tentative melody accompanied by a single chord reiterated 18 times. The theme ends just twelve bars later with four repeated cadences. As his confidence and strength grew, Jacob responded heartbreakingly to Beethoven's chromatic and somehow exploratory elaboration of these two ideas – simple tune and hesitant ending. He shaped the gentle melisma and off-beat decorations of the initial melody beautifully and with an expressiveness that gave every note profound significance. Each time the music's repeated elements returned, the achingly, sensitive and gentle pathos of his certain but soft touch on the piano keys became more searching. It became clear on a visceral level that as Jacob tenderly articulated these tentative embellishments and shifting harmonies he, with Beethoven, was saying, 'this is beauty, this is communication, this is feeling, giving, sharing, tenderness . . . this music, now, here, right now, for family, friends and strangers says everything I can and want to say about the meaning of life.'

The music reiterates its hesitations at its ending, repeating its last cadence four times over, deeply reluctant to stop – but finally and with the gentlest of flourishes . . . it is finished . . . definitely, unwillingly, quietly.

Why do I share this most bitter of autobiographical stories with you? Strangely, because it's the strongest argument for assessment I know. That final gift of my son was nothing less than his own assessment of the meaning of life – an unspoken, but beautifully articulated evaluation of the impact of creativity, community, communication and companionship on his existence, and his contribution to it. Most in the hall, including Jacob, understood the pathos of the occasion. Because they knew of its importance, his audience became both recipients and affirmers of this ultimate assessment. The 30 seconds of silence at the end of his performance was infinitely more deafening than applause.

****

Of course I deliberated long and hard whether to share this profoundly personal part of autobiography with you. It may seem disrespectful, over-emotional, trite or unnecessary – it may evoke a neutral response. By sharing this story, I have set the bar on assessment high – assessment *should* be about the point of things. The point of a lesson, the point of teaching, the point of education – the point of being. In the six years since Jacob's death, I and the rest of his family have had to consider these things very deeply. I am only beginning to find any sense of an answer. The purpose of existence has become simply – and as far as possible – to share the good bits of myself with others and in as loving a way as I can. The point of education is to help each child be and become the best beings *they* can be now – not in the future. The point of a school teacher is to be a continually learning individual who helps construct physical, emotional and social environments in which children can experience a wholesome and beautiful present that will sustain and influence them through life. Assessment decisions, I believe, need to be placed in this paradigm.

Autobiography is the theme of this book because it can be both a prime mover and assessment of our lives as educators. The closer I get to honest autobiography, the easier it is to compare my actions to the virtuous values I claim. You have to understand, therefore, that assessment for me is not about measuring, comparing, competing or grading academic achievements – there are other books that will help you do that. Assessment exists to tell us if we are helping a child fulfil their potential as a human being in the physical, natural, material, social, cultural, intellectual, inner and spiritual worlds they occupy – in the present. It concerns how far school education is helping raise children's horizons as they grow.

Assessment provides a vantage point from which we can make out the beauties and oppor-tunities that lie just beyond current understanding. It also helps identify the solid ground of confidence on which to stand before moving forward. Assessment should concern itself not only with how individuals are proceeding towards the fulfilment of academic targets, but also attempt to measure how far they are proceeding towards personal fulfilment.

These views on assessment arise from my lived experience as a teacher. Consider your story again. What parts of it colour your views on assessment? Have assessments in your personal journey been positive or negative experiences? How did receiving assess-ment affect you? What do you feel is worth assessing in your life? What about the lives of the children you teach? What would you choose to express the meaning of your life?

WHY ASSESSMENT?

Assessment is rarely out of the education news. Different opinions on what, who and how to assess have influenced a period of great change in UK education. Standard Assessment Tests (SATs), pre-school tests, baseline assessments of Reception children, entrance tests for Academies, Free or selective schools, Ofsted inspections, responses to Programme for Inter-national Student Assessment (PISA) and other international comparisons, extra assessments for newly qualified teachers and a raft of in-school preparatory assessments have ensured that UK children and their teachers are very heavily tested. UK children, however, are *not* the most tested in the world. Finland, Singapore, Hong Kong and China have more school tests, but the *impact* of those tests on child well-being varies significantly by country. In some countries – the UK and Singapore – school assessments are known to provoke high levels of anxiety among children (WHO, 2016; PISA, 2015). In other highly-tested countries like Finland, levels of school-related stress are low because the tests have few personal or life-changing consequences for the individual. It seems that teacher and societal *attitudes* to tests may be the factor that defines whether or not children find them stressful. If we want assessment to contribute to children's intellectual, physical and mental health and well-being, we should look carefully at what and how we assess and respond to assessments.

This book has focused on non-traditional approaches to education. It has offered arguments for a positive pedagogy, claimed that teaching creatively and for creativity should be central to the teaching of every curriculum subject and that the connecting cur-riculum is the most effective means of promoting both positivity and creativity in schools. It is necessary now to think about how these approaches can be assessed

ASSESSMENT WITHIN A POSITIVE PEDAGOGY

In a positive pedagogy, assessment must be affirmative. It should also add to challenge and rigour. I am in no doubt that assessment practice has improved immeasurably through my life in education and that in most schools, assessment helps produce more efficient deci-sions about pedagogy and curriculum than in the past, but efficiency is not enough. Assess-ment should be used to make a positive difference to the world, children and childhood (Scoffham and Barnes, 2011).

Positive assessment practice works on two levels: it informs all stakeholders about where education is making a difference and gives a sense of humane and professional ownership of the process. Assessment does not contribute to learning when it is reduced to a grid of summative ticks and marks or when it is removed from the interpersonal relationship between teacher and learner. Studies before and since Black and Wiliam's, seminal paper on assessment (1998) showed the importance of formative approaches that involve real and sympathetic interaction between teacher and learner. The need for a positive stance on assessment becomes even greater in a diverse society where judgements need to be sensitive to culture as well as individuals.

The examples of positive assessment practice throughout this chapter are intended to motivate new learning and help teachers regain a sense of professional control of education.

Self-assessment by children

Assessments are not only made by teachers. If we take education research, the CRC and children's rights seriously, it is clear that children benefit from assessing themselves, their peers and perhaps their teachers. Children's voices capture the impact of their most powerful experiences in words that add depth to the somewhat bland assessments of adults. Self-assessment involves asking children what they felt about an experience, how far they went towards meeting a target and why they thought something in their school experience was good or bad. In one school, for example, a child reported:

> The Sierra Leone project was one of the best parts of school in my life. My overall highlight of my time with Yusufu was one game, one song and one dance . . . when we performed the dance to the rest of the school they were all jealous of us and at the end of the dance the children clapped till their hands were red.
>
> (Private communication May 2017, Year 4 Ashley School, Harmony project)

In the same school after a project on open spaces, children summarised their feelings:

> *they are places to run and play; they connect us with nature;*
> *they make us feel calm;*
> *they are places to explore;*
> *we learn when we are outside.*
> *When I am in nature, I feel like I am at home.* (Ashley School, 2017).

You might use a simple table like Table 9.1 to help children assess in words, pictures or photographs responses to a particular unit of work or experience. The information shared provide evidence of the success or otherwise of a unit of work and help you plan new targets for individuals. The support children would need to understand and complete the 'How I have changed . . . ' section, is an important part of the process of self-evaluation.

Other stakeholders matter, too. Parents and carers, family, governors, children's younger and slightly older contemporaries, the local community, doctors and other health professionals, social workers, police and community leaders all have contributions to make.

Formative assessment

Schools usually divide assessment into summative and formative categories. Summative involves grades, marks, comparisons or summarising comments. Assessment becomes

▨ **Table 9.1** A simple self-assessment sheet (to be adapted according to the subject of assessment)

What we did . . .	What I liked best . . .
What I didn't like so much . . .	How I have changed . . .

formative when evidence from an evaluative process is used to *form* new responses, improved behaviours or choices of material, new ideas, methods or attitudes in either teacher or learner or both. Formative assessment can consist of a smile, encouragement, an illuminating or general question, a generative comment, discussion, dialogue, forward plan, reflection, performance, provocation or extension. They are commonly written. Effective formative assessment offers individuals guidance on their improvement and adds to a teacher's knowledge, understanding and practice. Certain teacher and pupil behaviours are especially conducive to affirmation (Black and Wiliam, 1998; Blythe, 1998; NACCCE, 1999; Clark, 2014). These are summarised in Table 9.2 and provide a guide to raising education standards within a meaningful learning context.

Including all children

Diversity itself is a huge resource for creativity and cross-curricular approaches; it is often the catalyst for new ideas and processes (Messiou and Ainscow, 2015). Using a range of assessment methods, therefore, reflects the diversity within and between us. Each child reacts differently to the events of school because each mind is different, and we know from successful multi-national organisations that when diverse minds genuinely collaborate in response to a challenge, creativity abounds. Authorities across the world now argue that such sources of creativity must be nurtured (NACCCE, 1999, 2014; PCAH, 2010; Rwanda Education Board, 2015). After spending a professional lifetime considering creativity, Csikszentmihalyi concludes:

> Centres of creativity occur . . . at the intersection of different cultures . . . Creativity generally involves crossing the boundaries of domains.
>
> Csikszentmihalyi, (2013: 9).

Engaging affirmatively with the contributions of students of all abilities and backgrounds positively affects feelings of social and psychological security and their disposition to participate and learn. The ways in which we engage should also reflect the diversity within

■ **Table 9.2** Behaviours conducive to affirmative assessment for children and their teachers

Teacher behaviours	Pupil behaviours
Establish a culture of success and positivity in the classroom	Work in pairs and small groups to discuss answers to questions/problems
Concentrate on specific problems encountered by individuals	Write down answers to questions and share them once everyone has had a chance to record their answers
Avoid negative comparisons with others	Vote for the best answer/choose the best answer from alternatives
Give individuals advice on how to improve	Know where you are strong/confident and where you are weak/unconfident
Provide individual targets and give clear guidance on what those targets are	Engage thoughtfully in challenges and questions
Provide an overarching rationale for the work children are doing	Think for yourself and share your thoughts with others
Help children assimilate new ideas into concepts they have already grasped	Talk about their understanding in your own words
Help children resolve contradictions between old and new knowledge	Assess yourself after knowing what your targets are
Plan regular opportunities for children to express or perform their understanding	Watch and listen carefully to others
Give plenty of time for children's answers – include paired and group discussion before answers	Engage in peer assessment once targets are understood
Think carefully about the questions you ask – open, provocative and stimulating questions	Discuss assessments with your peers and teacher – if you don't understand, say so
See each child as having potential and encourage them to avoid negative self-assessments	Give focused complements to others
Exhibit work that shows effort and insight, as well as other achievements	Be confident about questioning each other and the teacher
Encourage 'lasting relationships with those from different backgrounds' (HM Gov, 2018)	Do not be afraid of wrong answers

ourselves – we are all complex beings with sometimes contradictory layers of thought and consciousness of which we should be aware and use all of them. Since a high percentage of human communication occurs through facial expression and body language (e.g., Gladwell, 2006; Ekman, 2004), we will begin by considering the impact of wordless assessments.

Using wordless assessment

A smile is an assessment. Teachers easily (and often unintentionally) show their feelings about pupils' work through minute changes in expression and posture. From shortly after birth, children apparently innately assess the mood of their carers, through reading these non-verbal signals (Trevarthen and Delafield-Butt, 2014). Silent assessments do not just give emotional feedback – teachers may assess progress and standards in essential skills and knowledge across the curriculum without uttering a word. Indeed, in music (via sound and silence), art (colour, form and line) or PE (movement, interaction and form), the dominant media of expression are beyond words and perhaps *call* for initially wordless assessments. When a teacher communicates via applause, wrapped attention, a sympathetic smile, expression of wonder, delight, open-eyed surprise, intrigue or thought, the impact can be genuinely visceral, more powerful than words.

Every subject-discipline contains wordless elements. Observing a child's sense of direction, or ability to understand a map, the direction a river flows and where it is likely to be deepest are examples of fundamental geographical skills that require only limited language. How a child presents work in English or holds a book may tell a teacher something about their attitudes or difficulties. Noticing a child's experience of wonder or recognising when a group is overcome by awe, involves quiet assessment skills familiar to many experienced RE teachers. Others quietly extend science, mathematics or history through wordless interventions or the silent identification of misconceptions as children work.

We must be careful of wordlessness, too. Alone, wordless responses can be exclusive and unclear; therefore, they should be followed up with words and actions. A progressive consciousness of the impact of our silent responses should become part of teachers' professional development and research.

Assessing the inclusive social environment

You have seen that children are primarily social learners. Collaboration, it seems, is both generative of and results from creative activity. A key finding from Fredrickson's research on positivity and the human repertoire of abilities (2009) is that when we feel good, we form deeper, more prolonged, trusting, respectful and satisfying relationships. Positive states also promote the ability to make unusual and imaginative connections, to take risks and see the bigger picture. The good feelings that result from involvement in creative activity (Panksepp, 2004) are likely to promote better social relationships. This two-way connection between creativity and improved relationships was remarked upon consistently through the government-funded Creative Partnerships experiment in England between 2002 and 2011 (Roberts, 2006; CCE, 2012; Thomson, 2012). The same relationship is noticed in very young learners. Assessment of Early Years children has been a focus at Leuven University for many years (Laevers, 1994; Laevers and Heylen, 2004). Easy, relaxed, close and collaborative relationships describe Laevers' highest levels of assessed well-being and involvement.

John-Steiner (2001) also noted inter-relationships between creativity and collaboration in many leaders of creative change. Her work extends the reach of Vygotsky's concept of the Zone of Proximal Development (ZPD) towards creativity itself. If the ZPD applies to 'small c' creativity, a *group* collaborating on a task requiring thought, imagination, originality, inquisitiveness and persistence is more likely to develop improved learning attitudes than those working alone. Conventional and religious wisdom has claimed the same for millennia – when two or three minds are gathered together problems are solved more successfully.

Assessing an inclusive physical and emotional environment

The physical and emotional contexts of learning should be subject to assessment as much as its products and processes. Experienced teachers – 'those trained in the field' of pedagogy – have long experience in creating environments for learning and become experts at assessing and advising on their effectiveness (Csikszentmihalyi, 2015: 28). The Communication Trust (2017), for example, lists the following simple features of a classroom as "essential for effective communication in the classroom":

■ Good lighting
■ Comfortable temperatures
■ Not too many visual distractions
■ Low noise levels
■ Visual timetables
■ A variety of objects, picture and symbols to support communication
■ Wall and other displays to support learning

Similar checklists are offered to support school environmental audits. Advice to school leaders commonly focuses on environments with 'neat and uncluttered' spaces, 'clearly displayed learning goals', 'standards-based students work', wall displays and orderly routines – but none of these necessarily generate authentic or real-world learning contexts that include all children. High quality physical environments alone are insufficient.

My call for positive pedagogy asks more of an environment. It rests upon the assumption that a culture of learning can be established when all children in a class appreciate the personal relevance of the learning activities they share (Claxton and Lucas, 2010, 2015). I have argued in previous chapters that learning for primary-aged children should be practical, sensory, social, emotional and creative. A sense of relevance and authenticity also links students at levels beneath culture and language to provide opportunities to build new and lively cultures together in school. If you seek an environment for learning that is both affirmative and authentic, consider and discuss the features listed in Table 9.3.

ASSESSING CREATIVITY

An assessment vocabulary for creativity

Assessing creativity requires a clearly defined and agreed vocabulary. *Creativity Culture and Education* (CCE) and The *Centre for Real World* Learning (CRWL) help us by providing such definitions. Working with schools in a range of UK and international settings, the CCE and CRWL offer a distinctive vocabulary for the assessment of 'Creative Habits of Mind' (Spencer et al., 2012; Collard, 2014). Table 9.4 combines the CCE and CRWL frameworks with earlier work by Torrance and my own on the connecting curriculum. CCE's emphasis on *attitudes* like discipline, collaboration, persistence and questioning provides an important adjunct to *product*-focused aspects like usefulness, originality and value, represented in other studies (Wallas, 1926; NACCCE, 1999; Plucker, 2017). Additionally, a focus on creative *aptitudes* like Torrence's (1977) fluency, flexibility, elaboration, abstractness, 'resistance to closure' and my own (Scoffham and Barnes, 2011) on the ability to make multiple connections and broadens the scope of creativity. Imagination

---

■ **Table 9.3** A checklist for authentic learning

Features of a positive class environment	*Check*
The classroom has an atmosphere of security, support and trust	
There are plenty of examples of positive pupil/teacher relationships	
The curriculum is based on local environments, communities and the concerns of young people	
There are plentiful opportunities for good (ie genuinely inquisitive) questioning	
Children and teachers understand that there is rarely only one answer to a question	
Ideas for solutions and practice are expected to arise from multiple sources	
There are many different learning models	
There is frequent use of digital technologies across the curriculum	
Learning is and feels personalised	
Assessment is informal, transparent and affirmative	
Assessment is part of the daily life of the class and shared between children and teachers	
Achievement is widespread and understood by all	
A wide variety of learning behaviours are exemplified and highlighted	
There are constant opportunities to put new knowledge and skills into action	
Equipment and resources allow for many different choices and solutions	
There is frequent access to the outdoors	
There are frequently changing, multi-modal and interactive displays of all kinds of achievement	
Lessons offer a range of different situations and different people with whom to use language	

---

features in all definitions. You may like to choose ideas from the table to construct your own vocabulary for assessing children's creativity within particular projects.

Torrance and many others are unequivocal that creativity can be learned. Championed within an ethos of inclusion, security and positivity, the listed creative attitudes and aptitudes can be developed in all.

Assessing children's creativity can also be achieved through scoring individual characteristics of creativity (for example, on a scale of 1–10 where 10 is the highest imaginable response for the age group). Using the concepts introduced previously, you might want to assess how imaginative, original, valuable or useful, connection making and collaborative the results of a project were. Table 9.5 suggests how you might assess particular aspects of creativity.

▨ Table 9.4 A vocabulary for assessing creativity

Habits of Mind	Evidence in children's learning activity	Score or comment
Inquisitive	Wondering and questioning Exploring and investigating Challenging assumptions	
Persistent	Tolerating uncertainty Sticking with difficulty Daring to be different	
Imaginative	Playing with possibilities Making connections Using intuition	
Disciplined	Crafting and improving Developing techniques Reflecting critically	
Collaborative	Cooperating appropriately Giving and receiving feedback Sharing or presenting the 'product'	
Aptitudes		
Fluency	*Capacity to*: make divergent responses come up with ideas enter the 'flow' state	
Abstraction	*Capacity to*: tolerate ambiguity think 'outside the box' offer indirect interpretations work with symbols and non-concrete ideas	
Flexibility	*Capacity to*: change direction adapt ideas in the light of experience try out different solutions	
Elaborating	*Capacity to*: add extra and relevant detail offer explanations develop ideas beyond the obvious	
Resistant to closure	*Capacity to*: think about project after completed return to ideas continue learning beyond the immediate project	

(Continued)

Table 9.4 Continued

Habits of Mind	Evidence in children's learning activity	Score or comment
Connecting	*Capacity to*: link current activity to other activities relates activity to personal life involve others	
Aspects of creativity		
Product	Something to show, listen to or see An experience An idea, thought or action	
Originality	Novelty for the child Novelty for the group Novelty for the age range	
Usefulness	Of help or interest to someone Able to be used/appreciated 'A good idea/answer/solution	
Value	Valued by the individual Valued by the group Valued in the community	
Makes links	Connects two or more subject perspectives Connects to the 'real' world Connects people/places/things/ideas	

Table 9.5 Assessing creativity (choose relevant aspects of creativity from Table 9.4)

Aspects of creativity	Group score
Originality	1　2　3　4　5　6　8　9　10
Imagination	1　2　3　4　5　6　8　9　10
Value or usefulness	1　2　3　4　5　6　8　9　10
Connections	1　2　3　4　5　6　8　9　10
Collaborations	1　2　3　4　5　6　8　9　10

Assessing the *value* of a creative output returns us to a key theme of this book. Without values, we become directionless and aimless. Without values, education has little more than a functional, utilitarian meaning. Evaluating what we do – and taking the child's voice as seriously as the inspector's – is central to successful education practice. A successful school, I argue, is one that sustainably brings meaning to the life of children and teachers, humanity to relationships and purpose to learning. In this context values must be part of a continuing dialogue in the school, provoking questions like:

■   What was good about that experience/session/unit?
■   What didn't I/we like that?
■   Why didn't we succeed?
■   Why did we succeed?
■   What new and valuable links have been made?
■   How is this activity related to our core values?
■   How can we deepen our understanding of this value?
■   What should we do next?
■   What is right, good, beautiful, true?
■   What are the right things to be aiming at in this school?
■   What kind of children/teachers/community do we want to work towards?

ASSESSING CROSS-CURRICULAR WORK: ASSESSING UNDERSTANDING

A serious approach to cross-curricular learning requires a new approach to assessment:

■   One that is confident that the multiple subjects chosen are thoughtfully connected to the proposed theme or experience
■   Planning that simultaneously maintains subject integrity and sets challenging subject learning goals within an inter or multi-disciplinary context
■   An awareness of relationships or interdependence between the subjects chosen to illuminate an experience
■   A greater emphasis on measuring the degree of understanding

The first three of those points have been addressed throughout this book, but teaching for understanding requires more explanation.

Assessing understanding

A classroom where teaching for understanding is the goal has certain distinctive characteristics. The indicators involve the quality of relationships you have with the children, the ways you organise tasks, the way you teach and the ways you assess and communicate your observations. Table 9.6 suggests what these characteristics might look like in a classroom and offers a simple scale with which to assess understanding.

Research as part of Harvard Graduate School of Education's Teaching for Understanding (TfU) programme (Blythe, 1998; Project Zero, 2017) offers a novel means of assessing progress and achievement. TfU uses a performance-based method highly applicable to promoting and evaluating the creative and cross-curricular elements in

Table 9.6 Activities and assessments for unit of work on beauty

Year 3 (7–8-year-olds)		
OUG: Beauty		
ULUG (in the form of a question):	*What does beauty look like in nature, and how can I make something beautiful myself?*	
Generative experience:	*A collecting walk in the woods using themed journey sticks, drawings and colour swatches*	
Subject 1 – Science Skills: how to use magnifying glass and microscope, record visual details accurately, classify Knowledge: scientific vocabulary related to structures, patterns, forms in nature (plant and animal life) and classification of plant life Understanding: parts of leaves, flowers, plants, mosses, trees, and the life-processes of flora		
Subject 2 – Art and design Skills: drawing in pencil and pen, colour mixing, watercolour techniques, printing Knowledge: vocabulary of colour, of watercolour techniques, drawing conventions Understanding: pattern making, balance, symmetry, repetition		
Sessions 1–6	**Activities**	**Assessments**
Introduction session	Students engage in a collecting walk in a wooded area. Each group of five has three journey sticks and two colour swatches. Groups are invited to make themed journey stick collections: leaves, flowers, twigs, mosses, roots, bark, seeds, etc. Colour swatches, in shades of green, brown, blue, yellow, grey, white and orange, have double-sided tape to collect samples of natural colour. Children also use sketch books to collect drawings of the shape of real tress, the details of a fallen branch and a leaf.	**General Assessment – an introductory performance:** each individual makes an appropriate/accurate collection. **Formative Assessment:** teacher encourages and highlights inquisitiveness, collaboration and original responses.

Guided Enquiry *(four sessions)*	Groups pool their collections and decide on categories for classification; e.g.(a) leaves with serrated edges, palmate, ovate, cordate, lobed, pinnate, needles or (b) colours: dominant colours and shades. Groups examine samples from their collections through microscopes and magnifiers, noting patterns, structures, shapes and symmetry. They label and name the parts on a diagram of a leaf, flower or plant. Each child uses the microscope or magnifier to find a shape or pattern; they consider beautiful and explain why. They draw the pattern, shape, structure or impress their 'best' leaf, twig, seeds or flower into clay to make repeated patterns. Children transfer their best drawings onto polystyrene board then plan and make a repeating pattern based on what they have discovered about leaves. Others paint a detailed picture of one leaf/flower/twig or seed pod they have found.	**Formative Assessment – guided performances of understanding in science**: teacher guides with vocabulary, examples and questions. Teacher supports with techniques to use microscopes/ magnifiers and identification of patterns and symmetry, etc. Teacher encourages and highlights inquisitiveness, collaboration, tenacity and original responses. Teacher supports by demonstrating drawing painting, printing techniques.
Culminating Performance of Understanding *(sessions 5 and 6) – a culminating performance connecting several areas of learning creatively*	How can we present what we have found out about leaves, flowers and plants in an attractive engaging and creative way? Groups plan an interesting and accessible way of presenting their new knowledge to a younger (Year 2 class of 6-year-olds). Groups make their presentations. Class discussion after observing paintings by Rousseau, Hockney, Constable, Monet: What has this unit done to our understanding of what beauty is?	**Teacher supports:** imaginative methods and assesses creativity by scoring the originality, imagination, collaboration and usefulness of the presentations. **Performances of understanding:** Teacher assesses degree to which individuals have achieved the skills, knowledge and understandings. **Teacher assesses:** what qualities children have identified as contributing to perceptions of beauty.

children's work. TfU also uses a number of concepts useful to meaningful assessment:

- Overarching understanding goals
- Unit-long understanding goals
- Generative topics
- Performance of understanding

Overarching understanding goals (OUGs)

OUGs relate to the big ideas and values-led knowledge that a teacher would wish their students to gain from their whole experience of education. Elsewhere I have called them year-long goals. The goals expressed in school values statements might be considered 'overarching', but each teacher probably has their own personal hopes for their children too. Here are some OUGs from a Twitter sample collected in May 2017.

After a year in my primary class I would like to feel that all children are able to:

- Handle evidence to support their ideas
- Get along with their classmates when working in groups
- Form and develop good questions
- Listen carefully to others
- Feel confident they can achieve
- Know where they are most creative
- Understand the things that bind human beings together
- Love and care for the natural world
- Know that they can learn
- Identify one subject that is their 'special' subject

Unit-long understanding goals (ULUGs)

ULUGs are subsidiary, but feed into OUGs. In a cross-curricular and creative context ULUGs are the intended outcomes a unit of work that combines two or three subject-disciplines to answer a meaningful and important question. Questions to answer via a cross-curricular unit of work might be:

- How can art and music skills help me understand and think about sadness?
- How can skills and knowledge in history and geography help me feel I belong here?
- How do maths and science help us understand natural diversity in the wild area in the playground?
- How can the skills of science and history help me appreciate the church building next to our school?
- How can knowledge and skills in design/technology and geography help us make the school a safer place?
- How do modern foreign languages and citizenship help us build a better community?
- How can the knowledge and skills of RE and dance help me express wonder at the birth of a child?

Generative topics

The thematic contexts within which both OUGs and ULUGs are approached are called Generative topics. They may be visits, visitors or a series of activities. They might be an issue or theme like those illustrated in Chapter 5, or a big question like: How can we show love when looking after an animal? What does Darwin tell us about truth? How do people live sustainably in a given place? A generative topic may arise from an event, competition, production, exhibition, news item or other project. A topic is generative if it creates and sustains interest, engagement and enthusiasm for a number of weeks. Generative topics must be interesting to teachers too. They should have sufficient depth to be sustained, be seen as significant by all and contain the potential for multiple connections with life and curriculum.

Performances of understanding

When we are able to demonstrate our ability to understand and use the skills and knowledge gained from a unit of learning, we can be said to *perform* our understanding. Think of the first demonstration of your ability to skate, swim or ride a bike – it was a kind of performance – usually to an audience and with a sense of achievement, perhaps even prompting applause. At its basic level in education, a performance might be a matter of simply following a teacher's instruction, but with support new learning can be much more imaginatively demonstrated. When knowledge is transferred and applied in a completely new context, it becomes understanding. So a performance of understanding occurs when we – in a group or alone – show that we have understood something by applying it. Three kinds of performances are illustrated in the unit outlined in Table 9.6. These performances can indicate the degree to which a child or group can apply their learning and thereby help educators assess both the depth of learning and the effectiveness of teaching.

Planning and assessment become combined and mutually supportive when teaching for understanding. Table 9.6 shows the relationships between an overarching understanding goal (like being able to provide an answer to the question, *What is beauty?)* and a unit-long theme like *beauty in nature* within a generative topic like a forest walk. The table also shows how a two-subject approach can be used to deepen understanding of the experience. Note how throughout the six-week unit, teacher support, assessment and opportunities to demonstrate understanding blend to make the learning experience authentic, formative and positive. Later in the year the teacher might approach the same OUG (*What is Beauty?)* through the lens of mathematics or music or RE.

Subject-based assessment takes place throughout the processes described in Table 9.6, but culminating assessments may be confined to the degree of creativity of the group's presentation. The plan above would exemplify an inter-disciplinary mode of cross-curricular learning where the creative fusion of ideas is one of the aims of a unit. But as teachers we need to be assessing ourselves too. Table 9.7 is a checklist to use with a trusted colleague to support the implementation of a teaching for understanding approach.

CONCLUSION

This chapter has concerned the hows and whys of assessment. It has offered a deliberately humanistic approach to measuring what is important in education, perhaps more appropriate for a book on creativity. It has offered guidance on how you can collect evidence on the

▪ **Table 9.7** Teaching and assessing for understanding: observable classroom indicators

Is teaching and assessment focused around 'big ideas' or OUGs?	1	2	3	4	5	6	8	9	10
Are key questions prominently displayed and examined throughout the unit of work?	1	2	3	4	5	6	8	9	10
Are assessments made before the topic to ascertain prior knowledge/misconceptions?	1	2	3	4	5	6	8	9	10
Are focus exercises or other motivators used to engage students in exploring?	1	2	3	4	5	6	8	9	10
Do pupils have opportunities to demonstrate their understanding in some kind of performance (exhibition, dance, collection, talk, debate, video, song/music, quiz, learning walk, poem, recitation, play, etc.)?	1	2	3	4	5	6	8	9	10
Is feedback based upon transparent criteria and well-understood models or examples?	1	2	3	4	5	6	8	9	10
Is pedagogy flexible enough to help all participate, understand, contribute, learn and transfer their learning?	1	2	3	4	5	6	8	9	10
Do pupils have multiple opportunities to demonstrate understanding (by using the six facets: explanation, interpretation, application, perspective, empathy and self-reflection)?	1	2	3	4	5	6	8	9	10
Do students have the chance to rethink, revise and reflect on their work based on feedback?	1	2	3	4	5	6	8	9	10
Are students given the opportunity to self-assess, reflect and set their own targets for improvement?	1	2	3	4	5	6	8	9	10

degree of creativity and of connectivity in a child's experience. It has also suggested that it is possible to assess how far creative and cross-curricular approaches work to motivate, sustain and provide a foundation for lifelong, moral and meaningful learning.

REFERENCES

Ashley School (2017) available at: www.ashleyschool.org.uk/learning/year-groups/year-4 (accessed 25.10.17).

Black, C. and Wiliam, D. (1998) *Inside the Black Box: Raising Standards Through Classroom Assessment*. Arlington, VA: Phi Delta Kappa.

Blythe, T. (1998) *Teaching for Understanding Guide*. San Francisco, CA: Jossey Bass.

Clark, S. (2014) *Outstanding Formative Assessment*. Abingdon: Hodder Educational.

Claxton, G. and Lucas, B. (2010) *New Kinds of Smart: How the Science of Learnable Intelligence Is Changing Education*. Maidenhead: Open University Press.

Claxton, G. and Lucas, B. (2015) *Educating Ruby: What Our Children Really Need to Learn*. Carmarthen: Crown.

Collard, P. (2014) *Creativity, culture and education: Assessing creativity in education*, available at: www.wise-qatar.org/measuring-creativity-education-paul-collard#_ftn1 (accessed 24.10.17).

C:\Users\tmc242\AppData\Local\Microsoft\Windows\Temporary Internet Files\Content.Out look\NR3N7SV2\15031-1649_chRef Mismatch Report.docx - LStERROR_54

Communication Trust (2011) *All together now*, available at: www.thecommunicationtrust.org. uk/media/311/all_together_now_v_2.pdf (accessed 24.10.17).

Csikszentmihalyi, M. (2013) *Creativity: The Psychology of Discovery and Invention,* New York: Harper Perennial.

Czikszentmihalyi, M. (2015) *The Systems Model of Creativity: The Collected Works of Mihalyi Csikszentmihalyi.* New York: Springer.

Ekman, P. (2004) *Emotions Revealed: Understanding Faces and Feeling.* London: Phoenix.

Fredrickson, B. (2009) *Positivity: Groundbreaking Research to Release Your Inner Optimist and Thrive.* New York: Crown.

Gladwell, M. (2006) *Blink: The Power of Thinking Without Thinking.* London: Penguin.

HM Government (2018) *Integrated Communities Strategy Green Paper*, available at: https:// www.gov.uk/government/uploads/system/uploads/attachment_data/file/690819/Inte grated_Communities_Strategy_green_paper.pdf (accessed 16.03.18).

John-Steiner, V. (2001) *Collaborative Creativity.* Oxford: Oxford University Press.

Laevers, F. (ed.) (1994) *Defining and Assessing Quality in Early Childhood Education.* Leuven: Leuven University Press.

Laevers, F. and Heylen, L. (2004) *Involvement of Children and Teacher Style: Insights from an International Study on Experiential Education.* Leuven: Leuven University Press.

Lucas, B., Claxton, G. and Spencer, E. (2013) *Expansive Education: Teaching Learners for the Real World.* Maidenheaad: Open University Press.

Messiou, K. and Ainscow, M. (2015) Engaging with the views of pupils: A catalyst for power-ful teacher development? *Teaching and Teacher Education*, Vol. 5, pp. 246–255.

NACCCE (1999) *All Our Futures: Creativity, Culture and eDucation*, available at: http://sirk enrobinson.com/pdf/allourfutures.pdf (accessed 24.10.17).

Panksepp, J. (2004) *Affective Neuroscience: The Origins of Animal & Human Emotions.* New York: Oxford University Press.

PISA Singapore analysis (2015) Available at: www.compareyourcountry.org/pisa/country/SGP (accessed 24.10.17).

Plucker, J. (2017) *Creativity and Innovation: Theory, Research, and Practice.* Wako, TX: Prufrock.

President's Committee on Arts and Humanities (PCAH) (2010) *Reinvesting in Arts Education: Winning America's Future Through Creative Schools.* Washington, DC: PCAH.

Project Zero (2017) *Teaching for understanding website*, available at: www.pz.harvard.edu/ projects/teaching-for-understanding (accessed 24.10.17).

Roberts, P. (2006) *Nurturing creativity in young people: A report to government to inform future policy*, available at: www.creativetallis.com/uploads/2/2/8/7/2287089/nurturing-1. pdf (accessed 24.10.17).

Robinson, K. (2014) *Finding Your Element: How to Discover Your Talents and Passions and Transform Your Life.* London: Penguin.

Rwanda Education Board (2015) *Competence-based curriculum*, available at: http://reb.rw/file admin/competence_based_curriculum/syllabi/CURRICULUM_FRAMEWORK__ FINAL_VERSION_PRINTED.compressed.pdf (accessed 24.10.17).

Scoffham, S. and Barnes, J. (2011) Happiness matters: Towards a pedagogy of happiness and well-being. *The Curriculum Journal*, Vol. 22, No. 4, pp. 535–548.

Thomson, P., Hall, C., Jones, K. and Sefton-Green, J. (2012) *The Signature Pedagogies Project: Final Report.* Newcastle: CCE, available at: www.creativitycultureeducation. org/wp-content/uploads/Signature_Pedagogies_Final_Report_April_2012.pdf (accessed 24.10.17).

Torrence, P. (1977) *Creativity in the classroom, what research says to the teacher*, available at: https://eric.ed.gov/?id=ED132593 (accessed 24.10.77).

Trevarthen, C., and Delafield-Butt, J. (2014) The infant's creative vitality, in projects of self-discovery and shared meaning: How they anticipate school, and make it fruitful, in *The Routledge International Handbook of Young Children's Thinking and Understanding*. Routledge International Handbooks. Oxford: Routledge, pp. 3–18.

Wallas, G. (1926) *The art of thought*, Now available as a reprint by, Tunbridge Wells: Sollis Press (2014).

World Health Organisation (WHO) (2016) *Growing Up Unequal: The Health Behaviour of School Aged Children Report*. Geneva: World Health Organisation.

TEACHERS AND CHILDREN RESEARCHING CREATIVE CONNECTIONS

SUMMARY

This chapter introduces the idea of the teacher as a continual researcher. You will be given arguments as to why conducting your own education research is important and what it might look like. Through case studies and some challenging exercises, you will be shown that you are already a researcher, and how to make that research more rigourous and useful to others. Research builds your capacity to contribute to the learning community and helps engender the resilience you need to stay in education.

INTRODUCTION

When my school was inspected in the mid-1990s, Ofsted inspectors told us our children were 'over confident' and recommended that we should spend more time drilling children to raise the level of Standard Assessment Targets (SATs) results in English. We were hurt. As a staff, we had decided that confidence was a specific aim for our children and we believed that self-assured interaction and powerful personal experience of the world would result in deeper, more permanent learning than rehearsing for tests. Teacher research – our own and others' – would have given us confidence to argue that our community-based, cross-curricular, confidence-building approach successfully achieved our aims to make our school a place where all pupils felt a sense of belonging and where all were able to transfer new knowledge and skills confidently to real-world situations. Research would have given me and my staff the evidence to argue as professionals that what we felt was working indeed was – and that we had evidence to support it. We received our 'good' Ofsted grading, but felt bruised by the experience of inspection.

Resilience in a time of rapid change

Times have changed. During the past 30 years, the primary curriculum in England has been revised three times, two expensive curriculum reviews commissioned (and ignored) by government (NACCCE, 1999; Rose, 2006) and the recommendations of a comprehensive independent third review sidelined (Alexander, 2010). As the number of school children has risen, the total number of schools in which to teach them has fallen. Teacher recruitment has declined and teacher morale, under increasingly bureaucratic expectations, has been falling since the turn of the century. Teachers are leaving the profession ahead of retirement in ever greater numbers and retention even in the first five years after qualification is poor (Guardian, 2017; NUT, 2017; TES, 2017). More children from ethnic minorities and other parts of Europe are entering our schools, but local authority support for them has declined with cuts to provision since the financial crash of 2008. Local influence on education has steadily diminished as the variety of different types of school and governance has increased. Market forces, more rigourous summative assessment, heightened accountability and arguments about 'essential knowledge', school uniform and grammar schools have dominated education debates, while the high ideals enshrined in 'Every Child Matters' (DCSF, 2003) and 'extended schools' (UK Government, 2012) have faded. Austerity measures have impacted upon schools as poverty among children has risen (Independent, 2016; Child Poverty Action Group, 2017), and the results of cuts to education funding and teachers' pay are frequently reported (e.g. Independent, 2017). Against this background, it may seem difficult for teachers to be thinking of resilience.

My research (Scoffham and Barnes, 2011; Barnes, 2013) has suggested that happiness matters and that there are routes towards resilience even in the most difficult times. A fulfilling life in education may be more a product of values, creativity and friendships than of pay or conditions. Remunerations and resources are of course important in attracting and retaining teachers, but to encourage them to stay and grow they need friends, to be working in line with their values and to discover and fully utilise their own creative strengths. My tentative autobiographical and biographical research findings gave me hope. Since then I have redoubled my efforts to help teachers at home and abroad, develop the resilience that will support them through the changes and challenges that surely lie ahead. The process has started already if you want to know more about your strengths as a teacher and organiser of learning.

If you seek deeper understanding of your practice, it is probably because you want to improve it. Teachers who want to move toward what Whitehead calls an 'empathetic responsiveness' to children and education (Whitehead and McNiff, 2015: 250) can use action research techniques to analyse and learn from the multiple interactions and reactions that pepper every school day. Education research, especially at the outset, need not involve large numbers or complex questions. It does not require another person watching you or taking notes. It can be conducted by you, for you and be used to build your own confidence. Focusing on a single lesson, the responses of a small group or a single child are legitimate subjects for education research and can significantly help in evaluating practice, affirming your practice and building your capacity.

The principles underlying your research must be clear. Honesty and transparency are crucial, and in a classroom context where people and feelings matter, your own self-knowledge is an important starting point. We must return to our deep beliefs about education, the values that drive us and drove us to become teachers. Whitehead asserts that to live 'in the direction of our values', we must not simply be aware of them, but also acknowledge the contradictions and difficulties we experience in trying to live them. We might think our values are little more than grandiose ideals, but our deepest beliefs colour the mental narratives that accompany us even when we do not live according to our values. We may, for example, be led by a desire to be compassionate but find ourselves frustrated by our impatience and weakness in the face of realities of life. I might say I am concerned for every child's well-being, but find myself belittling or discouraging a child when I am tired, disappointed or anxious. Whitehead argues that we should examine the 'developmental possibilities' open to us after honestly confronting our values contradictions and inconsistencies. Only when we become aware of the flaws in our character can we decide on what, where and how we need to change (Whitehead, 2017). Indeed, the process of examining our own actions and motivations in the light of our professed values is a legitimate subject for research and personal development in all caring professions like teaching.

You may wish to sample this form of research for yourself. Revisit the values you identified in Chapters 1 and 2 and use Table 10.1 below to identify the contradictions and inconsistencies you find in your own practice.

■ Table 10.1 Researching personal values and inconsistencies

Your chosen value	Your values inconsistencies and values compromises	What could I do to address these inconsistencies?

Sharing the inevitable range of responses to Table 10.1 with colleagues will involve you in a 'values discussion'. You will find similarities and surprising differences in the reflections of those with whom you work or study. Secure and friendly conversation about similarities and dissimilarities can result in clearer, more nuanced and localised statements of values. Within a truly inclusive school, the decision to put those agreed values into action can provide direction, aim and profound meaning to school life. After thinking carefully about shared school values and the individual enthusiasms and skills of staff, you will be in a good position to choose suitable themes and questions to build a more connected and creative curriculum.

Connecting a curriculum to the lives of the school community is a demanding job. In primary schools, teachers are responsible for the learning of 30-plus children for six hours a day for over 40 weeks of the year. As society becomes more diverse, successful teaching becomes increasingly dependent on identifying and sharing fundamental and timeless human skills and values that run beneath all cultures and unite all subject-disciplines. The relationship between some of these values and the skills within a positive pedagogy is shown in Table 10.2. Such skills do not emerge once for all, but need constant tending, adaptation and enhancement for every class and individual through a lifetime in education. The values that drive and direct our teaching become more effective as we become experts in the domain of pedagogy.

There are many more cross-cultural skills and inclusive values, but self-assessing against the table above will suggest an agenda for personal development that can fruitfully last a lifetime in education.

Teachers continually assess themselves, they also continually research, but often do not recognise it. Stenhouse (1981: 104) described research as "systematic, self-critical

▨ **Table 10.2** Some fundamental and timeless teaching skills and the values that drive them

Some fundamental and timeless teaching skills: the ability to . . .	The values that direct and sustain inclusive teaching skills
• Read and respond constructively to the emotions of others	Empathy
• Understand and manage our own emotions	Self-control
• Understand others' points of view	Compassion, respect
• Use clear and accessible language	Communication
• Know how to act fairly	Equity, Rights
• Control without fear	Non-violence
• Maintain interest and engagement in all	Participation
• Provide security and confidence in others	Hope, optimism
• Be positive, laugh and be humourous	Joy
• Be consistently moral	Courage, honesty
• Believe in the ability of each child	Trust
• Engage in hard work for others	Selflessness, tenacity

inquiry made public", and this definition summarises what many pedagogs do informally on a regular basis. Each characteristic of this definition will be briefly examined in the context of primary teaching and learning.

Systematic inquiry

Teachers generally take a systematic approach to their job. Being systematic does not necessarily mean being efficient and machine-like. Neither does it mean being distant and uninvolved. Efficiency can be highly exclusive and work against human caring and sensitivity; machines do not usually allow for human variability. Teachers' preferred systems vary – some are more organised than others, but most develop a recognisable method in their daily interactions with children and their learning. Classroom exchanges provoke an inner stream of questions: Why did she say that? How shall I respond to that? What did I do wrong? How can I communicate that better? What shall I do if they finish too soon? How can I refocus them? Why didn't I think of that? Such internal interrogation becomes a reflex for teachers, but can also provide fruitful starting points for professional, formative research.

Case Study 10.1 Words and music

Katy, a Reception teacher in her first year, became aware that her class particularly enjoyed sessions where she used poems and songs with obvious rhymes in them. She asked herself a simple question: Why does rhyming seem to be so important? Katy decided to look out for answers to this question, to observe and note-take in class throughout the week. She noticed first that some children were 'good' rhymers, and some were not. Some enjoyed the fun of rhyming, anticipated rhymes, played, predicted and were able to make simple patterns with them. She also noted that some children seemed not to 'get' rhyme at all. As she observed she noted three commonalities amongst the poor rhymers: they all had difficulties with early reading skills and self-confidence, and many seemed unaware of the simple nursery rhymes she used at the beginning of each day.

She decided to read a little about rhyme and reading skills and found that other researchers had observed similar things. Some said that teaching rhyme to those who already found it difficult did not result in significant improvements to reading. The following week, Katy decided to teach two new rhyming songs and play rhythmic rhyming games with the class each day. The children showed great enjoyment in these activities. She also noticed that they settled down to other work more easily and that behaviour improved. She began to hypothesise that singing and playing rhythmic games regularly had a positive effect on the children's 'attitude and togetherness as a class'. "They just seemed happier," she said. Katy did another internet search, this time for articles on music and well-being, and found that others had observed the same things. She decided to use more singing and musical games throughout the rest of the term, and found that both she and her children were enjoying teaching and learning, and that reading ability was improving in many of the children with difficulties. Katy asked herself if it was the extra rhymes or the extra enjoyment that provoked these improvements.

In Case Study 10.1, classroom-based research conducted by the teacher herself – often called action or participant research – followed a simple structure. Katy was systematic in the following ways: she . . .

- Defined an issue to study
- Made focused observations
- Took notes
- Attempted to interpret the results in the light of the research of others
- Elaborated on her thinking
- Changed her classroom behaviour
- Observed the consequences
- Considered new interpretations of what she had observed
- Began to draw some generalised conclusions

Katy's practice as a teacher changed in the light of her discoveries during the everyday process of teaching. Sharing her observations in a staff meeting meant that her experience informed her colleagues.

Self-critical inquiry

Self-criticality comes easily to teachers – the daily and reflex judgements of children (expressed non-verbally or in words) makes self-criticism almost inevitable. Self-criticism does not have to be a negative attribute, however. New knowledge about the way the mind works, discussed in Chapter 8, throws light on how and why positive self-criticism combined with positive body language and positive facial expressions can be powerfully formative. 'Beating oneself up' about failures or an interaction gone wrong simply raises the heartbeat and provokes further feelings of anxiety or disappointment that can produce a downward spiral of negative feelings and actions. If criticality – from self or others – is sensitive, affirmative and perceived as formative, the resulting spiral can become an upward and virtuous one. The questions we should ask are therefore:

▨   How can I be positively self-critical?
▨   How can use criticality creatively and to enhance creativity?
▨   How can I encourage self-criticality in children without dispiriting them or creating anxiety?
▨   What are the best ways to engender systematic approaches, appropriate challenge and continued improvement in ourselves and our students?

Case Study 10.2 may help you think about developing affirmative forms of criticality.

Case Study 10.2 Design/Technology and History

Ahmed is a Year 3 teacher in Chester, UK. Eleven languages are spoken at home by the children in his class. His curriculum encourages him to use the local environment to make learning authentic and relevant. He has been leading a cross-curricular topic on the Romans in the area of Chester near his school. After visiting the museum and handling some fragments of real Roman pottery, the children were excited about the possibility of making Roman-style pots in their design/technology sessions. Using the museum's handling collection, Ahmed showed evidence that some Roman pottery was moulded and mass-produced. Using simple plaster moulds and clay, the children learned from an expert how to make copies of Samian ware dishes and hand-built oil lamps. As the children made their own copies, Ahmed reminded them they should have the same high standards of finish as the Romans themselves had. Whilst supporting the children to shape and smooth, join and add decorations, their teacher constantly raised the challenge for the children. How could they best hide the joints between clay additions? How could they smooth the inside and outside without weakening the pot? How could they make the rim comfortable to drink from, or apply the decorations more smoothly? In each interaction, Ahmed gently encouraged self-assessment, self-criticality. In the end, the pots were fired and painted and placed in a display for parents and governors. Six children were chosen by the class to take visitors around their exhibition and describe the processes, difficulties and solutions. Observing them, Ahmed heard his children describe in detail the difficulties and challenges they had overcome and the improvements they would now like to make. Their adult audience responded in feedback that they were impressed at the depth of what the children had learned about the Romans in the process. (Personal communication, October 2016)

As he was leading these lessons (the unit of work involved three History and three D/T sessions), Ahmed was careful to keep the targets for each subject in the children's minds. For history they had to ask the question, "How do we know the Romans used mass-production and international trade?" In design/technology, they asked, "How do we join, mould and finish a ceramic vessel and form an ergonomically, aesthetically pleasing shape?" Answering these questions involved a genuine challenge for each child, but the clear and supportive approach Ahmad adopted, ensured that self-criticality was built into process and product. He explained his aims to the parent helpers who volunteered to support these practical lessons and they became part of his aim to help his children develop a positive approach to self-criticality.

Making research public

At first publicising the results of your research may be as simple as talking about it with colleagues. Increasingly, multi-academy trusts, consortia of local schools, subject associations, special interest groups and teacher organisations like the Chartered College of Teaching (website) encourage teachers to share their classroom experience at meetings, in blogs, podcasts and newsletters. Despite the individuality of every child, many pedagogical problems and issues faced by teachers are common to all. Research into motivating, engaging and creating meaning for children and addressing guiding values like, sustainability, morality, community or living peacefully together in our world – should be the subject of continued and urgent research in education.

Case Study 10.3 Religious Education and PSHE

Sharmila teaches a Year 6 class in Birmingham, UK. They have been hearing about values in assemblies throughout the term, and she has developed some of the points introduced during her weekly RE and PSHEE sessions. In term three, she believed it was important to place her children's values thinking into a real-world context. Since there had been a lot in the news about refugees crossing the Mediterranean in crowded and dangerous boats, she felt it would be appropriate to follow up a school assembly on refugees with more focused work on values. Artist Bern O'Donaghue was invited to work on an installation project that involved each child making a small origami boat to represent one refugee. On one side of the boat, children were encouraged to write a family relationship word like mother, friend, uncle, cousin, nephew. On the other side, each was asked to write their own message to a refugee. Bern had told the children that adults would get to see these messages and others from different schools in an exhibition where these paper boats were to be brought together in a big display.

When the boats had been finished, Sharmila asked a group of children to examine all the sentences written by the members of their class (many had made three of four boats with different messages). In the light of their values work in RE, she asked the group to identify the values words their peers had used. They found that the words help, kind, care, hope, love, welcome, sorry and friend were by far the most common

> words used and made a graph from their tallies to show it to the rest of the class. Another group of 10 had the job of representing these values words in a visual way. They made paper picture frames with key values word boldly written on each one and then asked volunteers to make a 'mannequin challenge'/freeze-frame pose to illustrate what each valued might look like. These photos were displayed in big images around the school. (Personal communication, December, 2017)

Although the children in her class conducted the initial fieldwork, Sharmila's interest in researching values was inspired by this short project involving individual aims in RE, PSHE and Citizenship. She saw that there were ways in which pupils throughout the school could be helped to think more deeply about values across the curriculum – in geography, how a belief in hope could be illustrated in some sustainability projects in South Sudan, in English how love was expressed in a Shakespeare sonnet or poems by George Herbert and Ted Hughes, or in history in the ways that welcome was shown in three contrasting refugee events of the 17th century. Sharmila made her findings public by:

▨ Introducing the plans and results of her cross-curricular topics to the school staff
▨ Collecting, analysing and circulating the results
▨ Writing up a description of her project and some tentative conclusions in her teaching file
▨ Submitting an article to two subject-specialist journals

Doing it yourself

Think about classroom research that you could become involved in. You need a question to ask, a reason to be asking it and realistic, communicable ways of collecting evidence to answer the question. Table 10.3 suggests just a few questions to start you off, try in discussion to add a few questions and to agree on some relevant sources of evidence.

ACTING ON RESEARCH FINDINGS

Action research in your classroom is likely to change your practice. Your research may suggest, for example, that subject knowledge targets are not being met in some areas. A school in Manchester devoted a great deal of curriculum time to cross-curricular learning, but teacher researchers found that there were deficits in learning progression in some subjects, particularly mathematics, PE and music. Inspectors praised the school for its excellent spiritual, moral social and cultural development and its connections between the subjects, but teachers decided children would benefit from extra challenge in the subjects. Since they were agreed that they wanted to retain their experiential learning and cross-curricular focus, they devised a curriculum that offered a balance between cross-curricular learning and pure subject learning. Every term, teachers carefully planned a major and engaging educational experience that was to be interpreted through the eyes of two different curriculum subjects over three weeks. At the same time, the other 10 curriculum

■ **Table 10.3** Some starter research questions

Sample questions	Some ways to collect evidence
Why does involvement drama seem to help some of my children with barriers to communication?	*Observation* *Asking the children* *Asking the Teaching Assistant* *Asking parents* *Looking at class tests over the year*
Has conducting extra history and geography fieldwork affected behaviour in my class?	*Compare behaviour records from last year* *Ask. . . .*
Can pottery help my children with their mathematical skills?	
Which children are helped by a period of quiet reflection – and how?	
What difference does moving the classroom furniture make?	
Which places in school are most worrying for the children in my class?	
Where are the hidden boundaries in the school playground?	
What do children enjoy most in school?	

subjects continued to be taught excitingly and experientially but separately. This meant that through the year, every class had six well-planned and powerful learning experiences that became the foci for cross-curricular learning.

The *double focus* approach ensures that a challenging programme of learning discrete subject knowledge and skills remains at the heart of the curriculum, but that such learning is regularly put quickly into practice in real world and cross-curricular contexts. *Double focus* cross-curricular learning is illustrated in the Figure 10.1.

CONCLUSION

The inner voice of every teacher provides an ongoing narrative that powerfully affects their teaching. That voice – founded as it is upon a unique experience of life – is potentially a central source of creativity, professional development and meaning-making for each of us. Action research in the classroom is a way of making use of that voice to improve our teaching and build connections between ourselves, the curriculum and the learners in our schools. The questions we ask ourselves are probably similar to those our colleagues are asking. Seeking answers through research will support those around you, as well as you. Participant or action research is one means of taking control of our professional lives and making them more creative and fulfilling. Research of this kind uses our personal perspectives placed within professional standards policed by 'the field' (Csikszentmihalyi, 2015) of established teachers to serve the communities in which we live and work. Being part of a school community where such research is habitually created, shared and discussed builds

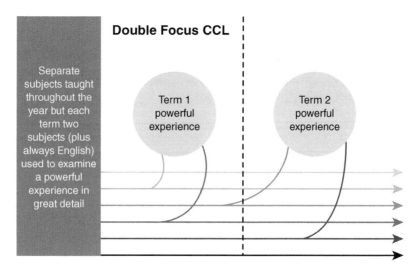

▨ **Figure 10.1** Double focus cross-curricular learning: the separate subject curriculum continues with six major cross-curricular projects for three weeks each

the capacity of teachers to do more, risk more, experiment more, achieve more and share more (Whitehead and McNiff, 2015).

REFERENCES

Alexander, R. (2010) *Children, Their World Their Education Final Report of the Cambridge Primary Review.* Abingdon: Routledge.

Barnes, J. (2013) *What sustains a life in education?* Unpublished PhD thesis, Canterbury Christ Church University, available at: https://create.canterbury.ac.uk/11386/1/barnesthesis.pdf (accessed 24.10.17).

Chartered College of Teaching website, available at: www.collegeofteaching.org (accessed 24.10.17).

Child poverty Action Group (2017) *Rights respecting schools*, available at: www.cpag.org.uk/child-poverty-facts-and-figures (accessed 24.10.17).

Czikszentmihalyi, M. (2015) *The Systems Model of Creativity: The Collected Works of Mihalyi Csikszentmihalyi.* New York: Springer.

Department of Children Schools and Families (DCSF) (2003) *Every child matters*, available at: www.gov.uk/government/uploads/system/uploads/attachment_data/file/272064/5860.pdf (accessed 24.10.17).

Guardian (2017, July 8th) *Almost a quarter of have teachers who qualified since 2011 have left profession*, available at: https://www.theguardian.com/education/2017/jul/08/almost-a-quarter-of-teachers-who-have-qualified-since-2011-have-left-profession

Independent (2016) Available at: www.independent.co.uk/news/uk/politics/child-poverty-increases-low-income-families-tory-cuts-conservative-government-austerity-a7340466.html (accessed 26.10.17).

NACCCE (1999) *All our futures: Creativity, culture and education*, available at: http://sirkenrobinson.com/pdf/allourfutures.pdf (accessed 24.10.17).

NUT (2017) *Teachers recruitment and retention*, available at: www.teachers.org.uk/edufacts/teacher-recruitment-and-retention (accessed 26.10.17).

Rose, Sir J. (2006) *Independent review of the primary curriculum*, available at: www.educa
tionengland.org.uk/documents/pdfs/2009-IRPC-final-report.pdf (accessed 24.10.17).

Scoffham, S. and Barnes, J. (2011) Happiness matters: Towards a pedagogy of happiness and
well-being. *The Curriculum Journal*, Vol. 22, No. 4, pp. 535–548.

Stenhouse, L. (1981) What counts as research? *British Journal of Educational Studies*, Vol. 29,
No. 2, pp. 103–114.

TES (2017) *Part-time secondary school teachers most likely to leave – and four other findings
on retention*, available at: www.tes.com/news/school-news/breaking-news/part-time-
secondary-school-teachers-most-likely-leave-and-four-other (accessed 26.10.17).

UK Government (2012) *Extended schools programme*, available at: www.gov.uk/government/
collections/extended-schools (accessed 24.10.17).

Whitehead, J. (2017) A living theory approach to changing perspectives in contemporary teaching. *Association for Teacher Education in Europe (ATEE) Conference*, Dobrovnik, Cro-
atia, October 23–25.

Whitehead, J. and McNiff, J. (2015) *Action Research for Teachers: A Practical Guide*. Abingdon: Fulton.

POSTSCRIPT
A connected, creative and positive life in education

A connected and positive experience of schooling has been my aim throughout a life in education. Personally meaningful and deep connections matter. They can be the human connections between my and my children's inner selves; collaborative, supportive connections between the separate members of a class; cultural connections between class and community; sustainable and globally informed connections between community and the world; and the knowledgeable connections made between and within the various subjects of the curriculum. Throughout this book, I have examined with you how to make such connections between our lives and the existing curricula in schools. I have tried to imagine with you what such an education might look like and why it might matter to our souls and planet.

Positivity matters equally. Through my ordinary life of disappointments, successes, heady joys and crushing sadnesses, I have found that meaning is not held in money, marketplace or measurement, but in making positive links between myself and other people, places, things and ideas. I discovered the importance of these connections through examining my unremarkable story and those of the people and things around me. I want to share my experience of the fulfilment I have found and – I hope – generated in a life in education. For me, creativity and positivity are inextricably linked. With many others, I was guided by teachers to discover undiscovered creative strengths within a broad and balanced curriculum where many options for creativity were available to me. Those interests were developed and nurtured in a curriculum that included fieldwork, friendships, visits, events, concerts, plays, play, whole books rather than decontextualized passages, written and actual contacts with members of the community, and the enthusiasm of the adults around me. Those with whom I still have contact remember the same primary school days with similar positivity to mine; each can identify a creative pleasure – sport, art, poetry, music, drama, design, technology and religion – born in those years.

Both western physicists and the followers of many traditional African religions claim that neither matter nor energy disappear. I have found meaning in the thought that the energy and commitment of my teachers and *their* teachers directed towards creating a better world, is currently entrusted to me. It is our responsibility – yours and mine – to direct the vast stores of energy generated by the good people who have touched our lives, to make the world of today's children a better place. What greater calling is there?

APPENDIX

The terms I have used throughout this book need definition and explanation. I have chosen the following nine terms that are particularly important to the treads and themes discussed:

a)   Subject-disciplines
b)   Thinking
c)   Inclusion
d)   Pedagogy
e)   Sustainability
f)   Values
g)   Diversity

a) The subject-disciplines I use this term to describe the subject-based mindsets that help us make sense of the world around us. School curricula are traditionally divided into the distinctive ways of thinking most valued by the culture. A culture that values the discipline of spirituality over all else would give spirituality precedence in its curriculum. The discipline of music was given high status in Balinese education because of its importance in Balinese culture (Gardner, 1993). In the UK, the dominant disciplines in primary education are English and mathematics – and science, though currently less prioritised in primary inspections (Ofsted, 2015). The 'foundation' subjects for England and Wales – history, geography, music, art and design, design/technology, religious education, physical education and modern languages, and Welsh language in Wales – are given less time. Personal, social, health and economic education (PSHEE) and sometimes citizenship appear in most schools.

Using the composite subject-discipline takes us beyond the term 'subject', which usually implies a politically or culturally selected 'core' knowledge. This combination subject and discipline is intended to include the unique history of a field of study; its gate-keepers and personalities; its specialised vocabulary, skills and attitudes; and the core values that distinguish it from other modes of thinking. Geography, for example, has its own story through time, its heroes, heroines and current experts. It also has a unique language (for example: north, east, south, west, valley, plain, coast, contour, land use, boundary), a core skill set (for example: map-making and reading, fieldwork, measuring weather, finding patterns in the landscape, etc.), central concepts (for example: place, maps, physical and human, climate, weather), attitudes (for example: environmental sensitivity, human/environment relationships), and values (perhaps sustainability, conservation and hope for the future). The key vocabulary and values of each discipline are often quite distinct from each other.

Every subject-discipline has its creative side. At its cutting edge, experts in each field use their abilities to test how far they can take its language, values and skills. At their innovative margins but also in day-to-day application, the subject-disciplines can be approached creatively as well as factually.

b) Thinking Thinking involves considering or reasoning about something. It is an active and conscious use of the mind. Many psychologists would link thinking with learning, indeed David Perkins goes as far as to say "Learning is a consequence of thinking" (Perkins, 1992: 12). The word thinking is used frequently in this book because of its powerful link with learning. When I first read Perkins' book *Smart Schools* (1992), I was a primary head teacher. I noted his confident association between learning and thinking and initially thought it obvious – then I looked around my school and at my own teaching. I asked myself 'How much *thinking*, reasoning, considering is going on?' I had to conclude that while there was plenty of listening, remembering, practising, repetition, writing, copying, learning by rote, applying formulas and silence – apart from maths problems, most thinking took the form of simple reinterpretation – very little serious reasoning was going on. Further, I noticed that the children who were considered to be 'doing well' were often those who memorised best; those with bad memories quickly interpreted this as an inability to think.

I vowed to make my school a 'thinking school'. Children and teachers were asked to use the school's immediate environment (10 streets around the school) as the basis of questioning and reasoning across the whole of the curriculum. There were no text or answer books for these local measurements or tables of statistics. There was no textbook to explain this street name or building function; no definitive answer to the 'why', 'when', 'where', 'who' and 'how' questions asked by the children as they photographed, mapped, drew and catalogued the familiar streets and gardens. Teachers were able to *see* that the children were thinking. Indeed, the children had to think in order to make sense of the streets, the little river, the park, the abandoned tannery, the telephone lines and manholes. Interestingly, different children began to shine; some surprising children became high achievers. More children began to ask questions, questions that became so complex we had to ask archaeologists and town planners, architects and conservationists to help us (teachers and children) think through the answers.

c) Inclusion Inclusion is not about special needs or newcomers to the school. Inclusion in the terms of this book is a moral stance involving all relationships within the school and community it serves. An inclusive school is one where all are able to participate and one where 'inclusive values' are lived. Booth (2005) argues that inclusive values "are concerned with equity, compassion, respect for diversity, human rights, participation, community and sustainability." Booth and Ainscow's *Index for Inclusion* (2011) makes the breadth and values basis of inclusion in schools clearer and more challenging to us all. This book follows Booth's call to teachers to base their work on the assumption that every child is of equal worth and has equal rights. School inclusion also includes each of the adults working in and visiting the school. An inclusive school community understands that every member can participate and make a contribution, each can be creative in their own way and all should experience achievement, know positive relationships and each find meaning or purpose. Inclusive values like fairness, hope, joy, beauty, compassion, respect and trust should not simply define the relationships in the school playground or corridor, they should be expressed in its curriculum and pedagogical choices too.

Inclusion is an important justification for choosing a cross-curriculum. Cross-curricular approaches allow for the participation of all. Children and teachers respond in a wide range of ways to the reality of the world around them – this is what makes them individuals. Gardner captured aspects of the range of discipline-based responses in his work on 'multiple intelligences', and much of his influence on Harvard's Project Zero is expressed in the cross-curricular nature of many of its projects.

An inclusive curriculum means one where interactions in every subject and between subjects should affirm what Bantu speaking people call *Ubuntu*. This single word expresses three important ideas:

■   All human beings are interconnected
■   Every action has implications for all those around
■   Personal identity is the result of the past and present lives of others

What an inclusive curriculum and pedagogy might look like will colour each case study and discussion in this book, but guidance and provocations will also be offered to encourage teachers to make inclusive decisions for their own curriculum and pedagogies.

d) Pedagogy I use the word pedagogy at times to describe the art and science of teaching. While the word is not commonly used in the UK, it is the usual word for what teachers are involved in throughout the rest of Europe. The word describes much more than the process of imparting knowledge. Pedagogy includes *how* the knowledge is imparted and its particular context. The context of pedagogy involves the physical, psychological, social, intellectual, cultural and spiritual environment in which learning happens.

The pedagogue is highly influential. They potentially have a huge influence on the atmosphere, activities and appearance of their classroom. The interpersonal context the pedagogue allows, encourages or enforces will affect the kind of relationships that are generated, affirmed or denied. The unwritten rules, ethos and the philosophies that provide what Jackson (1968) called the 'hidden curriculum' may more usually be the responsibility of the school head, but how that curriculum works out in an individual classroom is usually down to the teacher in charge.

Teaching itself may at times be the least of the roles fulfilled by the pedagogue. On occasion, a flexible and experienced pedagogue may be a learner, an elder, a facilitator, participant, mentor, carer, observer, researcher, player, enthusiast or thinker. The effective pedagogue will adopt many of these roles in a single day – that is why teaching can be called an art. The teacher versed in the art of teaching dances between a wide range of functions and responses. Their art is also to adapt or alter their role for different children, weave different roles together or dramatically or subtly contrast them in an ever-changing counterpoint.

Pedagogy can also be seen as a science. The successful and experienced teacher is constantly hypothesising and testing their ideas, habitually asking questions and seeking answers by experimentation, analysis and consultation with others. They tend not to be satisfied. There is never a day when learning to be a pedagogue is completed; teachers rarely get the chance to 'rest on their laurels'. Each day requires new roles, new skills, the construction or identification of new connections or the discovery new solutions because every mind is different and every mind is slightly different every day. Science is also advanced by research. Good pedagogues continue throughout their careers to use the research of their own daily experience to plan, adapt and evaluate what they do.

e) Sustainability Sustainability is not a word that simply applies to environmental decisions. In this book the concept is applied to our jobs, mental health and lifestyles too. My thesis "What Sustains a Fulfilling Life in Education?" (Barnes, 2013) was ultimately about how to stay (with joy and hope) in the profession of teaching. The question, 'can teachers and education itself sustain the pressures currently put upon it?' often arises in today's staffrooms. Sustain literally means to hold, maintain, support or endure, but sustainability has come to involve the ideal of attempting to "meet the needs of the present without compromising the ability of future generations to meet their needs" (UN, 1987). The concept of environmental sustainability should be taught and applied throughout the curriculum, but sustaining the best of oneself and aspects of school and community life worth preserving should also be taught. Social sustainability involves a different vocabulary and actions from sustaining an environment or the world's resources.

Sustainability in education involves activities, relationships and approaches designed positively to hold, support and engage the child *and their teacher* over time without compromising the needs of others and the future. A sustainable approach contributes to the development of resilience in both children and teachers to face the inevitable negatives of life. Sustaining what is wholesome about the life of an institution, culture or classroom may be as important as the sustainability of its physical environment, food choices or resources. For teachers and educational processes, sustainability can imply not just that an approach can be maintained without ill effects but will develop and increase in quality as time goes by. If a productive, fulfilling life in education is the aim, then teachers must feel valued and that their social, mental, intellectual, physical, economic and spiritual needs are satisfied by their job. There must be room for teachers' own creativity and plentiful opportunities to make supportive relationships amongst their peers. The values dominant in the school will define the extent to which these needs are met.

For children to feel sustained by school is surely a respectable aim. If a productive and fulfilling *experience* of education is the aim for all children, then they too must be valued and their inborn skills, preferences and identity nurtured. If a curriculum is to be weighted towards a series of positive encounters for each child, then necessary and inevitable negative experiences should be countered by genuinely positive ones. Curriculum and pedagogy are the routes that schools take to fulfil such aims. This book suggests that cross-curricular and creative pedagogies offer sustainable approaches relevant to new and established teachers. The continuity of experience and experiences that we find to be positive is perhaps what many of us aim at in our lives – working towards a sustainable existence within and beyond our lifespan and in the details of daily life in the school should be part of every school's vision.

f) Values This book uses Tony Booth's definition of values as its guide. Values, he argues, are:

> fundamental guides and prompts to action. They spur us forward, give us a sense of direction and define a destination.

> (www.indexforinclusion.org/avaluesframework.php)

Values *in action* are central to the message of this book. The relationships between our values and what we *do* tells us whether or not we are doing the right thing. For everyone, the connections between thought and action always involve moral choices. For the teacher, the realisation that every action is a moral action is especially demanding. Values control what and how we teach. The choices we and our schools make to exemplify, enrich, enervate or simplify the curriculum across all subjects are values-based decisions. Values are amoral; they are not necessarily good – indeed there are plenty of bad values to direct us. Some argue that deeply held beliefs in competition, hierarchy, authority, reward and punishment, selection, compliance and self-interest constitute exclusive and negative values. Whatever our viewpoint, the 'values discussion' needs to be held in schools and may be a critical factor in the sustainability and effectiveness of its programmes and our careers. This book argues that values should be discussed and agreed *often* in each educational institution and that different conclusions will be arrived at. The reader will be supported to think about, decide upon and discuss their own values as the first stage in the development of a values-based curriculum and pedagogy.

g) Diversity The understanding that each individual is unique flows through much of the guidance and most of the case studies in this book. Recognising and celebrating the differences – both within ourselves and between ourselves – does not just make us better citizens or build better communities; it also prepares us to be more connected and more creative.

REFERENCES

Barnes, J. (2013) *What sustains a life in education?* Unpublished PhD thesis, Canterbury Christ Church University, available at: https://create.canterbury.ac.uk/11386/1/barnesthesis.pdf (accessed 24.10.17).

Booth, T. (2005) Keeping the future alive: Putting inclusive values into action. *FORUM*, Vol. 47, Nos. 2 & 3, pp. 151–157.

Booth, T. and Ainscow, M. (2011) Index for Inclusion: developing learning and participation in *schools*. Bristol: CSIE.

Gardner, H. (1993) *Frames of Mind: The Theory of Multiple Intelligences* (2nd ed.). London: Fontana.

Jackson, P. (1968) *Life in Classrooms*. New York: Teachers College Press.

Ofsted (2015) *School Inspection Handbook,* available at: https://www.gov.uk/government/publications/school-inspection-handbook-from-september-2015

Perkins, D. (1992) *Smart Schools*. New York: Free Press.

United Nations (1987) *Our Common Future*. available at: www.un-documents.net/our-common-future.pdf (accessed 17.02.18).

INDEX

Page numbers in *italic* indicate a figure and page numbers in **bold** indicate a table on the corresponding page.